Battle for the Mind

We have still much to learn as to the laws according to which the mind and body act on one another, and according to which one mind acts on another; but it is certain that a great part of this mutual action *can* be reduced to general laws, and that the more we know of such laws the greater our power to benefit others will be.

If, when, through the operation of such laws surprising events take place, (and) we cry out . . . "Such is the will of God," instead of setting ourselves to inquire whether it was the will of God to give us power to bring about or prevent these results; then our conduct is not piety but sinful laziness.

George Salmon, D.D.

*A Sermon on the Work of the
Holy Spirit* (1859)

BATTLE FOR THE MIND

A PHYSIOLOGY OF CONVERSION
AND BRAIN-WASHING

by
William Sargant

with a Preface by
Charles Swencionis

MALOR
BOOKS

This is a Malor Book
Published by ISHK

P. O. Box 381069, Cambridge, MA 02238-1069

First Published in 1957 by Wm. Heinemann Ltd.
Second edition in 1959 by Pan Books Ltd.

This edition published in 1997 by ISHK

Sargant, William Walters.
  Battle for the mind : a physiology of conversion and brain-washing
/ by William Sargant : with a preface by Charles Swencionis.
    p.   cm.
  Originally published: New York : Doubleday, 1957.
  Includes bibliographical references and index.
  ISBN 1-883536-06-5
  1. Brainwashing,   2. Conversion—Psychology.   3. Rites and ceremonies.
  I. Title.
BF633.S3   1997
153.8'53—dc21
                              97-10363

Contents

Acknowledgements

The sources of all quotations are given as references at the end of this book. The author and publishers of *Battle for the Mind* thank those who granted permission for these quotations to be used.

All photographs and plates are reproduced by courtesy of The British Museum, London, and are copyright © The British Museum.

Preface

by Charles Swencionis

William Sargant asked how the brain could change rapidly to adopt whole new world-views. His interest was neither religious nor antireligious, but rather in how the brain could accommodate such rapid and far-reaching change. In cases like conversion and brain-washing, the meanings of many or most parts of one's world change. For the brain, this is a change not like the world revolving on its axis, but rather of changing its axis and drawing all new lines of latitude and longitude, or of great shifts in tectonic plates, so the parts of the world stand in new relations to each other. The brain has to change its connections and meaning systems. How can it possibly do this quickly?

Forty years after it was written, Sargant's *Battle for the Mind* makes disparate and complicated mental and behavioral phenomena understandable. His research in World War II showed that with enough battle exposure, every soldier eventually shows the symptoms of battle-fatigue, shell-shock, or what we know now as post-traumatic stress disorder (PTSD). He went further to look at similar processes in religious conversion, spirit possession, brain-washing, political conversion, and the consultation of oracles in the ancient world.

His basis was a Pavlovian theory, formulated more than seventy years ago. The theory he used is distinct from

Pavlov's famous theory of classical conditioning. It shares much with modern theories of PTSD, and even now could enlighten them. Sargant extended Pavlov's model to account for experiences that make people change their world view suddenly. They begin to see themselves as part of a new group, or become vulnerable to ideas very different from their usual assumptions.

The principles of how to do this were known by the czar's secret police and others long before Pavlov's time. How the brain might allow this is another matter.

Sargant asked how it could be that people would change long-standing, reasonable beliefs, drop their ordinary perspectives of common sense, and become open to ways of thought quite foreign to their previous lives. He found a pattern common to these situations. First, people were subjected to intense trauma. The trauma continued until people behaved in ways very different from what was usual for them. Their personalities showed signs of breaking down. New ways of thinking, applied intentionally or by accident, could then be easily accepted.

In brain-washing, trauma is applied through sleep deprivation, relentless pressure of an alternative ideology, and physical abuse. In religious conversion the trauma is internal, a conflict between fear of hellfire and damnation versus acceptance of the new religion. In spirit possession, there is no trauma, but pressure of a heightened emotional pitch can come from repetitive drum-beating, chanting, dancing, and drug or alcohol use. The mental set, environmental setting, expectation, and observation of others being possessed suggests to people how they should act. Consulting an oracle in the ancient world was not a rational process. Visiting an oracle involved sleep deprivation, chanting, drug use, solitary passage through tunnels and down pits and long exhausting sessions that could last over several days. When the oracle then announced a revelation, it could be seen with new eyes and perceived as having great importance.

Pavlov's Model of Brain Changes

Pavlov's dogs were almost drowned in a flood. At the last moment, an assistant rescued them, freed them from their cages, and led them to safety. Afterwards, they forgot or reversed training they had received before the trauma. Keepers they had shown affection to they now showed aggression toward. Keepers they had disliked they now showed affection for. They forgot their recent learning and had to be retrained.

This phenomenon interested Pavlov and he studied it. He theorized that there were three stages to this breaking down of neural organization and a fourth of reassembling the world. First, the animal is overloaded, through excessive exercise, excessive sensory stimulation, surgery, or sleep deprivation. This produces what Pavlov called the "equivalent" phase of brain activity. In the "equivalent" phase all outside stimuli, large or small, produce the same size response. You may see this in people who have been sleep deprived for a day or two. They lose judgment and perspective and react to a slight question or a major challenge with the same degree of irritability.

The second stage Pavlov called "paradoxical inhibition", in which weak stimuli produce strong responses and strong stimuli produce weak responses. Judgment is further impaired. One almost never observes people in this state in normal life. They are responding inappropriately, with four fire engines to a firecracker and no reaction to a real four alarm fire. This and the further stages are seen in soldiers, in civilians subjected to war, and people in normal societies subjected to rape, or other horrible traumas.

In the third "ultraparadoxical" stage many positive conditioned responses become negative and vice-versa. The dogs showed paradoxical responses to their keepers. They became friendly to keepers they formerly disliked and disliked ones they had been close to. In people, there can be feelings of possession, hypnosis-like states, and new commands and ideas become imperative.

The state of "transmarginal" collapse is even beyond the ultraparadoxical stage. In this stage, and after it, the dog seems to have unlearned recent and longstanding routines. Pavlov described this state as one in which there is inertness, temporary inhibition of most brain function, and isolation of functionally pathological points of the cortex.

A state of breakdown occurs in which the person or dog cannot function and has lost key markers by which they or it understood the world. Basic learning, basic assumptions about the world have been challenged. If the person or dog could change some of these assumptions, they could build a new map of the world, a different world, and function again if the trauma had not been too great. Parts of the cortex involved in the trauma become isolated from other parts of the brain they used to connect to and fire frequently and in a new manner.

Pavlov believed this overall process was the brain's attempt to avoid complete destruction: that it had to attempt to process trauma so great it called into question all it had ever learned. This is a model quite different from the classical conditioning for which Pavlov is usually remembered.

Implications for Social Processes

Traumatic, emotional events that people share bring them together, make them close. War buddies, school chums, and childhood friends are stock relationships for literature and film. Milder forms of the same techniques appear in hazing in college, which leads to life-long attachment to the alma mater and to friendships. Training exercises in sports activate "team spirit"; indoctrination in boot camp leads to loyalty; and corporate training sessions establish commitment to the company. More extreme versions exist in militant religious and political groups and in urban teenage gangs. These powerful techniques can bring about allegiance for a lifetime.

Walter Freeman suggests that the process of conversion is not an evil manipulation, but a social necessity, and that perhaps the same chemistry provides the mechanisms for transference in psychotherapy. The biological process may be the dissolution of existing neural connections by an electrochemical discharge in a brain, preceded by stress, and followed by a state of malleability. This could open the way for a new belief structure to facilitate social behavior. Such a mechanism could serve the function of allowing young adults to separate from their parents, form their own social units, and become parents themselves. That this mechanism exists at least in humans and dogs leaves open for investigation whether it evolved performing this social function, or whether it is an epiphenomenon.

Little is known about this mechanism Sargant described. It would be a mistake to wall it off into the corner of being only PTSD: one psychiatric syndrome in a list of many. This mechanism holds the possibility of explaining and understanding much of how people suddenly change direction in life, and some of the strangest religious and spriritual behavior ever described among human beings.

Could this explain the behavior of the snake-handling cults of the American South, flagellant bands offering supplication to God to avert the Black Plague in the fourteenth century, the strength of the Mau Mau movement in Kenya in the 1950's, and spirit possession in African traditions? Could this be why people believed so powerfully in the revelations of ancient oracles?

Current Models of PTSD

Current models of PTSD help us understand parts of how Pavlov and Sargant's mechanism works. Models of PTSD fall into roughly four categories: neurochemical; kindling; conditioning; and cognitive.

The neurochemical models suggest that PTSD can be understood as inescapable stress producing learned helplessness. The individual cannot escape repeated trauma and so learns that nothing he or she does matters. This produces chronic dysregulation in neurotransmitter systems. The neurotransmitter levels are no longer subject to normal checks and balances and may become set at abnormal levels. Some stress hormones are not secreted when they should be and others are in the bloodstream constantly at higher levels than normal. Mechanisms of reacting appropriately to stress have been burnt out. Stress alarms have been activated so frequently or extremely that they will no longer fire when needed and a lurking anxiety never leaves.

The kindling models suggest that trauma sets up a set of foci in the brain that fire frequently, repeatedly, and inappropriately. This reinforces memory of the trauma and interrupts ongoing processing. If memory of the trauma is either stored in certain circuits or foci, or these brain structures form an important part of the memory, trauma memories will be more active than other memories, and intrude on other thoughts and activities.

Conditioning models suggest that biological vulnerability, acted on by social trauma, causes intense fear, distress, or some other basic negative emotion. This leads to ongoing anxious apprehension, or psychological vulnerability. When this is acted on by social support and coping responses, it leads to full-blown PTSD.

Cognitive models suggest that an individual's world view is challenged by a traumatic event to the breaking point. So many assumptions formerly held of human nature and the ways the world should or does function become so untenable that the world view shatters.

Applications

If we understand how this mechanism works we could manipulate it consciously. Cynical, tyrannical uses to control human beings are obvious and have been a part of our past and present and will be a part of our future. Brainwashing has been used by cults, governments, advertisers, and professional training institutions. It may be a mainstay of all forms of even legitimate socialization into society.

Beneficial application is also possible. Treatment of PTSD should be possible by using a version of the process to bring victims back, to reintegrate them into society. It would be cruel and unethical to use trauma in such a process, but the use of drumming, chanting, music, and dancing does not seem out of place, if the patient wishes it and the process is under the patient's control.

Seeing Sargant's phenomenon only as PTSD ignores the healing aspect of its resolution. Granted that some traumas are so severe that people never recover, most are not this severe, and most people do recover. Understanding the process yields the possibility of individuals exerting greater control over their own healing process, directing where they want it to go, and which people they wish to strengthen their bonds with. People who are recovering from trauma have impaired understanding and choice, necessitated through Pavlov's process of breaking down existing neural connections. However, enlightened professionals who understand the process should be able to empower victims to a far greater degree than those who are ignorant of the process. It is quite possible that trauma victims themselves can control their healing to a far greater extent than we now foresee.

In these days of brain imaging, we may even investigate exactly what structures and circuits are involved. Such research could suggest drug treatments for PTSD that are more successful than current ones.

Our society is full of people convinced that they hold the best of all political, social, religious, and other positions. They (and perhaps we) have not a clue that these positions are not the result of rational choice, but some accident of social conditioning. Insight into this process and education that it exists might make people more capable of rational, informed choice in ideology, or even to reject ideology and dogma in favor of dealing with reality.

Perhaps most important, understanding Sargant and Pavlov's mechanism can give us insight into the formation of social bonds, the development of gangs and groups, and allow us to make more informed choices as individuals, as a society, and as a culture, how we want our own groups to develop.

Bibliography

Freeman, Walter J. *Societies of Brains: A Study in the Neuroscience of Love and Hate*. Hillsdale, NJ, Lawrence Erlbaum Associates; 1995.

Giller, Earl L. *Biological Assessment and Treatment of Posttraumatic Stress Disorder*. Washington, American Psychiatric Press; 1990.

Herman, Judith L. *Trauma and Recovery*. New York, Basic Books; 1992.

Jones, Jennifer C., & Barlow, David H. A new model of posttraumatic stress disorder: Implications for the future. In P.A. Saigh (Ed.), *Posttraumatic Stress Disorder*. Boston, Allyn and Bacon; 1992.

Krystal, John H., Kosten, T.R., Perry, B.D. *et al.* Neurobiological aspects of PTSD: review of clinical and preclinical studies. *Behavior Therapy*, 20:177-198; 1989.

Krystal, John H. Animal models for posttraumatic stress disorder. In Earl L. Giller, (Ed.) *Biological Assessment and Treatment of Posttraumatic Stress Disorder.* Washington, D.C., American Psychiatric Press; 1990.

van der Kolk, B., Greenberg, M., Boyd, H. *et al.* Inescapable shock, neurotransmitters, and addiction to trauma: toward a psychobiology of post-traumatic stress. *Biological Psychiatry*, 20:314-325; 1985.

Yehuda, Rachel, Southwick, Steven M., Perry, Bruce D., Mason, John M., & Giller, Earl L. Interactions of the Hypothalamic-Pituitary-Adrenal Axis and the Catecholaminergic System in Posttraumatic Stress Disorder. In Earl L. Giller, (Ed.) *Biological Assessment and Treatment of Posttraumatic Stress Disorder.* Washington, D.C., American Psychiatric Press; 1990.

Charles Swencionis, Ph.D.
Ferkauf Graduate School of Psychology
Albert Einstein College of Medicine of
Yeshiva University
Bronx, NY

November, 1996

Foreword

It must be emphasized as strongly as possible that this book is *not* concerned with the truth or falsity of any particular religious or political belief. Its purpose is to examine some of the mechanisms involved in the fixing or destroying of such beliefs in the human brain. Some critics will perhaps doubt whether it is possible to separate two parts of a whole in this way. But if a greater understanding of the problem is ever to be achieved, continued attempts must be made to do so.

Having beliefs of my own, and owing much to a religious upbringing, I am particularly anxious to give as little offence as possible to readers who may hold similar or quite different religious tenets. Yet history records the angry outcry even when Newton tried to disentangle the simple mechanics of gravity from its religious aspects. A deeply religious man himself, he was accused of trying to destroy religious faith in others. He could answer only that his work was concerned not with the ultimate question of why something happens, but with the immediate question of how it happens; and I must make the same plea for this very much humbler enquiry. Many people have pointed out, quite rightly, that the ultimate test of both religious and political values is not definable in terms of *how it happens*, but of *what is achieved*.

My concern here is *not* with the immortal soul, which is the province of the theologian, nor even with the mind in the broadest sense of the word which is the province of the philosopher, but with the brain and nervous system, which man shares with the dog and other animals. Yet it is through this material brain that emissaries of God or of the Devil—dictators, policemen, politicians, priests, physicians and psychotherapists of various sorts—may all try to work their will on man. It is not surprising therefore that arguments often arise as to who exactly is doing what. This study discusses mechanistic methods influencing the brain which are open to many agencies, some obviously good and some obviously very evil indeed; but it is concerned with brain mechanics, not with the ethical and philosophical aspects of a problem which others are very much more competent to discuss than I am. It must also be remembered that much of what is discussed here is still only a useful working hypothesis; a great deal of further research is needed before final conclusions are reached.

My choice of Wesley for special study in the technique of religious conversion was prompted by my own Methodist upbringing. I became convinced of the tremendous power latent in his methods, though these have now been abandoned by the Church which he built and strengthened by their use; and most people will agree with social historians who insist that his conversion of large areas of the British Isles helped to stave off political revolution at a time when Western Europe and North America were in a ferment, or in actual revolt, largely because of the anti-religious, materialistic philosophy with which Tom Paine, among others, was associated. John Wesley, and his methods, demand particular study at the present time from politician and priest alike, even if the hellfire doctrine he preached may seem outmoded. I have had to go outside my own field of medicine for some of the material used in this book and apologize in advance for any inaccuracies due to this. But if progress and synthesis are ever to be achieved, in this age of increasingly departmentalized knowledge, someone has to risk leaping over walls into other people's territory. And it must not be held against me that I do not discuss some types of purely intellectual conversion, but only those physical or psychological stimuli, rather than intellectual arguments, which seem to help to produce conversion by causing alterations in the subject's brain function. Hence the term "physiology" in the title.

I have to acknowledge the advice and help of more people than can be mentioned by name, who have visited or worked with me either at home or in the U.S.A. They are bound to find some of their viewpoints incorporated in my thinking, and I hope they would not wish it to be otherwise. In particular I have to thank Drs. Eliot Slater and H. J. Shorvon; some of our work done together in England during and after the war is reported in the earlier chapters of this book and has been already published in joint papers by scientific journals. All the material on war neuroses here quoted has appeared in such journals, and references are appended.

The Rockefeller Foundation made it possible for me to spend a valuable year at Harvard University and to see psychoanalytic teaching and treatment at close quarters. Let me emphasize that my discussion of psychoanalysis when illustrating some aspects of modern conversion and brain-washing techniques implies no denial of its very real value in the treatment of carefully selected patients. Another year spent, by invitation, at Duke University allowed me to study methods of religious revival, including the Christian snake-handling cults that flourish in the Southern States. I also owe much to Drs. Howard Fabing and George Sutherland with whom, while in the U.S.A., I frequently discussed the relation of Pavlov's work to problems of human behaviour.

My thanks are also due to Robert Graves. It was he who persuaded me, whilst on a visit to Majorca, to continue with this book, helped me to prepare the final manuscript, and also supplied Chapter 8 and some of the other historical references in support of my arguments.

And without the help of my wife, and my secretary, Miss M. English, this book could never have been written at all.

W. S.

Introduction

Politicians, priests and psychiatrists often face the same problem: how to find the most rapid and permanent means of changing a man's beliefs. When, towards the end of World War II, I first became interested in the similarity of the methods which have, from time to time, been used by the political, religious and psychiatric disciplines, I failed to foresee the enormous importance now attaching to the problem—because of an ideological struggle that seems fated to decide the course of civilization for centuries to come. The problem of the doctor and his nervously ill patient, and that of the religious leader who sets out to gain and hold new converts, has now become the problem of whole groups of nations, who wish not only to confirm certain political beliefs within their boundaries, but to proselytize the outside world.[1]

Great Britain and the U.S.A. therefore find themselves at last obliged to study seriously those specialized forms of neuro-physiological research which have been cultivated with such intensity by the Russians since the Revolution, and have helped them to perfect the methods now popularly known as "brain-washing" or "thought control". In August, 1954, the United States Secretary of Defence announced the appointment of a special committee to study how prisoners of war could be trained to resist brain-washing. He admitted the desirability of reviewing the existing laws, government agreements, and policies of military departments, with regard to prisoners captured by nations in the Soviet orbit. This committee reported back to the President in August, 1955.[2]

In Great Britain, too, the necessity for more vigorous research into the techniques of rapid political conversion has also been widely recognized. Several years ago, for instance, Mrs. Charlotte Haldane pleaded that research should be undertaken into the psychological mechanism of the process by which she, the wife of a famous British scientist, had been converted to a belief in the official Russian interpretations of Marxian dialectics; and into that of her sudden reconversion to the Western point of view, after failing to detect the falsity of the Russian system for so many years. Koestler and many others have described very much the same experience in their own lives.[3]

Many people are also bewildered at the spectacle of an intelligent and hitherto mentally stable person who has been brought up for trial behind the Iron Curtain, and prevailed upon not only to believe but to proclaim sincerely that all his past actions and ideas were criminally wrong. "How is it done?" they ask.

It is not always realized that this can be the political equivalent of that kind of religious conversion after which ordinary decent people suddenly come to believe that their lives have not only been useless but merit eternal damnation, because some religious particular has been neglected. The same psychological process may also be seen at work in a patient undergoing psychoanalysis: he can be persuaded that anomalies in his behaviour have been caused by an intense hatred of his father—even though he has always acted in a devoted and affectionate manner towards him.

How can people be induced to believe in what may contradict obvious fact?[1]

A general distinction should be made between the more
gradual changes of outlook and behaviour due to increasing age, experience and reason and the abrupt total
re-orientations of viewpoint, often brought about by others, which involve the surrender of strongly held beliefs
and the adoption of new beliefs often diametrically opposed to them.

This book will discuss some of the more important
mechanistic and physiological aspects of this problem, and
of how new ideas may be implanted and firmly fixed in
the minds even of those unwilling at first to receive them.
Interest in it was stimulated by chance circumstances eleven
years ago. World War II provided medicine with rare op-
portunities for studying the breakdown of normal persons
subjected to intense stresses. In England at the time of the
Normandy invasion in June, 1944, special arrangements
had been made to deal with a new crop of acute military
and civilian neuroses resulting from this operation. One
day while travelling to an emergency neurosis-centre, soon
after the start of the invasion, I stopped at an American
neuro-psychiatric hospital to visit a colleague, Dr. Howard
Fabing. He had just been reading a book by the famous
Russian neuro-physiologist I. P. Pavlov, called *Conditioned
Reflexes and Psychiatry*,[4] and strongly advised me to do the
same at once. This book consisted of a series of lectures
given by Pavlov not long before his death in 1936 at the
age of eighty-six; but they had not become available in
English until 1941. Stocks of the translation had been destroyed in the London Blitz that same year, but Dr. Fabing

had managed to secure a copy. Like several other neuro-psychiatrists of World War II, he had found Pavlov's observations on animals extremely useful for the better understanding of certain behaviour patterns observed when human beings break down under abnormal stress.[5]

Pavlov's clinical descriptions of the "experimental neuroses" which he could induce in dogs proved, in fact, to have a close correspondence with those war-neuroses which we were investigating at the time. Also, many of the physical treatments that had gradually been developed by trial and error during the war to relieve acute nervous symptoms, had obviously been anticipated by Pavlov as a result of his prolonged research on dogs.[4] It was now clear that what was needed was a much more careful study of certain of these findings, in their possible relation to human psychiatry, than had recently been given them either in England or in America.

So close were some of the similarities between these and canine neuroses that it seemed more improbable than ever that many current psychological theories about the origin of human neuroses and other abnormalities of behaviour were correct; unless it be conceded that Pavlov's dogs had subconscious minds, and also super-egos, egos and ids. And the part played by alterations in the function of the human brain itself had, it also seemed, been too summarily dismissed by some in their attempts to explain the reasons not only for neurotic and criminal behaviour but for all the constant mental turns, reconsiderations and adjustments which produce so-called "normal" behaviour in any given person, as he reacts to his environment.

When, late in life, Pavlov began comparing the results of disturbances of brain function noted in his animals with those noted in human beings, this phase of his work was little studied outside Russia, and many British and American psychiatrists still neglect it, although the relevant books have now been long available in both countries. The fact is that Pavlov continues to be known principally for his laboratory experiments on animals, for which he was awarded the Nobel Prize; and most psychiatrists prefer a broader basis to their work than his simple mechanistic and physiological approach. Moreover, there is a certain repugnance in the Western world to Pavlov's investigations. Cultural beliefs give man, in addition to his brain and nervous system, an independently acting metaphysical soul, which it is assumed helps to control his ethical behaviour and dictate his spiritual values. In this strongly and widely held view, animals have brains but no souls; which makes odious any comparison between the behaviour patterns of man and animals. And though studies of how animals' bodily systems function have admittedly been of great value in throwing light on the workings of the human machine, this view persists, even among some scientists, almost as a test of moral respectability.

In the United Kingdom, this prejudice against Pavlov has allowed many scientists to neglect his work; and in the United States the wave of Freudian psychoanalytic fervour which has swept the country, many years after its introduction and use in Europe, has had the same effect. Too many psychiatrists and psychologists in both countries have, in fact, blinded their eyes to Pavlov's thesis, though his viewpoint was irreproachably scientific. For Pavlov always insisted that experimental facts, however limited in their range, which can be repeatedly tested and checked, should take precedence over broader and vaguer psychological speculations.

Psychiatric research in Great Britain has, however, become far more realistic since World War II. Drugs and other physical methods of treatment gave such undeniable results, in the treatment of acute civilian and military war neuroses, that physiological aids to psychiatry were given a high research priority, and this policy has persisted. Indeed, it was the use of drugs in psychotherapy that first prompted the present study of Pavlov's experimental methods of changing the behaviour patterns in animals, and the mechanics behind historical techniques of human indoctrination, religious conversion, brain-washing, and the like.[6]

Early in the war, during treatment of the acute neuroses resulting from the Dunkirk evacuation, the Battle of Britain and the London Blitz, the value of certain drugs had become obvious in helping patients to discharge their pent-up emotions about the terrifying experiences which had caused their mental breakdown. This method had been used on a more limited scale in peacetime practice by Stephen Horsley and others.[7] As the war progressed, and after it was over, experiments with a wide range of such drugs were continued and a good deal was learned about their properties.[8]

A drug would be administered to a carefully chosen patient—by injection into a vein, or inhalation—and as it started to take effect, an endeavour would be made to make him re-live the episode that had caused his breakdown.

Sometimes the episode, or episodes, had been mentally suppressed, and the memory would have to be brought to the surface again. At other times it was fully remembered, but the strong emotions originally attached to it had since been suppressed. The marked improvement in the patient's nervous condition was attributed to the releasing of these original emotions. It was also found that the emotions which were most profitably released—or "abreacted", as the psychiatric term is—were those of fear or anger; little could be done by making, say, a melancholic patient weep and become more depressed.

Our first reading of Pavlov's book, in 1944, coincided with the learning of some more facts about these drug treatments. It was found that a patient could sometimes be restored to mental health not by his re-living a particular traumatic experience, but by stirring up in him, and helping him to discharge strong emotions not directly concerned with it. Thus, in some of the acute Normandy battle-neuroses, and those caused by V-bomb explosions, quite imaginary situations to abreact the emotions of fear or anger could be suggested to a patient under drugs; though as a rule these were in some way related to the experiences which he had undergone. Much better results could often, indeed, be obtained by stirring up emotions about such imaginary happenings than by making the patient re-live actual happenings in detail. For example, it might be suggested, under drugs, to a patient who had broken down as the result of a tank battle, that he was now trapped in a burning tank and must fight his way out. Though this situation had really never occurred, the fear that it might happen was perhaps a contributory cause of his eventual collapse.

Outbursts of fear or anger thus deliberately induced and stimulated to a crescendo by the therapist, would frequently be followed by a sudden emotional collapse. The patient would fall back inert on the couch—as a result of this exhausting emotional discharge, not of the drug—but he would soon come round. It then often happened that he reported a dramatic disappearance of many nervous symptoms. If, however, little emotion had been released, and he had only had his intellectual memory of some horrible episode refreshed, little benefit could be expected. But a falsely implanted memory might create a larger emotional discharge than the real and induce the physiological effects needed for psychological relief. A technique of deliberately stimulating anger or fear under drugs, until the patient collapses in temporary emotional exhaustion, was finally perfected with the help of Pavlov's findings. Especially important to this were some observations he made on the behaviour of his dogs after they had been almost drowned in the Leningrad flood of 1924; these will be discussed in later chapters.

One afternoon when this technique was being applied to the more normal victims of severe battle or bombing stress—it was less helpful in the treatment of chronic neurotics—I happened to visit my father's house, and picked up one of his books at random. It was John Wesley's *Journal* of 1739-40. My eye was caught by Wesley's detailed reports of the occurrence, two hundred years before, of almost identical states of emotional excitement, often leading to temporary emotional collapse, which he induced by a particular sort of preaching. These phenomena often appeared when he had persuaded his hearers that they must make an immediate choice between certain damnation and the acceptance of his own soul-saving religious views. The fear of burning in hell induced by his graphic preaching could be compared to the suggestion we might force on a returned soldier, during treatment, that he was in danger of being burned alive in his tank and must fight his way out. The two techniques seemed startlingly similar.

Modern Methodists are often confused when they read Wesley's detailed accounts of these successes; they do not consider that the reason for their preaching being ineffective, by comparison, may simply be because the present fashion is to address the intellect rather than stir up strong emotion in a congregation.

It now seemed possible, in fact, that many of the results which were being achieved by abreaction under drugs were essentially the same as those obtained, not only by Wesley and other religious leaders, but by modern "brain-washers", though different explanations would doubtless be given in every case. Also, it seemed as if Pavlov provided experimental evidence in his changing of animal behaviour, which helped to explain why certain methods of bringing about similar changes in man were successful. Without these experiences in a wartime neurosis centre there would have been no thought of connecting the physiological mechanics used by Pavlov in his experiments on animals with Wesley's mass conversion of the common people in eighteenth-century England and of going on to the present study.[6]

In the autumn of 1944, a period of illness enabled several weeks to be spent in following up these clues, studying case-histories of sudden conversion, and the means of inducing belief in divine possession used by various religious bodies throughout the world. Part of 1947-48 was spent in the United States, where an opportunity occurred of studying at first hand some of the revival techniques still practised in many parts of the country. These seemed relevant to this investigation because they are still extremely effective when used by skillful practitioners; in England they have practically died out.[9]

After ten years of intermittent study, the fruit of which was several articles, most of them published in scientific journals, a second period of illness enabled these to be re-arranged and consolidated for the present book. The crude mechanics of the techniques studied form only part of the picture; but because their importance is so often overlooked by those who believe in reasoned argument as far more effective than all other methods of indoctrination, it seems important that the Western world should be given some understanding of them.

To watch such methods in action and observe their devastating effect on the mind of ordinary people, is such a bewildering and horrible experience that one is tempted to turn one's back on what is a matter of fundamental importance for our cultural future, and shout defiantly: "Men are not dogs!"—as indeed they are not. Dogs, at least, have not yet conducted experiments on man. Meanwhile, however, a large part of the world's population is not only being reindoctrinated, but has had the whole medical system reorientated along Pavlovian lines—partly because the mechanistic and physiological approach to what is more commonly regarded in the West as the province of philosophy and religion has achieved such politically convenient results.

In succeeding chapters evidence will be provided for the general observations made above. It must be emphasized that this book is not primarily concerned with any ethical or political system; its object is only to show how beliefs, whether good or bad, false or truer can be forcibly implanted in the human brain; and how people can be switched to arbitrary beliefs altogether opposed to those previously held. Too technical a style has been avoided, because if politicians, priests, psychiatrists and police forces in various parts of the world continue to use these methods, ordinary people must know what to expect and what the best means are of preserving their former habits of thought and behaviour, when subjected to unwelcome indoctrination.

No claim is made that this book contains any facts that are basically new. Every subject discussed is available for further detailed study in specialist journals and books, to which references are given. But the net has been flung wider than by most previous writers on the subject, in an attempt to connect and correlate observations from many apparently unrelated and unconnected sources. The conclusion reached is that simple physiological mechanisms of conversion do exist, and that we therefore have much still to learn from a study of brain function about matters that have hitherto been claimed as the province of psychology or metaphysics. The politico-religious struggle for the mind of man may well be won by whoever becomes most conversant with the normal and abnormal functions of the brain, and is readiest to make use of the knowledge gained.

CHAPTER 1

Experiments in Animals

In the course of over thirty years of research Pavlov accumulated a mass of observations on various methods of building up behaviour patterns in dogs and then breaking them down again. He interpreted his findings in mechanistic terms which have since been frequently disputed by psychologists and psychiatrists. Yet the findings themselves have been confirmed again and again. Horsley Gantt attributed the absence of any important errors in Pavlov's work to his "painstaking methods, his adequate controls, his habit of giving the same problem to several collaborators working in separate laboratories or institutes, with whom he checked results and supervised experiments. . ."[4]

Pavlov had won the Nobel Prize, in 1903, for research on the physiology of digestion before turning to study what he called the "higher nervous activity" in animals. What changed his line of enquiry was a sense that he could learn little more about digestive functions until he had investigated the workings of the brain and nervous system, which often seemed to influence digestion. He then became so deeply absorbed in the implications of this new study that he concentrated on it until his death in 1936, at the age of eighty-six.

Pavlov was one of the Russian scientists of the old régime whose work Lenin thought valuable enough to encourage after the Revolution; and even though extremely cated connections between the main brain centres) might still swallow food placed within its mouth; but it needed a brain cortex and means of forming complicated conditioned responses, if it were to learn that food would be given only after an electric shock of a certain definite strength, or after a metronome had been heard beating at one particular rate and no other.

In discussing the "weak inhibitory" type, Pavlov pronounced that though the basic temperamental pattern is inherited, every dog has been conditioned since birth by varied environmental influences which may produce long-lasting inhibitory patterns of behaviour under certain stresses. The final pattern of behaviour in any given dog will therefore reflect both its own constitutional temperament and specific patterns of behaviour induced by environmental stresses.

Pavlov's experiments led him to pay increasing care to the need for classifying dogs according to their inherited constitutional temperaments before he subjected them to any of his more detailed experiments in conditioning. This was because different responses to the same experimental stress or conflict situation came from dogs of different temperaments. When a dog broke down and exhibited some abnormal pattern of behaviour, its treatment would also depend primarily on its constitutional type. Pavlov confirmed, for instance, that bromides are of great assistance in restoring nervous stability to dogs who have broken down, but that the doses of sedative required by a dog of the "strong excitatory" type is *five to eight times greater* than that required by a "weak inhibitory" dog of exactly the same body weight. In World War II the same general rule applied to human subjects who had temporarily broken down under battle and bombing stress and needed "front line sedation". The required doses varied greatly according to their temperamental types.

Towards the end of his life, when he was experimentally applying his discoveries about dogs to research in human psychology, Pavlov gave increasing attention to what happened when the higher nervous system of his dogs was strained beyond the limits of normal response; and compared the results with clinical reports on various types of acute and chronic mental breakdown in human beings. He found that severer and more prolonged stresses could be applied to normal dogs of the "lively" or "calm imperturbable" type without causing a breakdown, than to those of the "strong excitatory" and "weak inhibitory" types.

Pavlov came to believe that this "transmarginal" (it has also been termed "ultraboundary" or "ultramaximal") inhibition which eventually overcame even the two former types—changing their whole behaviour dramatically—could be essentially protective. When it occurred, the brain might have no other means left of avoiding damage due to fatigue and nervous stress. He found a means of examining the degree of protective "transmarginal" inhibition in any dog at any given time: by using his salivary gland conditioned reflex technique. Though the dog's general behaviour might seem normal, at first sight, the amount of saliva being secreted would tell him what was beginning to happen in its brain.

In these tests, the dog would be given a definite signal, such as the beating of a metronome at a certain rate, or the passing of a weak electric current into its leg, before being given food. After a time the signal would provoke an anticipatory flow of saliva, without the need of letting the dog see or smell the food. A conditioned reflex having thus been established in the brain between a signal and the expectation of food, the amount of saliva secreted could be precisely measured in drops, and any changes in the response of the brain conditioned reflexes and induced patterns, could be plainly registered.

Here let me digress by emphasizing the relevance of Pavlov's experiments on conditioned reflexes to the ordinary happenings of everyday human life. Much human behaviour is the result of the conditioned behaviour patterns implanted in the brain, especially during childhood. These may persist almost unmodified, but more often become gradually adapted to changes of environment. But the older the person, the less easily can he improvise new conditioned responses to such changes; the tendency then is to make the environment fit his, or her, increasingly predictable responses. Much of our human life consists also in the unconscious following of conditioned behaviour patterns originally acquired by hard study. A clear example is the way a car-driver builds up numerous and varied conditioned responses before being able to negotiate a crowded city street without paying much conscious attention to the process—this is often called "driving automatically". If the driver then gets into the open country, he will change to a new pattern of automatic behaviour. The human brain is, in fact, constantly adapting itself reflexly to changes of environment; although, as with car-driving, the first lessons in any given process may demand difficult, and even tedious, efforts of concentration.

Human and canine brains are obliged to build up a series of both positive and negative conditioned responses and behaviour patterns. Most people in business and the Armed Forces learn by experience to behave negatively in the presence of their superiors; and positively, even perhaps aggressively, in that of their juniors. Pavlov showed that the nervous system of dogs develops extraordinary powers of discrimination in building up these positive and negative responses. He showed that a dog can be made to salivate when a tone of 500 vibrations a minute is sounded, if this is a food signal; but not if the rate is only 490, and no food can therefore be expected.

Negative conditioned responses are no less important than the positive ones, since members of civilized societies must learn how to control normal aggressive responses almost automatically, though sometimes obliged to release them in a split second when a vital emergency arises. Emotional attitudes also become both positively and negatively conditioned: one learns an almost automatic revulsion from certain classes of people, and an automatic attraction to others. Even such words as Catholic and Protestant, Worker and Employer, Socialist and Conservative, Republican and Democrat, evoke very strong conditioned responses.

One of Pavlov's most important findings was exactly what happens to conditioned behaviour patterns when the brain of a dog is "transmarginally" stimulated by stresses and conflict beyond its capacity for habitual response. He could bring about what he called a "rupture in higher nervous activity" by employing four main types of imposed stresses.

The first was, simply, an increased intensity of the signal to which the dog was conditioned; thus he would gradually increase the voltage of the electric current applied to its leg as a food signal. When the electric shock became a little too strong for its system, the dog began to break down.

A second powerful way of achieving the same result was to increase the time between the giving of the signal and the arrival of food. A hungry dog might be conditioned to receive food, say, five seconds after the warning signal. Pavlov would then greatly prolong the period between a signal and the giving of food. Signs of unrest and abnormal behaviour might become immediately evident in the less stable of his dogs. He found, in fact, that the dogs' brains revolted against any abnormal prolongation of waiting under stress; breakdown occurred when a dog had to exert very strong or very protracted inhibition. (Human beings, too, often find prolonged periods of anxious waiting for an event more trying than when it finally comes.)

Pavlov's third way of producing a breakdown was to confuse them by anomalies in the conditioning signals given—continued positive and negative signals being given one after the other. The hungry dog became uncertain what would happen next, and how to face these confused circumstances. This could disrupt its normal nervous stability—just as happens with human beings.

A fourth way of producing a breakdown was to tamper with a dog's physical condition by subjecting it to long periods of work, gastro-intestinal disorders, fevers, or by disturbing its glandular balance. Though the three other means listed above had failed to produce a breakdown in a particular dog, this might be engineered later by using the same sort of stresses immediately after the removal of its sexual glands, or during an intestinal disorder. The advantage taken of debilitation and other changes of bodily function in human beings for their political and religious conversion will be discussed later. In some cases, Pavlov's findings may have been exploited; in others, anticipated.

Pavlov found not only that after castration or intestinal disorders a breakdown might occur even in temperamentally stable dogs; but also that the new behaviour pattern occurring afterwards might become a fixed element in the dog's way of life, though it had long recovered from the debilitating experience.

In the "weak inhibitory" type of dog new neurotic patterns thus implanted could often be readily removed again: doses of bromide might be enough to achieve this—though they did not alter the dog's fundamental weakness of temperament. But in "calm imperturbable" or "lively" dogs who needed castration, for instance, before they could be nervously disrupted, Pavlov found that the newly implanted pattern was more often ineradicable once the dog had recovered its normal physical health. He suggested that this was due to the natural toughness of the nervous systems in such dogs. The new patterns of behaviour had been difficult to implant without a temporarily induced debilitation; now they might be held with as much tenacity as the old.

The relevance of this last experiment to similar changes of behaviour in humans hardly needs to be emphasized: towards the end of a long period of physical illness, or after a period of severe debilitation (sometimes produced by enforced fasting), people of "strong character" are often known to make a dramatic change in their beliefs and convictions. If they then recover strength, they may remain true to the new orientation for the rest of their lives. Case-histories of people "converted" in times of famine or war, or in prison, or after harrowing adventures at sea, or in the jungle, or when brought to destitution by their own self-will, are frequent. The same phenomenon is often observed in both psychotic and neurotic patients who have suffered from glandular operations, fevers, loss of weight and the like, and only then developed their abnormal patterns of behaviour: if they had strong previous personalities, these new patterns may persist long after physical recovery.

Pavlov established that the ability of a dog to resist heavy stress would fluctuate according to the state of its nervous system and its general health. But once protective "transmarginal" inhibition had been induced, some very strange changes in the functioning of the dog's brain took place. And these changes could not only be measured with some precision by the amounts of saliva secreted in response to conditioned food stimuli, but were not liable, as when human beings have analogous experiences, to subjective distortions: there was no question, that is to say, of the dogs trying to explain away or rationalize their behaviour after having been subjected to these tests.

Three distinct and progressive stages of "transmarginal" inhibition were identified by Pavlov in the course of his experiments. The first he called the "equivalent" phase of cortical brain activity. In this phase, all stimuli, of whatever strength, resulted only in the same amounts of saliva being produced. The observation is comparable to the frequent reports by normal people in periods of intense fatigue, that there is very little difference between their emotional reactions to important or trivial experiences. And though the feelings of a normal, healthy person will vary greatly, according to the strength of the stimuli experienced, nervously ill people often complain that they become unable to feel sorrow and joy as acutely as before. As the result of fatigue and debilitation, in fact, a man may find to his chagrin that the excitement at receiving a legacy of ten thousand pounds is no higher than if it were one of sixpence; his condition then probably approximates to the "equivalent" phase of exhausted cortical activity identified by Pavlov in his dogs.

When even stronger stresses are applied to the brain, the "equivalent" phase of "transmarginal inhibition" may be succeeded by a "paradoxical" phase, in which weak stimuli produce livelier responses than stronger stimuli have done. The reason for this is not far to seek: the stronger stimuli are now only increasing the "protective inhibition"; but the weaker ones still produce positive responses. Thus the dog refuses food accompanied by a strong stimulus, but accepts it if the stimulus is weak enough. This "paradoxical" phase can also occur in human behaviour where the emotional stress is heavy, as will be shown in a later chapter. On such occasions, the individual's normal behaviour has been reversed to a degree that seems quite irrational not only to a detached observer, but to the patient himself—unless either of them happens to have studied Pavlov's experiments on dogs.

In the third stage of "protective" inhibition, which Pavlov called the "ultra-paradoxical", positive conditioned responses suddenly switch to negative ones; and negative ones to positive. The dog may then, for instance, attach itself to a laboratory attendant whom it has previously disliked, and try to attack the master whom it has previously loved. Its behaviour, in fact, becomes exactly opposed to all its previous conditioning.

The possible relevance of these experiments to sudden religious and political conversion should be obvious even to the most sceptical: Pavlov has shown by repeated and repeatable experiment just how a dog, like a man, can be conditioned to hate what it previously loved, and love what it previously hated. Similarly, one set of behaviour patterns in man can be temporarily replaced by another that altogether contradicts it; not by persuasive indoctrination alone, but also by imposing intolerable strains on a normally functioning brain.

Pavlov also showed that when "transmarginal inhibition" began to supervene in a dog, a state of brain activity similar to that seen in human hysteria might result. This can cause an abnormal suggestibility to the influences of the environment. His case-histories frequently include reports on hypnoidal or hypnotic states in dogs. Clinical reports on the behaviour of human beings under hypnosis, as well as in various conditions of hysteria, abound in description of abnormalities corresponding with those noted in Pavlov's "equivalent", "paradoxical" and "ultra-paradoxical" phases of breakdown in dogs. In states of human fear and excitement the most wildly improbable suggestions can be accepted by apparently sensible people; as in August, 1914, a rumour that Russian soldiers were travelling through England "with snow still on their boots" swept the country, and was so circumstantial that for a while it affected German strategy; or as in the earlier stages of the Second World

War, rumour continually reported the English renegade William Joyce ("Lord Haw-Haw") as having mentioned in a broadcast that the church clock of a particular village—the name of which always varied with the telling—was three minutes slow.

Summary of Above Findings

1. Dogs, like human beings, respond to imposed stresses or conflict situations according to their different types of inherited temperament. The four basic types correspond with those described as humours by the ancient Greek physician Hippocrates.

2. A dog's reactions to normal stress depend not only on its inherited constitution, but also on environmental influences to which it has been exposed. These alter the details of its behaviour, but do not change the basic temperamental pattern.

3. Dogs, like human beings, break down when stresses or conflicts become too great for their nervous system to master.

4. At the point of breakdown, their behaviour begins to vary from that normally characteristic of their inherited temperamental type and previous conditioning.

5. The amount of stress or conflict that a dog can master without breaking down varies with its physical condition. A lowering of resistance can be brought about by such things as fatigue, fevers, drugs, and glandular changes.

6. When the nervous system has been stimulated "transmarginally" (that is to say, beyond its capacity to re-

spond normally) for long periods, a dog's responses eventually become inhibited, whatever its temperamental type may be. In the two less stable types, the "weak inhibitory" and the "strong excitatory", breakdown will also occur sooner than in the two stronger types, the "lively" and the "calm imperturbable".

7. This "transmarginal" inhibition is protective and results in altered behaviour. Three distinguishable phases of increasingly abnormal behaviour occur:

a. The so-called "equivalent" phase, in which the brain gives the same response to both strong and weak stimuli.

b. The so-called "paradoxical" phase, in which the brain responds more actively to weak stimuli than to strong.

c. The so-called "ultra-paradoxical" phase in which conditioned responses and behaviour patterns turn from positive to negative; or from negative to positive.

8. When stresses imposed on the nervous system of dogs result in "transmarginal protective inhibition", a state of brain activity can also occur resembling hysteria in man.

* * *

Pavlov learned a great deal by observing the effect on his dogs of accidental occurrences, as well as of planned experiments. A crucial occasion was the Leningrad flood in 1924. We have already reported how in the "equivalent", "paradoxical" and "ultra-paradoxical" phases conditioned reflexes can be disorganized and reversed. It was the Leningrad flood that gave him the clue as to how the brain might also be wiped almost clean, at least temporarily, of all the conditioned behaviour patterns recently implanted in it. Just before his death, Pavlov told an American physiologist that the observations made on this occasion had also convinced him that every dog had its "breaking point"—provided that the appropriate stress was found and properly applied to its brain and nervous system.[16]

Pavlov had implanted a whole set of various conditioned behaviour patterns in a group of dogs—before these were one day accidentally trapped by flood water, which flowed in under the laboratory door and rose gradually until they were swimming around in terror with heads at the tops of their cages. At the last moment a laboratory attendant rushed in, pulled them down through the water, and out of their cage doors to safety. This terrifying experience made some of the dogs switch from a state of acute excitement to one of severe "transmarginal protective inhibition", as described earlier in this chapter. On re-testing them afterwards, it was found that the recently implanted conditioned reflexes had also now all disappeared. However, other dogs which had faced the same ordeal merely by registering increased excitement were not similarly affected and the implanted behaviour patterns had persisted.

Pavlov eagerly followed up the clue. In addition to the abnormalities induced, in the "equivalent", "paradoxical" and "ultra-paradoxical" phases by lesser degrees of "protective inhibition", lay a further degree of inhibitory activity on which he had accidentally stumbled, capable, it seemed, of disrupting for the time being all recently implanted conditioned reflexes. Most dogs which had reached this stage could later have their, old conditioned behaviour patterns restored, but it might need months of patient work. Then Pavlov let a trickle of water run in under the door of the laboratory. All the dogs, and especially those who had had their recent patterns abolished, were so sensitive to the sight that they could always be affected again by this means, although apparently normal again in other respects.[11] That some of the still sensitized dogs had resisted total breakdown did not shake Pavlov's conviction that appropriate stresses, properly applied, could have profound effects on all of them.

Application of these findings about dogs to the mechanics of many types of religious and political conversion in human beings suggests that for conversion to be effective, the subject may first have to have his emotions worked upon until he reaches an abnormal condition of anger, fear or exaltation. If this condition is maintained or intensified by one means or another, hysteria may supervene, whereupon the subject can become more open to suggestions which in normal circumstances he would have summarily rejected. Alternatively, the "equivalent" or the "paradoxical" and "ultra-paradoxical" phases may occur. Or a sudden complete inhibitory collapse may bring about a suppression of previously held beliefs. All these happenings could be of help in bringing about new beliefs and behaviour patterns. The same phenomena will be noted in many of the more successful modern psychiatric treatments, discovered independently of one another. All the different phases of brain activity, from an increased excitement to emotional exhaustion and collapse in a terminal stupor, can be induced either by psychological means; or by drugs, or by shock treatments, produced electrically; or by simply lowering the sugar content of the patient's blood with insulin injections. And some of the best results in the psychiatric treatment of neuroses and psychoses occur from the inducing of states of "protective inhibition". This is often done by continuing artificially imposed stresses on the brain until a terminal stage of temporary emotional collapse and stupor is reached, after which, it seems that some of the new abnormal patterns may disperse, and the healthier ones can return or be implanted afresh in the brain.

* * *

So far, the results of acute strain and breakdown in the nervous system have been discussed, rather than its day-to-day functioning. Now, Pavlov believed that the higher centres of the canine and human brain were in a constant flux between excitation and inhibition. Just as one has to inhibit intellectual activity by sleeping perhaps for eight hours, in order to maintain it at adequate strength for the remaining sixteen of the twenty-four, so smaller areas of the brain cannot be kept functioning normally except by a frequent switching on and off. Pavlov wrote:

> If we could look through the skull into the brain of a con-
> sciously thinking person, and if the place of optimal excit-
> ability were luminous, then we should see playing over the
> cerebral surface a bright spot with fantastic, waving bor-
> ders, constantly fluctuating in size and form, and surrounded
> by a darkness, more or less deep, covering the rest of the
> hemispheres.[4]

Pavlov was here speaking only figuratively. Things are not so simple as that, and recent research suggests that the picture seen would be far more complex, but he was emphasizing that when one area of the brain is in a state of excitation, other areas can become inhibited as a result. It is impossible to concentrate consciously and deliberately on two different lines of thought at the same time. Attention switches quickly between one and the other, as often as required. Shakespeare wrote that no man "can hold a fire in his hand by thinking on the frosty Caucasus". Pavlov challenged this dictum by showing as it were, that if one's nervous system can become sufficiently aroused by concentrated and ecstatic visions of the Caucasus, the pain stimuli of the burned hand may be inhibited. Sherrington, the great English physiologist, is said to have remarked that Pavlov's findings on this had helped to explain how the Christian martyrs could die happily at the stake.[11]

Pavlov was able to show that focal areas of inhibition in the brain—perhaps producing, for example, a temporary hysterical loss of memory, of eyesight, or the use of limbs in man—may be complemented by large areas of excitation in other parts of the brain. This provides a physiological basis for Freud's observations that repressed emotional memories often lead to a condition of chronic anxiety about apparently unconnected matters. The pathological condition may also disappear when the repressed memory is restored to consciousness, so that the local inhibition disappears and so does the complementary excitation elsewhere.

Pavlov noted that when one small cortical area in a dog's brain reached what he called "a state of pathological inertia and excitation" which became fixed, repeated "stereotypy" of certain movements would follow. He concluded that if this cerebral condition could affect movement, it might also affect thought, stereotypically; and that a study of such small cortical areas in the brains of dogs might account for certain obsessions in human thinking. As a simple example: it might explain why many people are plagued by tunes persistently running in the head, and others by distressingly lascivious thoughts that neither prayer nor the exercise of will-power seem able to dispel—though they may suddenly disappear for no ascertainable reason.

In the last years of his life, Pavlov made another important observation about these areas of "pathological inertia and excitation": he found that these small areas were subject to the "equivalent", "paradoxical" and "ultra-paradoxical" phases of abnormal activity under stress which he had thought applicable only to much larger areas of the brain. This discovery caused him a pardonable exhilaration: it might well explain physiologically, for the first time, certain phenomena also observed in human beings when they begin to act abnormally. It is a well-known characteristic of mentally unhinged people to include others in their obsessions. Thus, if a man who has always been sensitive to criticism loses control of his senses, he is likely to complain that, wherever he goes, everyone slanders and talks against him. And women who have always been nervous of sexual attack will often be convinced by internal sensations that some known or unknown person has actually interfered with them. Pavlov thought, in fact, that what psychiatrists call the phenomenon of "projection" and "introjection"—when a persistent fear or desire is suddenly projected outwards or inwards into seeming actuality— might be given a physiological explanation in terms of local cerebral inhibition.

Pavlov found that some dogs of stable temperaments were more than usually prone to develop these "limited pathological points" in the cortex when at the point of breaking down under stress. New behaviour patterns resulted from them: it might be a compulsive and repetitive pawing at the experimental stand—such as also follows interference with glandular function or some form of physical debilitation. Once acquired by a dog of stable temperament, patterns of this sort are, he found, very difficult to eradicate. Which may help to explain why when human beings of strong character suddenly "find God", or take up vegetarianism, or become Marxists, they often tend to become confirmed fanatics with one-track minds: a small cortical point has, perhaps, reached a state of permanent "pathological inertia".

Two years before his death Pavlov wrote prophetically:

> I am no clinician. I have been, and remain, a physiologist and, of course, at present so late in life would have neither the time nor the possibility to become one. . . . But I shall certainly not be erring now if I say that clinicians, neurologists and psychiatrists, in their respective domains, will inevitably have to reckon with the following fundamental patho-physiological fact: the complete isolation of functionally pathological (at the aetiological moment) points of the cortex, the pathological inertness of the excitatory process, and the ultra-paradoxical phase.[4]

He was right. Not only clinicians, neurologists and psychiatrist, but the ordinary people the world over have felt the impact of his simple type of mechanistic research—some of them to their cost. Further work may modify some

of the conclusions: but he has provided simple and sometimes convincing physiological explanations of much that
the Western world still tends to shroud in vaguer psychological theory.

It is admittedly unpleasant to think of animals being subjected to painful stress for the sake of scientific research.
Even though Pavlov was no sadist and as interested in curing his dogs' nervous breakdowns as causing them, some
of his experiments would hardly be tolerated in England
today. But, as the work has been done carefully, and reported accurately we should not let any legitimate feelings
blind our eyes to its value in human psychiatry or to its
possible significance in the political and religious fields.

CHAPTER 2

Animal and Human Behaviour Compared

We have repeatedly heard it argued that comparisons between the behaviour of man and animals, such as those made in Chapter 1, are invalid; because man has a soul, or at least a far more highly developed brain and intelligence. Yet since experiments on the digestive and glandular systems of animals have proved helpful in framing the fundamental laws which govern these systems in the human body, why not experiments on the higher nervous system? If the analogy between the human and canine digestion and glandular systems had been disallowed, and animal experimentation forbidden, general medicine might still be in the same backward state as modern psychiatry; the fact being that psychological theory has too often taken the place of scientific experiment as one of the main means of accounting for normal and abnormal patterns of human behaviour.

This chapter, it is hoped, will show that Pavlov's experiments on dogs are so remarkably applicable to certain problems of human behaviour that the remark "Men are not dogs" becomes at times almost irrelevant. The behaviour of the human brain, when subjected during World War II to strains and stresses, provided a remarkable opportunity for testing Pavlov's analogical conclusions. It will therefore be convenient to make a résumé of some of our own published wartime observations and others recorded and discussed in journals and books by Sir Charles Symonds,[17] Swank,[18] Grinker[19] and others.

In June, 1944, for instance, many shell-shocked patients were being admitted to emergency hospitals in England both from the Normandy beachhead and from blitzed London. Some of these showed all the usual symptoms of anxiety and depression observed in peacetime psychiatric practice. Others were in a state of simple but profound exhaustion, generally accompanied by a very marked loss of weight. Still others made gross and uncoordinated, yet regular, jerking and writhing movements, which were accentuated by temporary loss of speech or a stammer, or perhaps an explosive form of talking. One group of patients had reached various degrees of collapse and stupor.[6] It was in these acute cases that Pavlov's *Conditioned Reflexes and Psychiatry*, which we were then studying for the first time, proved most enlightening: parallels between their behaviour and that of Pavlov's dogs when subjected to experimental stresses leapt to the eye.

Roy Swank and his colleagues have, since 1945, published a series of papers based on their study of some five thousand combat casualties in the Normandy campaign, nearly all of whom were Americans.[20] His detailed findings point to the overwhelming influence of the fear of death, and of continued stress, on the development of combat exhaustion. He also emphasizes that the:

> . . . first reaction of the men to combat was fear. . . . By far the greater number of men controlled their fears, gained knowledge of combat and became confident, "battle-wise" troops.

It was only:

> . . . after a period of efficient combat which varied with the
> men and the severity of the combat, that the first evidence
> of combat exhaustion appeared.

The "protective inhibition" reported by Pavlov in his study
of dogs throws light on what then followed:

> The men noticed a state of constant fatigue, not relieved by
> several days of rest. They lost their ability to distinguish the
> various noises of combat. They became unable to tell friendly
> from enemy artillery and small bombs, and their location.

"Excitatory" symptoms could also become uncontrolled.
Thus:

> They became easily startled and confused, lost their confi-
> dence and became tense. They were irritable, frequently
> "blew their tops", over-responded to all stimuli; for example,
> they would "hit the dirt" on the slightest provocation
> whereas, before this, caution was reserved for selected ap-
> propriate stimuli.

Swank reports the final dramatic change from "excitation"
to "inhibition", also described by Pavlov in his dogs:

> This state of general hyper-reactivity was followed insidi-
> ously by another group of symptoms referred to before as
> "emotional exhaustion". The men became dull and listless,
> they became mentally and physically retarded, preoccupied
> and had increasing difficulty in remembering details. This
> was accompanied by indifference and apathy, and by a dull,
> apathetic facies. . . . The uniformity of the histories when

subsequently checked was an indication that, for the most part, these complaints were not exaggerated or fabricated.

He points out that, before being subjected to such stresses:

> . . . the average combat soldier was (probably) more stable than the average civilian, since obviously unstable individuals had been excluded prior to combat. . . . By and large, the men under consideration were from "high morale units" and were willing soldiers. It seemed evident that shirking played a small part and was almost entirely confined to men with short combat records.

Sir Charles Symonds, discussing his medical experiences in the Royal Air Force during the same war, similarly concluded that the tension resulting from a prolonged exercise of courage was a most important element in the development of emotional exhaustion.[17] These were our findings too, after we had dealt with several thousands of civilian and Service patients admitted to specialized neurosis units in the Emergency Medical Service hospitals.

The most interesting of all Swank's findings to this study of religious and political conversion, concerned the time-rate of breakdown under continued battle stresses (see diagram):

> Combat exhaustion may appear in as few as fifteen or twenty days, or in as many as forty or fifty days, instead of in approximately thirty days, as it did in the majority of men. One thing alone seems to be certain: practically all infantry soldiers suffer from a neurotic reaction eventually, if they are subjected to the stress of modern combat continuously and long enough.

In November, 1944, Swank still felt that an occasional soldier, "perhaps less than 2%", belonged to the group capable of withstanding combat stress for an inordinate length of time. But we find him reporting in 1946:

This seemed true . . . in November, 1944. Since then we have concluded that all normal men eventually suffer combat exhaustion in prolonged continuous and severe combat. The exceptions to this rule are psychotic (insane) soldiers, and a number of examples of this have been observed.

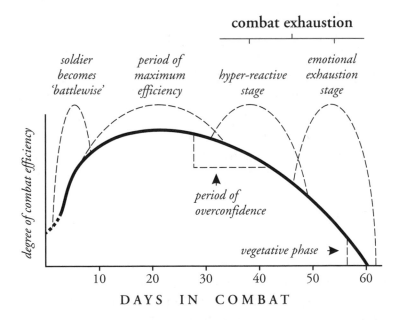

Portrayal of the relation of stress and the development of combat exhaustion to the combat efficiency (heavy black line) of the average American soldier.[21]

Since certain techniques of religious and political conversion can be made quite as fearful and as exhausting to the brain as active combat experiences, the importance of Swank's findings must be very heavily stressed. His statistical and clinical facts should be brought home especially to those who like to believe that the avoidance of breakdown in battle, or under brain-washing, is simply a matter of exercising sufficient will-power and courage. On the contrary, the continued exercise of will-power and courage may, in certain circumstances, exhaust the brain and hasten a final collapse. When dogs co-operate in experiments testing their tolerance to stress they are all the easier to break down: the loyal efforts they make prove their own undoing.

Normally, it seems, the human nervous system, like the dog's, is in a state of dynamic equilibrium between excitation and inhibition. But if subjected to excessive stimulation, it can pass into the same states of excessive excitation or excessive inhibition which Pavlov described in dogs. The brain then becomes incapable, for the time being, of its usual intelligent functioning. Numerous examples of this phenomenon have been reported in the medical literature: as when, for instance, hitherto normal front-line soldiers have passed into an intense "excitatory" state, running at random across no-man's-land, or dashing suicidally and uselessly into machine-gun fire. One man was reported in 1945 to have advanced twice under fire to help a friend whose leg had been blown off, but each time became so inhibited on arrival that he found himself unable to give first aid. Then he was suddenly overcome by acute excitement, banged his head repeatedly against a tree, and rushed wildly about calling for an ambulance; when the ambulance eventually arrived, he had himself forcibly strapped into it. Another soldier, after the death of a friend, tried to tackle a German tank single-handed; he had to be held down by his comrades and despatched to a psychiatric centre.[6] Uncontrolled cerebral excitation of this sort seems to be generally marked by an inhibition of normal judgment.

The state of "protective" inhibition, noted by Pavlov in dogs subjected to acute stress, also appears to be found in combat casualties; they often develop stupor, or loss of memory, loss of the use of limbs, fainting attacks, etc. Others become literally paralysed with fear. Others succumb to simple nervous exhaustion, and these are usually men of stable personality who, in addition to mental stress, have been deprived of food and sleep for long periods. Sir Edward Spears has described its occurrence in World War I:

> These were very bad times, when the trench, choked with dead and wounded, collapsed under the bombardment, when men worked with frenzy to dig out a comrade, pulled him out with his face collapsed, then dug no more. At such times often had come a stupor, a kind of overpowering sleepiness, merciful but which the officer had to conquer. . .[22]

In some cases, the inhibition seemed limited to small focal regions in the brain. One patient, for instance, is reported as stammering only at the mention of an officer who had called him a coward. Dumbness, succeeded by stammering during recovery, was common. Such frequent disturbances of what Pavlov termed "man's secondary signalling system" may be explained, as he suggested, by its greater sensitivity to excessive stimulation, consequent on its more recent evolutionary development. Other forms of focal brain inhibition were seen in patients with fixed, rigid faces, complaining of a lump in the throat; or with a bent back and weak, but not completely paralysed, legs. Such complete paralysis was uncommon though the gait was often slowed down. Pavlov noted a similar progressive inhibition in dogs submitted to bombardment of stimuli; it started in the mouth and the fore parts of the body, and took some time to reach the hind legs.[6]

Patients often showed areas of both focal excitation and focal inhibition. There might be rigidity or inhibition of facial movements or speech, combined with severe tremors of the body and hands. Or a paralysis of speech might be combined with neck jerkings. Acute anxiety was often marked by inability to swallow. The upper part of the body might shake violently while the lower part remained still. A set or grinning face might be accompanied by tremors, jerks, and writhings of other parts of the body.

Sudden changes from excitation to inhibition, or contrariwise, were sometimes reported in these "fluctuating" cases. One man, for instance, had lain trembling in a ditch, half paralysed with fear, when his company was ordered to attack. But as soon as his officer taunted him with: "A girl would put up a better show", he suddenly became wildly excited, shouted "Come on boys!" leapt out of the trench to the attack, and then fainted. Other soldiers ran about shouting in panic, this phase being followed by a sudden dumbness. One man had fallen down paralysed and speechless in a village street which was under bombardment; but when picked up by his comrades, suddenly began to shout and struggle.[6]

It is important to note that in many cases of breakdown under intolerable stress, reported by various writers, no motive of immediate gain could be discerned. On the contrary, it often occurred just when normal behaviour would have been much more likely to secure the victim's personal safety. These sudden states of total inhibition or collapse after severe stresses, recall Pavlov's "transmarginal" phase in dogs. Other examples of this extreme form of inhibition were observed when men arrived at the hospital in almost complete hysterical stupor. Similar inhibitory states were later induced experimentally, when we made patients relive their battle or bombing experiences, under drugs, and they grew very excited.

These abnormal mental states may be succeeded in humans, as in Pavlov's dogs, by what he termed a "dynamic stereotypy"—that is, a new functional system in the brain which requires increasingly less work by the nervous system to maintain it. The repetitive pattern of movements or thoughts thus exhibited by some patients did not yield easily to simple methods of treatment, such as removal to hospital and rest. Further strong stimuli might be needed to disperse the new and highly abnormal patterns now implanted. But one group of patients reacted better to heavy sedation with drugs than to re-stimulation, among them some in states of confused excitement, who had heard imaginary noises and voices, and were now developing fresh fantasies. Unlike the typical peacetime patient who suffers from similar hallucinations, they quickly improved after a period of deep sleep and complete rest induced by sedatives—as Pavlov's "strong excitatory" type of dog had also done when given large doses of bromide soon after an acute breakdown.

Such responses to stress, of course, occurred only in a small proportion of soldiers and civilian defence workers in the Blitz. The remainder were able to enjoy periods of rest, between their ordeals, long enough to fend off a collapse; "breaking-point" being reached only after repeated or long continued periods of stress. The exception was when a sudden enormous strain had been imposed on the nervous system; for example, a very near miss in a bomb explosion. In such cases, soldiers and civilians alike, although behaving to all outward appearances in a deliberate and conscious manner, might retain very little memory if any of their subsequent behaviour, because "transmarginal inhibition" had abruptly supervened; later, they might with equal suddenness regain consciousness and worry about where they had been during the two or three previous hours. Some memories of this lost period might return spontaneously later, or be recovered under sedatives which relaxed the inhibition.

The "equivalent" phase of "transmarginal inhibition", described by Pavlov in his experiments on dogs, seemed frequent among our patients in the war. Normally energetic and active people would sit about complaining that nothing interested them any longer, that they had ceased to feel joy or sorrow whatever might happen. This phase would gradually pass off after rest and treatment but, in some cases, persisted for a long time.

Fascinating examples of human behaviour corresponding with Pavlov's "paradoxical" phase were also seen. Before reading the accounts of his experiments on dogs, we were at a loss to understand a case like the following. A patient of normal previous personality had been subjected to very severe bombing stress. When asked to hold out his hands and let the doctor see whether they had a tremor, he obeyed; but suddenly found himself unable to lower them again while he was being watched. This worried him, but what he found worse, he said, was that he could lower them if he stopped trying to do so, or thought about something else; he might, for instance, automatically lower them to feel in his pocket for a matchbox. In fact, the strong stimulus directed to making him do something which he wanted produced no response, yet a smaller undirected stimulus remained effective. In a short time this condition, to his great relief, passed off. We also had many patients suffering from severe fright—paralysis of the limbs; the harder the man tried to move them, the more paralysed they became. Yet if he stopped worrying about the difficulty, he might suddenly find it would improve. This "paradoxical" phase seems to occur as frequently in mental as in physical experience. A simple instance is a condition which most brain-workers are liable to while over-working: they try to remember names or words, but cannot do so until they have stopped trying.

Both in peace and war, normally aggressive people may all at once develop uncharacteristic feelings of cowardice, and feel for a while the uselessness of going on. And people who normally enjoy life the most may suddenly feel the strongest desire to die. Sudden unexplained aversions to people previously loved or admired are also met with in these "paradoxical" and "ultra-paradoxical" phases, so is extremely aggressive behaviour, alternating unpredictably with abject submission.

During the Blitz a series of bombs fell in the grounds of our hospital near London, and several civilian patients were killed by one direct hit. The hospital contained many patients already under treatment for acute war neuroses, and paradoxical reversals of behaviour under stress now kept appearing and disappearing. A bomb explosion might make a patient suddenly unable to move an arm, as described above. He was then given an intravenous injection of barbiturate to relax the functioning of his brain—whereupon he would immediately recover the use of his arm. But he might also recover it without the help of drugs when he calmed down again after the raid. Many of these sudden switches from aggression to submission, or vice versa, also occurred with no obvious reason for the change.

Pavlov's findings, that severe focal excitation on one area of a dog's brain could cause profound reflex inhibition of other areas, seemed most applicable to these instances of human behaviour. Patients would be admitted with trembling hands and blank, exhausted or "bomb-happy" faces. Yet they might then presently come to the doctor and demand their discharge to return to their civilian or military duties. Usually the doctor would suppose that the patient was "shooting a line", and tell him to stop being foolish and to go back to his ward. But it was plain to the doctor who had studied Pavlov's experiments that such requests could be prompted by a temporary fixation on the idea of having to get out of hospital and back to duty at all costs; and that it had caused a reflex inhibition of all thoughts about his deplorable physical and nervous state—which would certainly prevent him from undertaking any work whatsoever. If he was then quietly told that his return to duty must be postponed and given the reasons for this, he might suddenly realize again how things really were and become more co-operative. The expression "bomb-happy" was a useful coinage: it perfectly described how a bombing, with its consequent fear reactions, could destroy the power of integrated thinking about the past, present, or future in survivors who had caught the full brunt. Yet sedatives correctly administered on the spot or in specialized centres and hospitals could quickly restore them to normal habits of thought; which suggested that the symptoms elsewhere ascribed to moral cowardice or simple malingering had often been produced merely by the temporary failure of normal brain function.[23]

It is important to observe that such states of abnormal behaviour in hitherto normal people, though rapidly dispersible under prompt and proper sedation, would also disperse after a time of their own accord. In a few weeks or months, little external evidence of such behaviour remained. Fewer really incapacitating war-neuroses in persons of previous mental stability appear to persist ten years after World War II than after World War I. Yet, as with Pavlov's dogs after the Leningrad flood, sensitivity to what brought about their nervous disruption is doubtless still latent in men who seem well readjusted to ordinary civilian life. Any event which reminds them of their original neurosis may affect them as strongly as the sight of water flowing in under the laboratory door affected Pavlov's dogs.

Further evidence of the applicability of Pavlov's canine findings to problems of human psychology was found in the detailed response of our patients to treatment. Pavlov found heavy sedation extremely valuable in helping dogs which had broken down under imposed stresses. He obtained entirely different responses to treatment from dogs classified according to the four basic temperaments; and widely varying doses of sedatives were needed for the "strong excitatory" and the "weak inhibitory" dog of the same body weight. We found the same thing in patients given emergency "front-line" sedation when they broke down under severe bombing stresses; they could be classified in the same groups and the amount of sedative needed would vary considerably.

The value of heavy emergency front-line sedation in preventing acute neuroses from becoming chronic had been repeatedly observed quite early in the war.[24] But the need for differential dosage was not yet generally appreciated, and in most centres fairly standardized doses were prescribed for all types of persons breaking down under battle or blitz stresses. But as soon as Pavlov's findings became available and we reconsidered this point, we decided that the nervous system of man responded to extreme stresses in much the same way as that of dogs.

Under severe and prolonged stresses people of a "strong excitatory" or "weak inhibitory" temperament would, as already described, reach states of uncontrolled excitement or paralysed inhibition. The other two temperamental types—namely, the "lively", or "controlled excitatory", able to fight back giving as much punishment as he took; and the "phlegmatic" type, seemingly unmoved by most ordinary stresses—also occurred in men as well as in dogs. The predominance of "inhibitory" symptoms when the victim finally breaks down (an important matter when we come to consider political conversion and brain-washing) was shown by a 1942 finding and report that, around the time of Dunkirk and the London Blitz, no less than 144 out of 1,000 consecutive admissions to a crisis centre for civilian and military patients near London had suffered from temporary losses of memory.[25] Such loss of memory is often a simple inhibitory response of the brain to overwhelming stresses it cannot deal with by any other means; and a peace-time psychiatrist rarely meets more than one or two cases of this particular hysterical complaint in the course of a year.

The need for varying the sedation dosages in humans, according to whether they were very "strong excitatory" or "weak inhibitory", became very clear in the following kinds of circumstance. Most soldiers who broke down on the Normandy beachheads were, at first, given immediate front-line sedation, and only those who did not respond to this treatment were returned to neurosis centres in England. By then, three to seven days of sleep had already been induced by heavy doses of sedation. The patients sent back for treatment in our hospitals were found to have an abnormally high percentage of psychotics or neurotics in their family histories. Many had themselves suffered from pre-war nervous breakdowns and consulted other psychiatrists; their symptoms usually suggested the "weak inhibitory" type of Pavlov's classification. But when the casualty clearing stations on the beachheads temporarily overflowed, patients were sent to us before a reasonable period of heavy sedation could be allowed them. These showed far more acute and severe excitatory reactions than the former batch, but many of them responded well to the large doses of sedatives prescribed, and could soon return to at least modified duties. Yet the same doses administered to the "weak inhibitory" patients had (as in Pavlov's dogs) served only to aggravate the inhibition, so that many arrived with paralyses or inhibitory stammers, or even in deep hysterical stupors.[6] Experience shows that inhibitory responses in men of this temperament can, in fact, be helped by sedation, but only with much smaller doses than those benefiting the "strong excitatory" types. Pavlov had explained this phenomenon as follows:

> The best therapy against neuroses, in agreement with the findings of this clinic, are bromides. . . . But the dose should be regulated accurately—for the strong type five to eight times greater than for the weak type.

And again:

> Formerly we came to an erroneous conclusion here; not regulating the dose of bromide correspondingly to the type we thought that its administration in weak animals was never helpful, and that in large doses it was injurious . . . a most important part of the therapy is the exact dosing corresponding to the precise type of nervous system.[4]

The tendency of physical debilitation to hasten a breakdown under imposed stresses had been noted by Pavlov in his dogs; and the same phenomenon was observed again and again in our patients. Those with previously stable temperaments could often be distinguished from the unstable types by noting whether or not they had lost weight before first reporting sick. During the Blitz, civilians would often start complaining of neurotic symptoms, and be unable to understand why they had developed such severe anxieties about bombing when they had hitherto remained unaffected by it for weeks or months. In such cases it was frequently found that they had lost from fifteen to thirty pounds in weight before this ever-increasing sensitivity to bombing stimuli became noticeable. But once these abnormal reactions set in after a severe loss of weight, they could not necessarily be dispersed by fattening the patient up again, though this was done in the general interests of his health, and were as likely as not to remain fixed.

The most stable types might collapse only after a loss of thirty pounds in weight, caused by lack of nourishing food, lack of sleep, and similar debilitating factors characteristic of wartime. But patients who reported similar symptoms without any loss of weight, and had therefore put up less fight were likely to be chronically neurotic types, unlikely to respond to any routine treatment.

Very many of the more spectacular reactions to war stresses could be labelled as "anxiety hysteria". Indeed, one of the commonest final reactions to stress, in patients of previously stable temperament, as opposed to the unstable, was the development of hysterical responses. Pavlov gave the same label to similar responses in his dogs, at the point of breakdown under imposed stresses, and constantly diagnosed hypnoidal or hypnotic states in them.[4] The frequency of hysterical reactions to severe imposed stresses in both humans and animals is of the greatest significance here. Descriptions of hysteria in all psychiatric textbooks record bizarre symptoms which do not become always understandable except by analogy with Pavlov's mechanistic experiments on dogs. The mental aberration characteristic of hysteria is often similar to a form of "protective inhibition", and so is hysterical paralysis. Even in peacetime hysteria, something approaching the "bomb-happy" phase of acute war neurosis can be discerned.

Once a state of hysteria has been induced in men or dogs by mounting stresses which the brain can no longer tolerate, "protective inhibition" is likely to supervene. This will disturb the individual's ordinary conditioned behaviour patterns. In human beings, states of greatly increased suggestibility are also found; and so are their opposite, namely, states in which the patient is deaf to all suggestions, however sensible. Hysteria has produced sudden and unexplained panics in most wars; often among troops famous for their battle-record. Among the finest fighters of the ancient world were: Caesar's veteran legionaries, and from the bravest of these he chose his Eagle-bearers. Yet after ten to thirteen years of continuous campaigning in Gaul they also could break down suddenly. Suetonius[26] records two cases of hysterical Eagle-bearers running away on different occasions. When Caesar tried to stop them, the first attempted to strike him with the sharp butt of the Eagle, the second left the Eagle in his hand and rushed on. But these are extreme cases; hysteria was also evidenced in the susceptibility to rumours of Londoners during the Blitz. Brain exhaustion led them to believe stories about "Lord Haw-Haw's" broadcasts from Germany which they would have at once rejected as untrue when in a more relaxed and less exhausted state. The anxiety engendered by the Fall of France, the Battle of Britain, and the Blitz created a state in which large groups of persons were temporarily able to accept new and sometimes strange beliefs without criticism. The mechanism of increasing states of suggestibility will be discussed repeatedly in later chapters; since this is one of the means of indoctrinating ordinary people both religiously and politically.

Critical faculties may become inhibited in these states of anxiety hysteria. "He whom the gods wish to destroy, they first of all drive mad." Thus some soldiers and civilians in acute states of breakdown cannot be reassured by any remark however sensible; others accept reassurances, however foolishly phrased. Police forces in many parts of the world rely on this inhibition of critical faculties and normal judgment to obtain full confessions from prisoners subjected to debilitation or emotional stresses, without the need to injure them physically (see Chapter 9). The same phenomenon can also be turned to curative use by psychiatrists, as will be shown in due course. It enables them to suggest new attitudes to life, and new patterns of behaviour, in the hope that they will replace harmful ones.

Pavlov has drawn attention, in his lectures, to many other similarities between canine and human neuroses. Why varieties of neurotic behaviour in time of war have been stressed here, is because they have been so accurately reported by so many psychological "field-workers", and because they occurred among ordinary types of person rather than among the predominately neurotic and psychotic personality types who are admitted to psychiatric hospitals in peacetime. Pavlov was also presumably dealing with ordinary dogs. In both cases the brain was being subjected to unavoidable stresses. The dog isolated on his experimental stand, the soldier in his trench or lonely foxhole, and the civilian in a fire brigade or rescue squad, all had to take whatever came to them, and their ordeals were similar. In peacetime society an opportunity for escape is generally given those who find themselves in situations that make too great demands on their nervous system; hence the rarity among average people of strikingly abnormal behaviour under stress. And the civilian population, even in modern warfare, usually comes off better than the soldier; during the Blitz, for instance, Londoners who had begun to develop anxiety symptoms during bombing could often arrange to be evacuated or obtain a period of rest. But for the soldier it was generally a case of "They must conquer or die who have no retreat".

In inducing experimental neuroses in his dogs, Pavlov found it necessary, as a rule, to secure their co-operation. In human beings, neuroses are also commonest among those who try to overcome the stresses to which they are exposed. Like the dog on the experimental stand, who refuses to co-operate in an experiment, soldiers who run away before the first shot is heard may keep their nervous system intact, and thus avoid severe breakdown, until they are caught up by difficulties which they have hitherto escaped. There is something to be said for the Chinese Taoist philosophy which enjoins the avoidance of stress, as opposed to the philosophies of aggressive daring that still persist in Europe and North America.

Pavlov's findings also illuminate many varieties of abnormal behaviour noted in common forms of nervous and mental sickness. William Gordon[27] published a very interesting paper on this subject in 1948. He pointed out that the mature brain builds up systems of positive and negative conditioned responses by which the individual adapts himself to his environment, mostly basing his present behaviour on past experience, and that mental health is determined by the efficiency of such adaptation. In so severe a mental disorder as schizophrenia, a partial or complete reversal of most previous conditioning is observed. Gordon, like Pavlov, believes that schizophrenia results from the "ultra-paradoxical" phase of brain activity. He points out that schizophrenics are often described as having lost all interest in their former pleasures and pursuits, and then suddenly developing depraved, suicidal or anti-social behaviour. This change can sometimes be explained by showing that the patient now responds positively to his former negative conditioning, and negatively to his former positive conditioning.

How devastating a sudden reversal of one's positive and negative conditioning can be is described by Gordon in a series of apt illustrations. The human being develops eating habits in which a number of stimuli involving smell, vision, hearing, and taste all acquire strong positive conditioning, while others acquire equally strong negative responses. Some smells, for instance, may make a human mouth salivate—as with Pavlov's dogs—in anticipation of food; others cause nausea and a temporary loss of appetite. But mentally sick patients will suddenly start eating foods to which they previously had a repugnance, and refusing other foods which they used to enjoy.

Children are trained to urinate and defecate at definite times and in appropriate places. As Gordon points out, the sight or touch of the chamber-pot becomes a strongly *positive* conditioned response in the young child; whereas clothes, bedding, floors and furniture become *negatively* charged. But when the patient falls mentally sick, it is often observed that clothes, bedding, floors, etc., become positive for urination and defecation, and that it is almost impossible to make him use the lavatory-pan, commode or bed-pan provided, because these will now all elicit negative responses. Gordon also emphasizes the apparent "purposefulness" and "deliberateness" of the new activities.

Numerous other instances occur in very varied fields of human behaviour. Faulty conditioning in childhood, or a sudden reversal of conditioning brought about by nervous or mental sickness later in life, can cause havoc to the sexual function, which may become shamelessly erotic in the previously inhibited or totally inhibited in those of normal tendencies.

Obsessional thinking becomes particularly distressing when the "paradoxical" and "ultra-paradoxical" phases of brain activity supervene. The most conscientious of mothers can suddenly be obsessed with a fear that she may do harm to the child whom she loves more than all the world. People most afraid of dying can become obsessed with the idea that they may throw themselves from a window or on the live rail of an electric railway. They realize the abnormality of these thoughts, but the more they struggle against them, the stronger they tend to grow. The Christian Church has always been greatly exercised with the problem of how to exorcize evil thoughts which persist against one's will. One way sometimes recommended, is not to bother about having evil thoughts; there is another, which is to use prolonged prayer *and* fasting until point of temporary debilitation is reached, when a priest or holy man may be able to alter the behaviour patterns in the penitent's mind.

In a letter written to a brother Jesuit in May, 1634, Father Surin, an exorcist of the nuns of Loudun, describes in a religious setting what seems to be most distressing "paradoxical" and "ultra-paradoxical" brain disturbance brought on by the strain and anxiety of his psychotherapeutic exertions:

> The extremity in which I find myself is such that I have scarcely one free faculty. When I wish to speak, my mouth is closed; at mass I am suddenly stopped; at table I cannot convey the morsel to my lips; at confession I forget in a moment all my sins; and I feel that the devil comes and goes as in his own house, within me. Directly I awake, he is with me at prayer; he deprives me of my consciousness when he pleases; when my heart would expand itself in God, he fills it with rage; when I would watch, he sets me asleep; and . . . boasts that he is my master.[28]

It is not the purpose of this book to document all the possible occurrences in human beings of "equivalent", "paradoxical" and "ultra-paradoxical" phases with particular case-histories. This chapter has, however, suggested that, though "men are not dogs", it would be foolish indeed to continue to disregard entirely experimentation on the higher nervous activity of dogs as irrelevant to human psychology, or to the question of how a man's thoughts and beliefs can be effectively changed.

CHAPTER 3

The Use of Drugs in Psychotherapy

In the summer of 1940 we were already prescribing barbiturates, both in strong doses orally administered, as sedatives for overwrought Dunkirk survivors, and in small
intravenous doses to produce a semi-drunken state which
helped them to release some of their inhibited emotions of
terror, anger, frustration and despair. The value of the treatment, which had been in limited use before the war, was
confirmed during the subsequent London Blitz.[23] It has
since come to be called "drug abreaction"; the term "abreaction" dating from the time of Breuer and Freud's early
studies in the treatment of hysteria, when they observed
that some patients were helped by "just talking it out".[29]
Freud had found that "affectless memories, memories without any release of emotion", were almost useless; meaning
that unless a doctor could get his patients to relive the
emotions originally associated with a repressed experience
that had caused a neurosis the mere fact of his remembering the experience would not constitute a cure. Sadler consequently defined abreaction as a process of reviving the
memory of a repressed unpleasant experience and expressing in speech and action the emotions related to it, thereby
relieving the personality of its influence.[30]

In World War I, much the same abreactive treatment had
been successfully used, but for the most part with hypno-

tism not drugs; and it was then established that the experience responsible for a neurosis might also be one which the patient remembered intellectually, but the emotional associations of which he had repressed. Freud came to accept this finding as it became more and more obvious that neurotic symptoms could be caused by even well-remembered incidents in a patient's past.

In both World Wars abreaction, whether under drugs or hypnosis, had a definite place in the treatment of acute combat neuroses. Millais Culpin[31] wrote:

> Once the man's conscious resistance to discussing his war experiences was overcome, great mental relief followed the pouring out of emotionally charged incidents. It was as if the emotion pent up by this conscious resistance had by its tension given rise to symptoms. The memory, usually of a nature unsuspected by me, then came to the surface, its return being preceded perhaps by congestion of the face, pressing of the hands to the face, tremblings, and other bodily signs of emotion.

In 1920, William Brown[32] had suggested that emotional abreaction was often a far more efficient means of curing a war-neurotic than simple suggestion under hypnosis. "Suggestion removes the symptoms, but abreaction removes the cause of the symptoms by producing fully adequate reassociation." It is hoped to show, however, that suggestion may also have an important part to play in effecting cures by abreaction.

Published reports on the value of drug abreaction in the handling of Dunkirk and Blitz neurosis casualties caused this treatment to become widely adopted in Great Britain.

Further interest was then aroused among American psychiatrists by Grinker and Spiegel's later use in 1942 of the same treatment in North Africa, though they renamed it, somewhat confusingly, "narcosynthesis".[19] Moreover, Harold Palmer, a British psychiatrist, had been getting interesting results in the same theatre of war by the use of ether instead of barbiturates;[33] improving on a technique for the treatment of hysterical symptoms first described by Penhallow at Boston in 1915,[34] and used by Hurst and his collaborators during the First World War.[35]

When, in 1944, we also began using ether to induce abreaction, as recommended by Palmer, instead of barbiturates, we immediately noticed a great difference in our patients' behaviour. In most cases, ether released a far greater degree of explosive excitement, which made their recital of events extremely poignant or dramatic.[36] Another most striking observation was that sudden states of collapse, after emotional outbursts induced by ether, were far more frequent than after those induced by hypnosis or barbiturates.

It then occurred to my colleague Dr. H. J. Shorvon and to myself that this collapse phenomenon, which we were now repeatedly observing, might correspond to Pavlov's "transmarginal inhibition", which occurs when the cortex has become momentarily incapable of further activity. We remembered how, in some of Pavlov's dogs, the Leningrad flood had accidentally abolished the recently conditioned behaviour patterns implanted by him. Was the same thing happening in some of our patients who had suddenly collapsed in this way? If so, we might also expect others to become more suggestible or show reversal of previous patterns of behaviour and thought, because a "paradoxical" or

"ultra-paradoxical" phase of brain activity was being produced. This proved to be so in some cases at least.[6]

Under ether, certain patients would easily be persuaded
to relive experiences of terror, anger, or other excitement.
Some of them might then collapse from emotional exhaustion and lie motionless for a minute or so, unmoved by
ordinary stimuli; and, on coming round, would often burst
into a flood of tears and report that their outstanding symptoms had suddenly disappeared. Or they would describe
their minds as now freed of the terror aroused by certain
obsessive pictures; they could still think of these, if they
wished, but without the former hysterical anxiety. When
simple excitement at the recital of past experiences did not
reach the phase of "transmarginal inhibition", and collapse,
little or no change or mental improvement might be observed in the patient; if, however, the abreactive treatment
was repeated, and drugs were used to increase the amount
of emotional stimulation until collapse supervened, sudden improvement could occur.

Such a drastic technique was not always necessary. Some
patients, for instance, suffering from a recent loss of
memory, required only a small dose of barbiturate, injected
intravenously, to relax their brains; and this would send
the memory flooding back without further effort. Ether
proved most useful in cases where this treatment was not
enough; for instance, where abnormal behaviour had become so organized and fixed as to resemble the "stereotypy" described by Pavlov in his dogs. Such conditions could
become persistent, disabling, and resistant to simpler curative measures. But the massive excitement aroused under
ether, ending in a state of "transmarginal inhibition" and

collapse, could disrupt the whole vicious self-sustaining pattern of behaviour and induce a rapid return to more normal mental health.

Reports, originally published in 1945, on two cases of this sort, will serve as an illustration.[6] A soldier in his twenties had been admitted to an aid-post on the Normandy beachhead, weeping, speechless, and paralysed. He had had four years' Army service as a truck-driver before this and never reported sick with nerves, until he had been suddenly converted into an infantryman and sent up to the front line, where mortar fire and shelling produced a rapid breakdown. Proving unresponsive to a fortnight's sedation treatment in France, he was evacuated to England, and on admission to our War Emergency Hospital still appeared to be mentally slow, tense and apprehensive. More sedatives were given, followed a week later by insulin treatment designed to increase his weight. Yet his mental condition did not change. He walked slowly, with bent back and rigid features, and his apprehensiveness and slowness of thinking made it difficult for us to get his story out of him.

At this stage an intravenous barbiturate was administered and he was asked to describe what had happened. The drug made him much more relaxed mentally, and he described being under mortar fire for eight days in the same section of the front line. Then he had been taken across a river into a wood and ordered to the attack. In the wood, he had become increasingly nervous, and begun to tremble and shake. Several men were killed by mortar fire near him; whereupon he lost his voice, burst into tears, and became partially paralysed. Eventually, two wounded men helped him back to an ambulance. "I felt sort of stunned. I laid down crying. I could not speak, I could cry and make sounds." But the barbiturates induced very little emotion as he gave this recital, and no change was observed in his condition either immediately afterwards or on the next morning.

That afternoon, however, he was given another abreaction and this time ether was used instead of a barbiturate. When taken over the same ground again, he told the story this time with far greater emotion, and at last became confused and exhausted, tried to tear off the ether mask, and over-breathed in a panic-stricken way until the treatment was stopped. When he came to and rose from the couch, an obvious change had occurred in him. He smiled for the first time and looked relieved. A few minutes later he said that most of his troubles had gone away with the ether. A week later, he was still saying: "I'm a different fellow. I feel fine." This improvement was being maintained a fortnight afterwards.

Another case illustrates a similar dispersal of a brain "stereotypy" by the use of ether. Here, however, it will be seen that the use of ether in itself was not sufficient to induce complete abreaction; after a preliminary failure, the flame of the patient's excitement was deliberately fanned until he was brought to the necessary point of collapse. The stereotypy of his behaviour pattern then broke up and he greatly improved.[6]

This soldier had spent four and a half years in the Army as a driver-mechanic, and had landed in Normandy a fortnight after D-day. His symptoms came on gradually after he had been in action for several weeks. He, too, was given a week's sedation treatment in France, did not respond, and found himself evacuated to hospital in England. He was now depressed and apathetic, complaining of dizziness and inability to stand the noise of gunfire or aircraft. He could not rid his mind of the thought of his friends who had been killed in France. What kept recurring in his imagination was a scene in which one of his comrades had died with a hole through his head; the chin of another had been blown off, and blood was spurting from the hand of a third.

Though given further sedation, and insulin treatment to restore his weight, he complained a fortnight later that he felt worse than ever—the scene in which his friends had been killed or injured persisted in his imagination. He was then given ether to make him relive this scene, and he got emotionally excited enough to say he thought that the next head to go would be his own; but he did not reach the phase of collapse. On regaining consciousness, he wept and said he felt no better. He could "still see it all in his mind". So he was given a second ether treatment. This time he was made to relive another frightening experience which had taken place some days before the one now fixed in his mind. He had been subjected to mortar fire and dive-bombing in a churchyard, and when the therapist suggested to him under ether that he was back there again, he began clawing at the couch, imagining that he was in a ditch. The therapist deliberately played on his fears by giving him realistic comments on the ever worsening situation until, reaching a climax of excitement, he suddenly collapsed and lay almost as if dead. "Transmarginal inhibition" had supervened. This time, on regaining consciousness, he smiled and said: "Everything has gone. Everything is different. I feel more open, Doctor. I feel better than I did when I came here."

When asked if he remembered his friend's face being blown off, he grinned and said: "I seem to have forgotten about it. France is not worrying me now." When again questioned about this incident, he said: "Yes, and the fellow with the hole in his head, but it has lifted from my mind." When asked why this had happened, he answered: "I can't explain it." He then discussed the whole scene quite freely and without the usual display of emotion. Later in the day, he said: "I feel a lot better. It has gone out of my system. I know all about it, and it doesn't stick in me. It doesn't affect me in the same way." He then began to improve rapidly.

The most remarkable feature in this case was that the experience chosen as a means of stirring up enough excitement to destroy his abnormal behaviour patterns, was not the particular one which had been haunting him. In other words, the emotional explosion cleared away a whole chapter of recent emotional history and its associated behaviour patterns which had been building up, due to the patient's growing inability to stand up under continued battle stress.

The longer that abnormal patterns of behaviour persist, the more difficult, naturally, they are to remove again by such simple methods as those just described. But a third case shows that a six-months' stereotypy of thought, accompanied by depression and hysteria, can sometimes be relieved in the same way.

A woman in her fifties stated on admission to hospital, in 1946:[36] "I keep on going funny, and seeing different

incidents, with rocket-bombs, that I have been through."
She had been a full-time air-raid warden in a heavily
bombed London area throughout the war. The main neurotic symptoms had not set in until 1945, when her job
was drawing to a close. Her helmet had then been blown
off by a severe rocket explosion and something had hit the
back of her head. A lump came up but she disregarded it
and continued to help in the work of rescue. "I saw terrible sights; plenty of people cut to pieces under the debris." Fifty people, in fact, had been either killed or injured.
A few months later, the incident began to haunt her. As
soon as she closed her eyes to take a rest, she saw people
cut and bleeding. The same sort of pictures plagued her
dreams. This had been going on for six months before she
entered the hospital. She was depressed and worried, unable to concentrate; she had also lost considerable weight
and complained of giddiness, feelings of unreality, disturbed
sleep and a weakness in the legs which had practically im-
mobilized her. A neighbour said that from being a very
energetic and bright person, she had become listless, for-
getful and "flat".

Under ether, she relived the rocket-bomb incident with
great emotion and intensity, describing how she was buried under the debris with her husband, until rescued by a
brother. She interrupted her recital by frantically shouting
for her husband. "Where are you? Where are you?" She
repeated this several times at the top of her voice, at the
same time groping with her fingers as though searching
for him among the debris. The climax came when she described his rescue, at which point she suddenly fell back,
collapsed and inert. On regaining consciousness, she found

she had complete use of her limbs, and a clear mind, with no fears or visions. The improvement was maintained, and insulin treatment restored her weight.

Nevertheless, we did not always find it essential, in abreaction, to make a patient recall the precise incident which precipitated the breakdown. It would often be enough to create in him a state of excitement analogous to that which had caused his neurotic condition, and keep it up until he collapsed, he would then start to improve. Thus imagination would have to be used in inventing artificial situations, or distorting actual events—especially where the patient, while remembering the real experience which had caused the neurosis, or reliving it under drugs, had not reached the "transmarginal" phase of collapse necessary for disrupting the new morbid behaviour pattern. Among the patients from whose cases the above important finding could be deduced was a soldier in a tank regiment whom we could bring to the point of emotional collapse, under ether, only by persuading him that he was trapped in a burning tank and must try to get out at all costs. This had never actually happened, though it must have been a persistent fear of his throughout the campaign.

Some neurotic patients are clearly helped towards recovery when forgotten memories are brought back to consciousness. Both Freud and Pavlov, in their researches on the working of, respectively, the human and the canine brain, suggest that repressed emotional incidents may create severe generalized anxiety in some temperamental types. And Janet had also emphasized the importance of re-exciting patients while trying to bring back such memories to consciousness.[37] Yet our experience in World War II suggested that the arousing of crude excitement might often be of far greater curative virtue than the reliving of any particular forgotten or remembered experience. Indeed, the amount of excitement stirred up seemed to be the determining factor in the success or failure of many attempts to disrupt newly-acquired morbid behaviour patterns. Emotion that did not carry the patient to the point of "transmarginal inhibition" and collapse might be of little use—which is a finding of close relevance to the main theme of this book, namely, the physiology of religious and political conversion. Of equal relevance to the same theme were the increases of suggestibility, and the sudden reversals of behaviour witnessed in neurotic patients when the "ultra-paradoxical" phase of inhibition had presumably been reached: negative conditioned responses becoming positive, and positive, negative.

One more point must be made in this context: many patients who have been subjected to repeated abreactions, during a period of months and even years, on the psychotherapist's couch, are known to become increasingly sensitive to the therapist's suggestions. He may then be able to change their previous behaviour patterns without too much difficulty: they respond more willingly when he attempts to implant new ideas in them, or new interpretations of old ideas, which they would have rejected without hesitation before they developed a "transference" to him.

To be plain: it is hoped to show that there are remarkable basic similarities between, first, the behaviour of many neurotic patients during and after abreaction; next, the behaviour of ordinary people subjected to fear-provoking sermons by a powerful preacher; and lastly, the behaviour of political suspects in police stations and prisons where confessions are elicited and habits of "right thinking" implanted. Moreover, normal groups can be stimulated in peacetime by preaching, or mob oratory, as surely as neurotic individuals can be by drugs during abreactive treatment in a wartime hospital. Subsequent chapters will review a variety of methods used in different contexts to achieve similar effects. Yet let one finding be emphasized without further delay: some types of people are peculiarly resistant to "abreaction" under hypnotism or drugs, and to the more peaceful religious and political methods of conversion. The over-conscientious and meticulous person, for instance who feels obliged to dot every "i", cross every "t" and mind all his "p's" and "q's", rarely becomes too excited even under ether; and some melancholic patients are also too deeply depressed to let their pent-up emotions be discharged by drug-stimulation.

Abreaction under drugs is perhaps too solemn-sounding a phrase for a familiar phenomenon: when a man has something to get off his chest which has been worrying him, he is likely to take several stiff drinks and expect them to loosen his tongue for him. Conversely, drink is used in business, in journalism, and the intelligence services to force indiscreet admissions from people who find it difficult to keep a secret. And after successes on the battlefield or football field, many tongue-tied victors use drink to discharge their repressed emotions in a socially acceptable manner. *In vino veritas.*

Emotions can also be discharged by vigorous dancing. It was with wild hysterical dances that Britain greeted the Armistice in 1918. Negro jazz came as a godsend to the war-neurotics of the period—the waltz and the two-step were not invented for the release of strong emotions—and the curative treatment lasted well into the 'twenties. Some primitive tribes use dancing for the same purpose. Abreaction by drink—first beer, later wine—and wild rhythmic dancing, was also the object of the ancient rites in honour of Dionysus; but the Greeks had their own word for it— *catharsis* or "cleansing". Abreaction is a time-worn physiological trick which has been used, for better or worse, by generations of preachers and demagogues to soften up their listeners' minds and help them take on desired patterns of belief and behaviour. Whether the appeal has more often been to noble and heroic deeds, or to cruelty and folly, is a matter for the historian rather than the physiologist to decide.

Chapter 4

Psychoanalysis, Shock Treatments
and Leucotomy

It seems then, that the efficacy of abreactive techniques, though ascribed in the past to various agencies invoked by the abreactor, often depends on powerful physiological forces unchained in the process. To realize this, one has only to consider how many sufferers from inhibitory neuroses have been helped by sudden non-specific emotional shocks. People have been relieved of hysterical blindness by a sudden loud clap of thunder; others have recovered the use of their legs after a strong emotional fright induced by a sudden blow on the head.

In Great Britain during the last ten years, fairly intensive research has been in progress on the value of different drugs available for psychotherapy; especially those capable of inducing cerebral excitement in various types of neurotic illness. Nitrous oxide (dental gas)[38] high carbon dioxide and oxygen mixtures,[39] such drugs as methedrine (similar to benzedrine, but given intravenously),[40] and various combinations of all these have been tested.[8] As already mentioned, ordinary peacetime neuroses do not yield to treatment so dramatically as those that were treated during the Normandy fighting and the London Blitz. Only in the exceptional case, where a hitherto stable person has been unbalanced by a severe psychological shock or intolerable stress, is wartime experience repeated. Yet peace yields plentiful examples of what happens when the normal, or abnormal, brain is subjected to constant abreactive treatment; and these may help towards a better understanding of brain-washing and the traditional techniques of religious conversion.

Animal experimentation, it must be once more repeated, showed that when the brain was stimulated beyond the limits of its capacity to tolerate the stresses imposed, "protective inhibition" finally supervened. When this happened, not only could previous behaviour patterns implanted in the brain be suppressed, but former positive conditioned responses could become negative, and *vice versa*. Similarly, the administration of too exciting, or too frequent, brain stimuli may sometimes cause human victims to reverse their previous patterns of behaviour. And others are likely to become more suggestible, accepting whatever they are told, however nonsensical, as the inescapable truth.

All these effects can be observed when peacetime psychiatric patients are subjected to repeated abreactions with or without drugs. And the more ordinary the previous personality, the readier may be his response and more confident his talk about "seeing things in a new light". After some particularly severe abreaction, a patient will sometimes "box the compass" in his views on religion or politics, or in his attitude to family and friends; or these attitudes may chop and change with alarming rapidity. Suggestibility in many can be enhanced, temporarily at least, by repeated abreaction. The patient may come to accept various types of simple reassurance from the psychotherapist, which he would never have accepted from his lawyer, or minister, or family physician, when in a more quiet frame of mind.

Moreover, just as Pavlov's dogs remained sensitive to the original cause of their mental disruption—namely, water seeping in underneath the laboratory door during the Leningrad flood—so patients tend to become highly sensitized to the therapist who causes them repeated emotional upheavals. Psychoanalysts have called this the formation of positive or negative transference towards themselves. Here again Pavlov provides a possible physiological explanation for what has hitherto been explained in more complex psychological terms. It is precisely by inducing the "transference" phenomenon that Freud and his psychoanalytical school explain the success of their treatment methods. Though it is now generally admitted that not all mental illnesses are due to sex trauma, they still in practice encourage the patient to harp on early sexual excitements and associated sex guilt feelings and thus help to arouse in him the emotions necessary for successful abreaction.

Some techniques of psychotherapy do, in fact, show that methods of political and religious conversion have their counterparts in ordinary psychiatric practice, and that the patient can be made to "see the light", whatever the particular doctrinaire light may be, without recourse to drugs or specially induced debilitation, or any other artificial aid to abreaction. Drugs speed up the process by bringing about the required physiological changes in brain function; but these can also be produced by the use of repeated psychological stimuli.

A patient under psychoanalytic treatment, for instance, is made to lie on a couch, where daily for months, and perhaps years, he is encouraged to indulge in "free association of ideas". He may also then be asked: "What does 'umbrella' mean to you?"—"Uncle Toby." "What does 'apple' mean to you?"—"The girl next door." These answers may perhaps also be found to be of sexual significance. He has to go back over his past sexual peccadilloes, and relive other incidents which aroused intense anxiety, fear, guilt, or aggression, especially in childhood. As the analysis proceeds, and emotional storms perhaps mount, the patient becomes more and more sensitized to the analyst. So-called "transference situations", both positive and negative, are built up physiologically; often assisted in the early stages of treatment by the fatigue and debilitation resulting from the anxiety aroused. The patient's tension and dependence on the therapist may be greatly increased. A stage is finally reached when resistance weakens to the therapist's interpretations of a patient's symptoms, and he may start to accept them much more readily. He now believes and acts upon theories about his nervous condition which, more often than not, contradict his former beliefs. Many of the individual's usual patterns of behaviour may also be upset by this process, and replaced by new ones. These changes are consolidated by making the patient's behaviour as consistent as possible with the new "insight" gained. Attempts are then made, before treatment ends, to reduce the patient's emotional dependence on the therapist. As one patient personally analysed by Freud remarked to me:

For the first few months I was able to feel nothing but increasing anxiety, humiliation and guilt. Nothing about my past life seemed satisfactory any more, and all my old ideas about myself seemed to be contradicted. When I got into a completely hopeless state, he [Freud] then seemed to start to restore my confidence in myself, and to piece everything together in a new setting.[1]

Psychoanalytic treatment is much slower in bringing about what more violent or intensive methods often achieve in the psychiatric, political or religious field. And although some therapists are loath to admit that their form of treatment can ever amount to a conversion experience, this seems a most likely explanation for what may happen not only to some of their patients but even to doctors themselves when undergoing analysis for training purposes. For, if the treatment has been successful, they can become firmly indoctrinated with Freudian principles to the exclusion of most others. They may even have dreams of the particular Freudian orientation expected by their teachers, to confirm their faith. What is more, the same type of person (or even the very same patient) who attends a Jungian analyst, often completes his psychoanalysis with a Jungian type of "insight", after having dreamed Jungian "collective subconscious" dreams. Evidence for this has been provided by a well-known psychiatrist. He told the writer how as a much younger man, he came to England in the 'twenties and submitted to the experiment of three months' analysis from a Freudian, followed by three months' analysis from a Jungian practitioner. His contemporary notes show that dreams he had under Freudian treatment varied greatly from those he had under Jungian treatment; and he denies having experienced the same dreams before or since. Among the aims of therapy, in fact, seems to be a disruption of the patient's previous behaviour patterns, helped by the arousal of strong emotions. The increased suggestibility of the patient may help the therapist not only to change his conscious thinking, but even to direct his dream life. Analysis is often considered complete only when the therapist's points of view have been thoroughly absorbed and resistance—or so-called "negative transference"—to the therapist's interpretations of past events has broken down.

The ability to dream special types of dreams for a particular therapist is also seen among more primitive peoples. Bengt Sundkler in *Bantu Prophets in South Africa*[41] points out how Bantu native Christian pastors place very great importance on making those seeking conversion, or having recently been converted, dream the right kind of "stereotyped" dreams. He reports that:

> . . . some missionaries have felt humiliated and even scandalized because of the stress laid upon dreams by Africans. Missionaries are almost shocked that such an important spiritual revolution as conversion would seem to be due in many cases to some absurd dream rather than the conscious decision of the will. . . . The most striking symbols recurring in the (stereotyped) dreams quoted by Allier are: light, shining clothes, group of Christians on the other side of the river calling the dreamer to pass over. . . . Characteristic (also) are the clear and distinct impressions as recorded by the dreamer. The length, or rather shortness, of the green grass as seen in heaven is always commented upon. Minute detail in dress and outfit is often pointed out.

Sundkler gives many other interesting details about the artificial production of such dreams:

> Some Zionists know of what they refer to as the "gift of dreams". . . . Others again have to be trained and schooled in dreaming in order to achieve the right stereotyped dream. . . . Prophet X attached much value to the dreams of his neophytes. After an initial general confession of sins, he would tell them to go home for three days and later return to relate to him all they had dreamed during that time. They would not fail to have very significant dreams, he assured them. The one great thing waited for and expected in the dreamer is the revelation of Jehovah, or the Angel, or Jesus, always appearing in shining white robes.

It is also pointed out that, as in other psychotherapeutic disciplines, the stereotyped dreams produced have as their corollary the giving of "stereotyped and standardized interpretations", and that:

> In the name of the "freedom of the Holy Spirit" the sect thus exercises a totalitarian control over the individual, which does not even shun the hidden depths of the person's subconscious mind. The individual is malleable and the sect is moulding him into a standard type.

It is not surprising that the ordinary person, in general, is much more easily indoctrinated than the abnormal. Even intensive psychoanalysis may achieve very little in such severe psychiatric disturbances as schizophrenia and depressive melancholia, and can be almost equally ineffective in certain settled states of chronic anxiety and obsession. A person is considered "ordinary" or "normal" by the community simply because he accepts most of its social standards and behaviour patterns; which means, in fact, that he is susceptible to suggestion and has been persuaded to go with the majority on most ordinary or extraordinary occasions.

People who hold minority opinions, even though these may be posthumously proved correct, are often called "mad", or at least "eccentric" during their lifetime. But that they can hold either advanced or demoted views distasteful to the community as a whole, shows them to be far less suggestible than their "normal" contemporaries; and no patients can be so difficult to influence by suggestion as the chronic mentally ill. Ordinary persons also have much greater powers of adaptation to circumstance than most eccentrics or psychotics. During the London Blitz, ordinary civilians became conditioned to the most bizarre and horrifying situations; they would go calmly about their work though well aware that neighbours had been buried alive in bombed houses around them. They realized that to worry about the victims when nothing more could be done to extricate them, would lead to their own nervous collapse. In fact, those who broke down during the London Blitz were for the most part abnormally anxious or abnormally fatigued persons who could no longer adapt themselves to the unusual horrors and stresses.

This point cannot be too strongly emphasized in its relevance to the phenomenon of political or religious conversion. It is a popular fallacy that the average person is more likely to resist modern brain-washing techniques than the abnormal. If the ordinary human brain had not possessed a special capacity of adaptation to an ever-changing environment—building up ever-changing conditioned reflexes and patterns of responses and submitting for the time being when further resistance seemed useless—mankind would never have survived to become the dominant mammal. The person with deficient powers of adaptation, and excessive rigidity in behaviour or thought, is always in danger of breaking down, entering a mental hospital or becoming a chronic neurotic.

It is also noteworthy that stage hypnotists, to demonstrate their powers of suggestion, make a practice of choosing from among the most ordinary volunteers who offer themselves. The hearty and well-built young soldier or the easy-going athlete is likely to prove an easy subject. Hypnotists are, however, careful to attempt nothing with the suspicious and anxious neurotic.

The higher incidence of hysterical phenomena among ordinary people under the acute stresses of war, compared with that among the same sort of people under the minor stresses of peacetime, or among chronically anxious and neurotic people either in peace or war, is further evidence (if any were needed) for the point we have been making, namely that among the readiest victims of brain-washing or religious conversion may be the simple, healthy extravert.

Modern Shock Treatments and Leucotomy

Before being able to change behaviour patterns of thought and action in the human brain with speed and efficiency, it is apparently in many cases necessary to induce some form of physiological brain disturbance. The subject may have to be frightened, angered, frustrated, or emotionally disturbed in some way or another, because all such reactions are likely to cause alterations in brain function which may increase his suggestibility or make him liable to forgo his normal conditioning. Psychotherapeutic techniques that involve merely talking to the patient generally prove ineffective in curing severer states of mental disorder, even when strong emotions can be aroused. In most such severe cases of mental illness normal behaviour patterns have already been disrupted and abnormal ones either established or on the way to being so. Far better results may then be achieved by a combination of psychotherapy with one or another of the newly introduced modern shock treatments, or with operations on the brain. The history of psychiatric treatment shows, indeed, that from time immemorial attempts have been made to cure mental disorders by the use of physiological shocks, frights, and various chemical agents; and such means have always yielded brilliant results in *certain types of patient*, though also applied indiscriminately and deleteriously to patients who could not respond to that particular treatment.

During the last twenty years, a variety of shock treatments have been used, each discovered independently of the others. But the similarity between their effects is fascinating when viewed in the light of Pavlov's physiological experiments on dogs and the findings made on combat casualties in World War II. It has already been shown that some of the most rapid and dramatic cures under drug abreaction and other psychotherapeutic treatments, occur when states of excitement produced in the brain go on to reach the phase of protective inhibition and collapse, and the brain is thereby freed of some of its recently acquired patterns of behaviour and thought. Electric shock treatment, which has proved most helpful in dispelling certain states of severe mental depression, is simply the artificial inducement of an epileptic fit. This is done by passing an electric current through the brain, the strength of the current being no greater than is necessary to cause the fit.[42] A series of four to ten fits, given once or twice weekly, may shorten such attacks of depression to a few weeks only, where the illness would probably have lasted a year or two, or even longer. Yet, unless a full epileptic fit is produced, this electrical treatment is without effect. A so-called "sub-shock", meaning an electric shock which causes no convulsion in the brain, is worse than useless. A full convulsion means that the brain goes on convulsing to the point when it can do so no longer, but becomes temporarily exhausted and inhibited. There are similarities between a convulsion and a very severe emotional abreaction under drugs that are striking.

It is very difficult indeed to make severely depressed patients abreact and discharge pent-up emotions under drugs. And the emotions then are not aggressive, as when stronger temperamental types are treated, but consist largely of self-abasement and self-blame. However, after a series of electrically induced convulsions, this abnormal condition, which shows evidence of "paradoxical" or "ultra-paradoxical" brain activity, soon breaks up. The patient begins to show a normal aggressiveness against the world again, rather than against himself, ceases to feel responsible for everything that has gone wrong, and may even round angrily on the doctor who is treating him. At this point he again becomes amenable to ordinary forms of suggestion and psychotherapy. The mind being as it were, freed from its inhibitory strait-jacket, his delusions of guilt and impending catastrophe disperse and fade away.

A significant clue to the problem was provided by a depressed American patient who was attending revival meetings in an endeavour to cure herself of severe mental depression associated with feelings of religious guilt. She found she could not work up sufficient enthusiasm to participate in the group excitement which was transfiguring almost everyone else present—until a course of electric shock treatment enabled her to do so. This suggested that certain states of abnormal brain activity respond far more readily to repeated electrically induced convulsions than to abreaction with or without drugs similarly designed to produce a temporary disturbance of brain function. Both methods, however, may turn out to work on the same physiological principles. Attendance at revival meetings had relieved another American patient from two previous attacks of depression, but not from a third much severer attack. This responded only to electrical shock treatment.[9]

Already before World War II, schizophrenia, especially in the early stages of the disease, was being successfully treated by insulin shock therapy.[43] This method is to give a patient large doses of insulin to lower the amount of sugar in his blood, thus producing a state of mental confusion and excitement. For an hour or more, perhaps, he lies in a semiconscious state, twitching, jerking, and perhaps talking incoherently, until a deep coma supervenes. When using this treatment for the relief of schizophrenia, the psychiatrist may keep the patient in coma for half an hour.

Sugar is then administered by means of a stomach-tube or intravenous injection, and he quickly wakes up. Symptoms may disperse after a course of such treatments given daily and with little additional psychotherapy. So here is one more treatment involving an initial stage of often uncontrolled brain excitement, and ending in temporary brain inhibition and stupor.

Both electric shock and insulin shock treatments tend to disperse recent abnormal behaviour patterns, though seldom proving efficacious in cases where these are too long established. The useful fields of these various treatments are now becoming more clearly differentiated; for instance, it is generally recognized that severe cases of early schizophrenia may respond best to the more complicated insulin therapy, combined sometimes with electric shock treatment, whereas states of mental depression perhaps brought about by prolonged petty anxiety, can often be cured by electric shock alone; and war neuroses, again, with depressive symptoms caused by more violent mental stress, may respond to much less severe abreactions under drugs.[44]

Among the different types of patient who do not respond at all readily either to psychotherapy or any of the modern shock treatments, is the obsessional neurotic, who feels the urge to carry out certain repetitive actions—as Dr. Johnson had to touch certain fingerposts when he walked down Fleet Street. These are often harmless: an Oxford Classical professor of the 'twenties anxiously asked the late Dr. William Brown, whether his compulsion always to walk up and down the room, when he lectured, in sequences of seven steps, was dangerous. Brown, with tongue in cheek, put his mind at rest: "When you find yourself walking in multiples of seven, come to me again! Simple sevens are all right."[45] There are, indeed, progressive degrees of obsession. A mother, for instance, may worry continually that she may have dropped an open safety pin in a milk bottle, and that the bottle will be returned to the dairy, but not washed properly, and that the next child who drinks milk from the bottle will swallow the safety-pin. She may be perfectly aware of the wildly improbable nature of this repetitive fear, but nevertheless feels compelled to examine every empty milk bottle five or six times before the milkman collects it. In all other respects she may be a sensible and efficient housewife. Others, with minor symptoms of the same illness, make sure before going to bed that all gas taps are turned off and all doors properly locked, repeating the process two or three times. They are sometimes likely, of course, to rationalize their behaviour by saying that "all sensible people make several security checks; it is worth the trouble".

Obsessional neurotics are also inclined to be excessively careful of their appearance and the tidiness of their houses, to wash their hands unnecessarily often and to be meticulously rigid in their brain patterns. Neighbours can usually set their clocks by the time when the obsessional neurotic walks down the street to work and returns again. This is the type of person who boasts that in thirty years he has never been late for work, and never more than a minute or two early. He is, however, likely to plague his spiritual adviser with minor worries and compulsive religious doubts which he cannot dispel. The obsessional neurotic is usually unsuggestible, and the despair of the psychotherapist or stage hypnotist.

When he finally becomes so chronically ill and compulsive that he is a burden to himself and his associates, little sometimes can be done to help him by psychiatry—short of a brain operation called "leucotomy", which will presently be discussed. This resistance to treatment will be found extremely relevant when the mechanism of conversion and brain-washing are discussed in later chapters. Some obsessional patients have undergone psychoanalytic treatment for as many as fifteen years, on and off. They tend to include their treatment in the same obsessional pattern, hoping that one day some subconscious memory will finally be unearthed and explain everything.

A study of obsessional neuroses, however, shows how stubbornly certain types of brain can cling to their established behaviour patterns. Abreactive treatments are often without effect and an obsessional patient may be given as many as twenty or thirty electric convulsion treatments; but though these result in mental confusion, and he may even temporarily lose much of his memory for recent events, as soon as the treatment is over and memory begins to flood back, old obsessions are liable to return in full force.

The more disquieting symptoms of an obsessional neurosis very often disappear gradually by themselves in the course of time; and may only be acute while associated with depression. If this can be made to lift, the obsessional neurotic will be benefited by electric shock treatment. But when subjected to simple psychological abreaction, even if depression is not present, he generally finds it impossible to "let himself go". If suffering from bomb-shock, for example, he may discuss meticulously whether the explosion occurred at five or ten minutes past three in the afternoon.

He will also interrupt attempts to excite him trans-marginally by an insistence on absolute accuracy in whatever he is saying, and is proof against suggestion even under ether. If, therefore, a simple medical means of breaking up chronic obsessions is ever discovered, one of the final weapons will have been forged for the armoury of the religious and political conversion practitioners. Meanwhile, their methods are much more successful with the healthy-minded majority. They often fail with the eccentric unless they can first physically debilitate and exhaust him to a point where his beliefs become less firmly held and he sees that his only hope of survival lies in submission; he may then sometimes be totally switched and re-indoctrinated. Many human eccentrics may approximate to Pavlov's stronger dogs who acquired new behaviour patterns only when they had first been debilitated by castration, hunger, or induced gastric disorders which made them lose a great deal of weight. Once re-indoctrinated, they were fattened up, and the new behaviour patterns became as firmly fixed as the old; indeed, Pavlov could not get rid of them again.

Obsessional symptoms in humans often occur after a debilitating loss of weight, a severe fever, or some operation or disease that alters glandular function. Attempts are now made sometimes to treat such patients by putting them on a weight-reducing diet, or giving them drugs to make them lose their appetite: hoping that the resulting debilitation will help disperse the obsessional behaviour patterns which were acquired in similar circumstances.[1] The history of religion contains many records of sinful obsessional thinking being relieved by purges, vomitories or starvation, after simpler methods had failed. Though it was found that every dog had his eventual "breaking-point", and the same truth may be presumed in human beings, even debilitation cannot be relied upon to alter obsessional patterns of thought and behaviour once they have become firmly established by time.

In a clinical account of religious and political conversion, it is impossible to avoid classifying the human subjects according to basic temperamental types, each of which may call for a different type of physiological and psychological treatment. The stronger the obsessional tendency, for instance, the less amenable will the subject be found to some of the ordinary techniques of conversion; the only hope is to break him down by debilitation and prolonged psychological and physiological measures to increase suggestibility. Individual or mass hypnosis is also ineffective when used on several types of neurotics and psychotics; as a rule it can be confidently used only where there is evidence of suggestibility present.

In the present state of medical knowledge the only hopeful treatment of some chronic obsessional, chronic schizophrenic and chronic anxious or depressive patients, who respond to no form of shock therapy, psychotherapy or drug treatment is a surgical one to which, as a rule, recourse is only had when all else fails: the newer modifications of the operation called "prefrontal leucotomy". These can have such interesting effects that they deserve mention in this context.

The operation, in its now many varied forms, throws considerable light on the cerebral mechanisms by which patterns of human thought and behaviour are implanted or eradicated. It was first introduced, in 1936, by the Portuguese neurologist Moniz,[46] who received the Nobel Prize for his success in enabling so many chronically ill patients to leave mental hospitals and return to their work and families; and the after-effects of such operations on the thought processes have been carefully studied in the case of British patients who have undergone it up to ten years ago, or more. Some fifteen thousand patients have now been treated in Great Britain alone.

Leucotomy is reserved for patients suffering from severe and persisting states of anxiety and tension, produced in some cases by real and unpleasant facts, and in others by hallucinations or delusions; but in either case resisting dispersion by non-surgical treatments. The operation, especially in its recently improved and modified forms can greatly diminish the tension, while not always eradicating the thoughts that created it. One can, in fact, by this means diminish excessive anxiety arising from both normal and abnormal thinking, without affecting other thought processes or the intelligence itself to any marked degree; and with a reasonable chance that a favourable result will be permanent. The operation has been greatly refined in recent years and now causes far less change in the general personality.

To watch the progress of such patients after operation is to realize that, once their anxiety about a real or imaginary idea has been diminished, the idea itself has a tendency to diminish in importance. A patient may, for example, be confined in a mental hospital because he is obsessed by the delusion that he has an abnormally shaped face which everyone who sees it will laugh at. After leucotomy, he may still believe in his abnormal face, but cease to regard it as such a social disability. This will enable him to leave hospital, return to work, and carry on as many people do who have real facial disfigurements. And, a few months later, it may be found that the delusional idea about the face has also vanished or become much less important to him for want of the continued emotional reinforcement of his anxiety about it.

It is said that leucotomy tends to make people matter-of-fact and conventional so that they lose their personality. And it is true that the result is, in general, to make them more ordinary members of a group, open to suggestion and persuasion without stubborn resistance; for they will have ceased to feel as deeply about their ideas and can therefore think more logically, and examine new theories without emotional bias. As an instance: one patient with a Messianic delusion had proved wholly unamenable to intensive psychoanalytic treatment, but after leucotomy was now able to discuss his Messianic claims with an intelligent male nurse and let them be argued away. Genuine religious conversions are also seen after the new modified leucotomy operations. For the mind is freed from its old strait jacket and new religious beliefs and attitudes can now more easily take the place of the old.

Religious feelings in man may be destroyed if *too extensive* an operation is performed in the frontal lobes. Rylander has described such patients in Sweden, while Ström-Olsen and Tow[47] have noted others in this country. One of Rylander's patients was:

> . . . a Salvation Army worker, a very high-ranking officer. She married a clergyman. For years she lay in hospital, con-

stantly complaining that she had committed sins against the Holy Ghost. She complained of it for weeks and months, and her poor husband did his best to distract her, but without success. Then we decided to operate upon her. . . . After the dressing had been taken off, I asked her, "How are you now? What about the Holy Ghost?" Smiling, she answered, "Oh, the Holy Ghost, there is no Holy Ghost."[48]

However using more modern types of operations, and much more limited cuts in the frontal lobes, symptoms of anxiety and obsessional rumination can be lessened without producing too many undesirable effects on ordinary religious beliefs. John Pippard after a careful examination of over a hundred patients who had been followed up for from one-and-a-half to five years after operation, reported recently:

> . . . the religious attitude is not directly affected by rostral (modified) leucotomy, but is liable to be affected in the re-integration of the personality after operation, as indeed it may be in the reintegration after psychotherapy or other treatment. . . . Personality deficits are negligible after 95 per cent of rostral leucotomies which have given good symptomatic relief, compared with only 44 per cent of standard (more extensive) leucotomies. Positively undesirable changes were present in only 2 of 114 cases, compared with 29 per cent of standard leucotomies.[49]

Whether it be a mistake to convert mentally agonized persons into more ordinary ones, who have not such overwhelmingly strong feelings one way or another, will of course always remain a moot point for some people. At all events, the success of leucotomy is a reminder of the uselessness of the merely rational approach to many patients suffering from fixed ideas; and of the consequent unhappy recourse, throughout history, to lunatic asylums, prisons, concentration camps, gallows or the stake as a means of removing from society all individuals who cannot otherwise be made to accept the beliefs accepted by the more ordinary and suggestible majority.

CHAPTER 5

Techniques of Religious Conversion

In approaching this subject, we shall try to find out what it is that is common to many religions in the methods of sudden conversion employed by their priests and evangelists. We shall endeavour to bring this into relation with what we know of the physiology of the brain. We must beware of being distracted by what it is that is being preached. The truths of Christianity have nothing to do with the beliefs inspired by the rites of pagan religions or of devil-worshippers. But the physiological mechanisms, of which use has been made by religions on each side of this gulf, will bear the closest examination.

The leaders of successful faiths have never, it may in fact be said, dispensed entirely with physiological weapons in their attempts to confer spiritual grace on their fellow men. Fasting, chastening of the flesh by scourging and physical discomfort, regulation of breathing, disclosure of awesome mysteries, drumming, dancing, singing, inducement of panic fear, weird or glorious lighting, incense, intoxicant drugs—these are only some of the many methods used to modify normal brain functions for religious purposes. Some sects pay more attention than others to a direct stirring up of emotions as a means of affecting the higher nervous system; but few wholly neglect it.

The evidence already presented suggests that the physiological mechanisms which make possible the implantation or removal of behaviour patterns in men and animals are analogous; and that when the brain breaks down under severe stress, the resultant behaviour changes, whether in man or in an animal, depend both on the individual's inherited temperament, and on the conditioned behaviour patterns which he has built up by a gradual adaptation to environment.

It has also been pointed out that those who wish to disperse wrong beliefs and undesirable behaviour patterns and afterwards implant saner beliefs and attitudes are more likely to achieve success if they can first induce some degree of nervous tension or stir up sufficient feelings of anger or anxiety to secure the person's undivided attention and possibly increase his suggestibility. By increasing or prolonging stresses in various ways, or inducing physical debilitation, a more thorough alteration of the person's thinking processes may be achieved. The immediate effect of such treatment is, usually to impair judgment and increase suggestibility; and though when the tension is removed the suggestibility likewise diminishes, yet ideas implanted while it lasted may remain. If the stress or the physical debilitation, or both, are carried one stage further, it may happen that patterns of thought and behaviour, especially those of recent acquisition, become disrupted. New patterns can then be substituted, or suppressed patterns allowed to re-assert themselves; or the subject may begin to think and act in ways that precisely contradict his former ones. Some temperamental types seem relatively impervious to all emotional stresses imposed on them. Others retain their beliefs, once firmly implanted, with a tenacity that defies the severest psychological and physiological shock treatments, and even brain operations especially designed to disrupt them. But such resistance is unusual.

With these facts in mind, one can hope to understand more clearly the physiological mechanisms at work in some types of sudden religious conversion; hence the repetitive summary. Methods of religious conversion have hitherto been considered more from psychological and metaphysical angles than from physiological and mechanistic ones; but techniques employed often approximate so closely to modern political techniques of brain-washing and thought control that each throws light on the mechanics of the other. It is convenient to start with the better documented history of sudden religious conversion which has this in common with political conversion, that an individual or group of individuals may adopt new beliefs or patterns of behaviour, as a result of illuminations bursting upon the mind suddenly and with great intensity, often after periods of intense emotional stress. But since political prisons publish no available clinical reports on the physiological changes noted in those whom they have subjected to intolerable mental stress, it will be convenient to quote those observed in analogous combat-casualties, and then compare them with those observed in sudden religious converts. Two conveniently parallel texts are John Wesley's *Journal* of 1739, and Grinker and Spiegel's report on their treatment of acute war neuroses in North Africa in 1942. Grinker and Spiegel[19] describe the effects of abreaction of war experiences under barbiturate drugs as follows:

The terror exhibited . . . is electrifying to watch. The body becomes increasingly tense and rigid; the eyes widen and the pupils dilate, while the skin becomes covered with a fine perspiration. The hands move convulsively. . . . Breathing becomes incredibly rapid or shallow. The intensity of the emotion sometimes becomes more than they can bear; and frequently at the height of the reaction, there is a collapse and the patient falls back in the bed and remains quiet for a few minutes. . .

Wesley reports under the date April 30th, 1739:

We understand that many were offended at the cries of those on whom the power of God came; among whom was a physician, who was much afraid there might be fraud or imposture in the case. Today one whom he had known many years was the first who broke out "into strong cries and tears." He could hardly believe his own eyes and ears. He went and stood close to her, and observed every symptom, till great drops of sweat ran down her face and all her bones shook. He then knew not what to think, being clearly convinced it was not fraud nor yet any natural disorder. But when both her soul and body were healed in a moment, he acknowledged the finger of God.[50]

Grinker and Spiegel report:

The stuporous become alert, the mute can talk, the deaf can hear, the paralysed can move, and the terror-stricken psychotics become well-organized individuals.

Wesley can also record:

I will show you him that was a lion till then, and is now a lamb, him that was a drunkard, and is now exemplarily sober; the whore-monger that was, who now abhors the very "garment spotted by the flesh".[50]

The main difference lies in the explanations given for the same impressive results. Wesley and his followers attributed the phenomenon to the intervention of the Holy Ghost: "It is the Lord's doing and it is wonderful in our eyes." Grinker and Spiegel, on the other hand, believed that their results demonstrated the correctness of Freud's theories in which they had themselves believed. As will be shown later, almost identical physiological and psychological phenomena may result from religious healing methods and conversion techniques, equally in the most primitive and the more highly civilized cultures. They may be adduced as convincing proofs of the truth of whatever religious or philosophic beliefs are invoked. But since those beliefs are often logically irreconcilable with each other, and since the similarity of the physiological and psychological phenomena produced by their invocation are all that they may have in common—we find ourselves confronted with a mechanistic principle deserving the most careful examination.

Just as we have hitherto selected Pavlov's experiments on dogs to illustrate one aspect of our larger problem, and war neuroses of World War II to illustrate another, so here John Wesley's methods and results will be selected as typical of those seen in an effective and socially valuable religious setting. Nobody can doubt their religious efficacy or social value; for his preaching converted people by the thousands, and he also built up an efficient system for perpetuating these beliefs.

Harold Nicolson, writing in 1955, says:

> Finally a revivalist of genius appeared in the person of John Wesley. On the death of Wesley in 1791, heathenism returned for a short while to England. The Church almost reverted to the condition which Bishop Butler denounced in 1736. . . . Bishop Butler did not foresee the great flame that John Wesley was so shortly to kindle or that, after a temporary reaction, the Evangelicals would receive from Wesley's hand a torch that was to smoke and flicker for some eighty years.[51]

It is now generally admitted that he made great numbers of ordinary English people think less about their material well-being than their spiritual salvation, thus fortifying them, at a critical period of the French Revolution, against dangerous materialistic teachings of Tom Paine. The powerful influence of the Methodist revival still permeates England in the form of its "nonconformist conscience". Moreover, it was descendants of those who fostered this powerful religious movement in England who later pioneered the great Trade Union Movement of the present era.

The eighteenth century, like the twentieth, considered itself an "Age of Reason"; the intellect was, in fact, held to be far more important than the emotions, when habits of thought and behaviour needed to be dictated. Wesley's great success was due to his finding that such habits were most easily implanted or eradicated by a tremendous assault on the emotions. Most Wesleyan ministers now confess themselves bewildered when they read the detailed reports of his conversions; after blinding their eyes to the tremendous power still latent in the technique he employed. All evidence goes to show that there can be no new Protestant revival while the policy continues of appealing mainly to adult intelligence and reason and until Church leaders consent to take more advantage of the normal person's emotional mechanism for disrupting old behaviour patterns and implanting new.

Wesley's own efforts as a preacher were relatively ineffective until his own heart became "strangely warmed" at a meeting in Aldersgate Street in 1738. He had previously gone for help, in a state of severe mental depression, to Peter Böhler, a Moravian missionary, having returned a total failure from being the pastor of the newly-founded colony of Georgia. Hitherto he had always believed that spiritual salvation could be achieved only by the performance of good works, as opposed to faith alone. His sudden conversion transformed him into one who puts faith beyond everything, enabling him to cast all his fears aside; and he found a sudden ally in his brother Charles, who had been with him in Georgia and whom Peter Böhler had also been trying to change. Charles was likewise suffering from acute mental depression, induced both by his own Georgia experiences and by physical debilitation after a second attack of pleurisy. These sudden conversions of both brothers, with an interval of only three days between them, to a belief in the certainty of salvation by faith, rather than by good works, are probably described in one of Charles Wesley's famous hymns:

> Long my imprisoned spirit lay
> Fast bound by sin and nature's night;

Thine eye diffused a quickening ray—
I woke, the dungeon flamed with light;
My chains fell off, my heart was free,
I rose, went forth, and followed Thee.

The reader may find some difficulty in realizing the immense contemporary importance of the religious problem which Peter Böhler had helped the Wesley brothers to solve. To put faith before works implied a total reorientation of their religious position: as radical as the change from political Conservatism to Communism would be today.

Once habituated to the new pattern of thought, John Wesley set about implanting it in others. With the help of his brother Charles, whose hymns were addressed to the religious emotions rather than the intelligence, he hit upon an extremely effective technique of conversion—a technique which is used not only in many other successful religions but in modern political warfare.

First of all, Wesley would create high emotional tension in his potential converts. He found it easy to convince large audiences of that period that a failure to achieve salvation would necessarily condemn them to hellfire for ever and ever. The immediate acceptance of an escape from such a ghastly fate was then very strongly urged on the ground that anybody who left the meeting "unchanged" and met with a sudden fatal accident before he had accepted this salvation, would pass straight into the fiery furnace. This sense of urgency increased the prevailing anxiety which, as suggestibility increased, could infect the whole group.

Fear of everlasting hell, which was as real to Wesley's own mind as the houses and fields in which he preached, affected the nervous system of his hearers very much as fear of death by drowning did Pavlov's dogs in the Leningrad flood. Monsignor Ronald Knox quotes this autobiographical account from John Nelson (later one of Wesley's most able lieutenants) describing his own conversion:

> As soon as he (Wesley) got upon his stand, he stroked back his hair, and turned his face towards me where I stood, and I thought fixed his eyes upon me. His countenance struck such an awful dread upon me, before I heard him speak, that it made my heart beat like the pendulum of a clock; and when he did speak, I thought his whole discourse was aimed at me.[52]

Wesley learned in time that to capture an audience he had first to gauge its intellectual and emotional capacity. He reports that on a tour of Ireland in 1765:

> I rode to Waterford, and preached in a little court, on our "great High-Priest that is passed into the heavens" for us. But I soon found I was got above most of my hearers: I should have spoken of death or judgment. On Tuesday evening I suited my discourse to my audience . . . and deep attention sat on almost every face.[53]

He fills his *Journal* with day-to-day notes on the results of his preaching. For example:

> While I was speaking one before me dropped down as dead, and presently a second and a third. Five others sunk down in half an hour, most of whom were in violent agonies. The "pains" as "of hell came about them, the snares of death overtook them." In their trouble we called upon the Lord, and He gave us an answer of peace. One indeed continued

an hour in strong pain, and one or two more for three days; but the rest were greatly comforted in that hour, and went away rejoicing and praising God.[54]

Wesley also reports:

About ten in the morning, J— C—, as she was sitting at work, was suddenly seized with grievous terrors of mind, attended with strong trembling. Thus she continued all the afternoon; but at the society in the evening God turned her heaviness into joy. Five or six others were also cut to the heart this day, and soon after found Him whose hands made whole; as did one likewise who had been mourning many months, without any to comfort her.[54]

This took place at Bristol; but in Newgate Prison, where many who heard him preach were soon due to die by public hanging, his message was, not unnaturally, even more effective:

Immediately one, and another, and another sunk to the earth; they dropped on every side as thunderstruck. One of them cried aloud. We besought God in her behalf, and He turned her heaviness into joy. A second being in the same agony, we called upon God for her also; and He spoke peace unto her soul. . . . One was so wounded by the sword of the Spirit that you would have imagined she could not live a moment. But immediately His abundant kindness was showed, and she loudly sang of His righteousness.[54]

With such preaching methods it is not enough to disrupt previous patterns of behaviour by emotional assaults on the brain, one must also provide an escape from the induced mental stress. Hellfire is presented only as the result of *rejecting* the offer of eternal salvation won by faith. Emotionally disrupted by this threat, and then rescued from everlasting torment by a total change of heart, the convert is now in a state to be helped by dwelling upon the complementary gospel of Love. The punishment for backsliding from a state of grace must always be kept in mind; but once conversion has taken place, love rather than further fear can be used to consolidate the gain. On December 20th, 1751, Wesley wrote:

> I think the right method of preaching is this. At our first beginning to preach at any place, after a general declaration of the love of God to sinners, and His willingness that they should be saved, to preach the law,* in the strongest, the closest, the most searching manner possible.
>
> After more and more persons are convinced of sin, we may mix more and more of the gospel, in order to beget faith, to raise into spiritual life those whom the law hath slain. I would not advise to preach the law without the gospel, any more than the gospel without the law. Undoubtedly, both should be preached in their turns; yea, both at once, or both in one. All the conditional promises are instances of this. They are law and gospel mixed together.[55]

Political brain-washing similarly points to a new path to salvation after fear, anger, and other strong emotions have been excited as a means of disrupting the old bourgeois thought patterns. If the Communist gospel is accepted, love may also be substituted for fear; but severe penalties of relapse await deviationist backsliders.

---

* The "law" in this context includes the certainty that hellfire awaits the unsaved sinner.

As Pavlov's experimental findings in dogs and experiences in the treatment of war neuroses would lead one to expect, the effect of getting too emotionally involved, either positively or negatively, with Wesley's preaching was to increase markedly the likelihood of being converted. It often happened, quite unexpectedly for the person concerned, that when he had been roused to the greatest pitch of indignation and anger by the proceedings, he suddenly broke down and accepted every belief demanded of him. For it has been shown in previous chapters that anger, as well as fear, can induce disturbances of brain function which make a person highly suggestible and reverse his conditioned behaviour patterns, or even wipe the "cortical slate" clean.

Thus Wesley reports on Sunday, July 1st, 1739:

> The first that was deeply touched was L— W—, whose mother had been not a little displeased a day or two before, when she was told how her daughter had exposed herself before all the congregation. The mother herself was the next who dropped down, and lost her senses in a moment; but went home with her daughter, full of joy, as did most of those that had been in pain.

And on Friday, June 15th, 1739, he had also reported:

> Some sunk down, and there remained no strength in them; others exceedingly trembled and quaked; some were torn with a kind of convulsive motion in every part of their bodies, and that so violently that often four or five persons could not hold one of them. I have seen many hysterical and many epileptic fits; but none of them were like these in many respects. I immediately prayed that God would not suffer those who were weak to be offended. But one woman was of-

fended greatly, being sure they might help it if they would—
no one should persuade her to the contrary; and was got
three or four yards when she also dropped down, in as violent an agony as the rest.

Again, on July 30th, 1739:

> One of these had been remarkably zealous against those who
> had cried out and made a noise, being sure that any of them
> might help it if they would. And the same opinion she was
> in still, till the moment she was struck through, as with a
> sword, and fell trembling to the ground. She then cried
> aloud, although not articulately, her words being swallowed
> up. In this pain she continued twelve or fourteen hours,
> and then her soul was set at liberty.

These phenomena were commonest when Wesley first
began preaching after his own conversion, and when he
addressed congregations unused to his methods. But he
was recording them more than thirty years later, still convinced that, to be effective "sanctification" should be sudden and dramatic. He had originally rejected this theory
when made by Peter Böhler, but on re-reading his New
Testament found that the effective conversions reported in
it had, in fact, been sudden ones.

Wesley took the trouble to check his results scientifically:

> In London alone, I found 652 members of our Society who
> were exceedingly clear in their experience, and whose testi-
> mony I could see no reason to doubt. And everyone of these
> (without a single exception) has declared that his deliver-
> ance from sin was instantaneous; that the change was
> wrought in a moment. Had half of these, or one-third, or

one in twenty declared it was *gradually* wrought in *them,* I should have believed this, with regard to *them,* and thought that some were gradually sanctified and some instantaneously. But as I have not found in so long a space of time, a single person speaking thus, I cannot but believe that sanctification is commonly, if not always, an instantaneous work.[56]

This did not mean, of course, that a period of intense anxiety, depression, self-questioning, and indecision, often enhanced by physical debilitation due to a variety of causes, had not preceded the "sanctification". Such "softening-up" processes can all contribute to the disturbances of brain function which occur when stresses become too great and a protective mechanism starts to come into play. Wesley's appeal was most successfully made to the poor and uneducated; but we find him reporting in 1742:

I could not but observe that here the very best people, so-called, were as deeply convinced as open sinners. Several of these were now constrained to roar aloud for the disquietness of their hearts and these generally not young (as in most other places), but either middle aged or well stricken in years.

In 1758, a powerful revival started at Everton. Cambridgeshire farm-workers are by no means an easily excited group but the Rev. John Berridge had also stumbled on the basic mechanics of the sudden conversion process. Though accused by his religious detractors at the near-by Cambridge University of exhorting his audience to "Fall! Won't you fall! Why don't you fall! Better fall here, than fall into hell!" He had no hesitation in inducing the final

Early print by Heemskerck of a Quaker Meeting, showing quaking.

A Hogarth contemporary print (1747) of
Wesley (or one of his preachers) going in the
death cart with a condemned man to Tyburn.

The following series of photographs show some of the physiological mechanisms of conversion discussed in this book. They are seen in a wide variety of religious settings in quite different parts of the world, and they are helping to implement or maintain quite different types of religious beliefs.

In primitive religions, rhythmic drumming is very commonly used to stimulate group excitement and emotional release.

Paul Hartmann from *Dieux d'Afrique* by Pierre Verger

Paul Hartmann from *Dieux d'Afrique* by Pierre Verger

Rhythmic dancing and hand clapping is also common (above).

Priests, too, may help to whip up the excitement (left).

Paul Hartmann from *Dieux d'Afrique* by Pierre Verger

Acute states of excitement may then occur
in participants, which are often attributed
to the intervention of a god.

The final phase of exhaustion and collapse may
then supervene.

Transmarginal exhaustion and collapse (below).

Paul Hartmann from *Dieux d'Afrique* by Pierre Verger

Isles of Rhythm by Earl Leaf, A.S. Barnes

Voodoo trance and possession.

Dance and Drama in Bali by Beryl de Zoeta and Walter Spies, Faber & Faber

Technique used in Bali which makes those taking part believe they are possessed by the spirits of monkeys.

Terminal exhaustion phase of religious trance dancing in Bali.

state of collapse in his converts, for the number of "groaners, sighers, tumblers and convulsionists" also caused dismay at the University. In *Simeon and Church Order,* Charles Smyth reports him as writing:

> And now let me make one Reflection. I preached of Sanctification very earnestly for six Years in a former Parish and never brought one Soul to Christ. I did the same at this Parish for two Years, without any Success at all; but as soon as ever I preached Jesus Christ, and Faith in His Blood, then Believers were added to the Church continually; then People, flocked from all Parts to hear the glorious Sound of the Gospel, some coming six Miles, others eight, and others ten and that constantly . . .

Berridge told them:

> . . . very plainly, that they were Children of wrath, and under the Curse of God, though they knew it not; . . . labouring to beat down Self-Righteousness; labouring to show them that they were all in a lost and perishing State, and that nothing could recover them out of this State, and make them Children of God, but Faith in the Lord Jesus Christ.[57]

By this method, Southey writes: "this man produced a more violent influenza of fanaticism than had ever followed upon Whitfield's or Wesley's preachings."[57]

Some persons tend to minimize the importance of psychological factors, emotional doubts, physical debilitation, and the like, in religious conversions, and to emphasize them when excusing the victims of similarly induced political conversion. But successful "brain-washing" also demands the rousing of strong emotions, and these need not have any particular relevance to the new faith provided that they are sufficiently disruptive. For example, Arthur Koestler's *Arrow in the Blue*[58] describes his conversion to militant Communism in these words:

> Though I had been steadily moving towards the Communist position for more than a year, the final decision to become an actual member of the Party was again a sudden one. . . . This time the event that clinched the issue was of a more profane nature. More precisely, it was a whole series of grotesque events, crowded into one December evening in 1931.

Koestler goes on to explain how, one Saturday afternoon, he went to fetch his car from a garage where it had been under repair for nearly three weeks. Delighted to get it back, he drove straight from the garage to a friend's flat where a poker party was in progress. Koestler loved poker, was not too expert at it, but seldom lost heavily. That afternoon, however, he lost the equivalent of several months' salary; far more than he could afford:

> Dejected, I drove to an after-dinner party of the radical bohemia, where I promptly got drunk, as under the circumstances was only to be expected. The party lasted till two or three in the morning, and I paid no attention to the fact that it had turned very cold, and that I had no anti-freeze in my radiator. When I left, the engine-block of the newly-repaired car had burst and a thick icicle was sticking out of one of the cylinder-heads—a sight to make any motorist weep, even if the car was not his own.

More trouble was still to come:

On seeing my dismay, a girl who had been at the party and who had always got on my nerves, offered me the hospitality of her nearby flat; this again leading to the consequences which were to be expected. I woke up in the morning with a super-hangover mixed with self-reproach, anxiety and guilt next to a person whom I disliked, financially broke, and with a bust-up car.

Koestler comments:

> In my experiences the "language of destiny" is often couched in vulgar slang. The series of grotesque misadventures on that Saturday night looked as if they had been arranged by a crude jester; but the face of a clown, bending close against your own, can be very frightening. By the time I got back to my flat my decision was made, though I hardly felt it to be mine; it had made itself. Pacing up and down in my bedroom, I had the sudden impression that I was looking down from a height at the track along which I had been running. I saw myself with great clarity as a sham and a phoney, paying lip-service to the Revolution which was to lift the earth from its axis, and at the same time leading the existence of a bourgeois careerist, climbing the worm-eaten ladder of success, playing poker and landing in unsought beds.

The pattern of Koestler's life underwent a total change, and he remained a loyal Communist until six years later, when he experienced an equally intense reconversion. In *The God That Failed* [3] the phenomena were seen to follow a series of emotional shocks, when captured and imprisoned during the Spanish Civil War:

> The experiences responsible for this change were fear, pity, and a third one, more difficult to describe. Fear not of death,

but of torture and humiliation, and the more unpleasant forms of dying . . . and finally, a condition of mind usually referred to in terms borrowed from the vocabulary of mysticism, which would present itself at unexpected moments and induce a state of inner peace which I have known neither before nor since . . .

In *The Invisible Writing* [59] he also says:

On the day when Sir Peter [Chalmers] and I were arrested, there had been three occasions when I believed my execution was imminent. . . . On all three occasions I had benefited from the well-known phenomenon of a split consciousness, a dreamlike, dazed self-estrangement, which separated the conscious self from the acting self—the former becoming a detached observer, the latter an automaton, while the air hums in one's ears as in the hollow of a seashell. . . . Much worse was another episode on the same day; being photographed for the rogues' gallery against a wall in the street, hands tied, in the midst of a hostile crowd.

This last incident had revived claustrophobic panic feelings experienced during a surgical operation in his childhood. Koestler reports:

This, together with the other events of the same day, and of the next three days with their mass executions, had apparently caused a loosening-up and displacement of psychic strata close to rock-bottom—a softening of resistances and rearrangement of structures which laid them temporarily open to that new type of experience that I am leading up to.

These clinical observations become still more interesting when he gives in non-religious terms the same sort of mystical experience that floods the literature of religious conversion. The fact is that mystical experiences, like sudden conversions, do not always arise from purely religious influences and stresses; they can sometimes be induced by chemical means—such as, for instance, mescaline, ether, and laughing gas.

Koestler's detailed accounts of his two conversions, and the quasi-mystical experiences that accompanied the second of these, show how varied are the emotional and physiological stresses that can help towards conversion. His stresses include a severe alcoholic hangover, a broken-down car, heavy financial loss, a disagreeable sexual entanglement; civil war, capture, threats of sudden death by shooting, and the revival of a childhood panic. In each case, the new troubles were heaped on the old until their combined weight perhaps proved more than could be tolerated by his nervous system, and a change in brain patterns seems to have occurred.

Koestler's *The Invisible Writing* should be read for a full description of his non-religious mystical or dream-like type of experience in prison:

> Then I was floating on my back in a river of peace under bridges of silence. It came from nowhere and flowed nowhere. Then there was no river and no I. The I had ceased to exist.

He also says:

> The coming-back to the lower order of reality I found to be gradual, like waking up from anaesthesia. . . . Whether the experience had lasted for a few minutes or an hour, I never

knew. In the beginning it occurred two or even three times a week, then the intervals became longer. It could never be voluntarily induced. After my liberation it recurred at even longer intervals, perhaps once or twice in a year. But by that time the groundwork for a change of personality was completed.[59]

Experiences of this sort can be induced by a wide range of stresses on the brain. What is more, feelings of divine possession and subsequent conversion to a religious faith can be helped on by the use of many types of physiological stimuli. It should be more widely known that electrical recordings of the human brain show that it is particularly sensitive to rhythmic stimulation by percussion and bright light, among other things, and certain rates of rhythm can build up recordable abnormalities of brain function and explosive states of tension sufficient even to produce convulsive fits in predisposed subjects. Some people can be persuaded to dance in time with such rhythms until they collapse in exhaustion. Furthermore, it is easier to disorganize the normal function of the brain by attacking it simultaneously with several strong rhythms played in different tempos. This leads on to protective inhibition either rapidly in the "weak inhibitory" temperament or after a prolonged period of excitement in the "strong excitatory" one.

Rhythmic drumming is found in the ceremonies of many primitive religions all over the world. The accompanying excitement and dancing is also maintained until the same point of physical and emotional collapse has been reached.[60] Alcohol and other drugs are often used to heighten the excitement of religious dancers and this too hastens the breakdown, after which feelings of being freed from sin and evil dispositions, and of starting life anew, may occur. Belief in divine possession is very common at such times, and so is the mystical trance—essentially similar to that experienced by so many Christian and other saints in cramped cells or under martyrdom, and vouchsafed to Koestler when threatened with shooting by the Franco forces.

The Voodoo cult in Haiti shows with what ease suggestibility can be increased by subjecting the brain to severe physiological stresses. Voodoo has numerous deities, or *loa*, some of them African tribal gods, brought to the West Indies by slaves, some of them saints whom Catholic priests later taught the slaves to invoke. The *loa* are believed to descend and take possession of a person, usually while he or she is dancing to the drums. The possessed person then behaves as the particular deity should behave; the different habits of *loa* being a matter of tradition. As with soldiers who continue fight after being temporarily stunned by an explosion, or football players who get kicked on the head in the early stages of an exciting match, the possessed have no recollection, when they come to themselves again an hour or so later, of what has seemed to others an intelligent and effective performance.

The case of men and women who have been worked up into a state of suggestibility by Voodoo drumming shows the power of such methods. Though apparently unconscious, they carry out all the detailed behaviour expected of the particular deity by which they believe themselves possessed. A Voodoo priest increases excitement and suggestibility by altering the loudness and rhythms of the drums just as in a religious snake handling cult, which I observed myself in the United States, the preacher used the tempo and volume of singing and hand clapping to intensify the religious enthusiasm, and emotional disruption was finally induced by thrusting live poisonous snakes into their hands. After a terminal collapse into stupor, both groups of participants may awake with a sense of spiritual rebirth.

In 1949, Maya Deren went to Haiti on a Guggenheim Fellowship to study and film Haitian dancing. In the *Divine Horsemen*[61] she has published a detailed account of the physiological and psychological effects of the drumming on her own brain, ending in her apparent possession by Erszulie, the Goddess of Love. She tells how the drums gradually induced uncontrollable bodily movement, until as a climax she felt possession coming on her:

> My skull is a drum; each great beat drives that leg, like the point of a stake, into the ground. The singing is at my very ear inside my head. This sound will drown me! "Why don't they stop! Why don't they stop!" I cannot wrench the leg free. I am caught in this cylinder, this well of sound. There is nothing anywhere except this. There is no way out. The white darkness moves up the veins of my leg like a swift tide rising, rising; is a great force which I cannot sustain or contain which, surely, will burst my skin. It is too much, too bright, too white for me; this is its darkness. "Mercy!" I scream within me. I hear it echoed by the voices, shrill and unearthly: *"Erszulie."* The bright darkness floods up through my body, reaches my head, engulfs me. I am sucked down and exploded upward at once. That is all.

She also tries to convey some of the strange feelings and impressions that came upon her while dancing in a trance around the peristyle of the Voodooan meeting-house, behaving as the Goddess Erszulie is supposed to behave on such occasions:

> If the earth is a sphere, then the abyss below the earth is also its heavens; and the difference between them is no more than time, the time of the earth's turning. If the earth is a vast horizontal surface . . .

Such feelings expressed in ordinary language are incomprehensible and even nonsensical to readers who have never experienced the "paradoxical" and "ultra-paradoxical" phases of brain activity induced by intolerable stress; "white darkness", for instance, makes no more sense to them than would the intense mystical joy excited by flagellation.

Maya Deren enjoyed feelings of spiritual rebirth as she recovered from her trance:

> How clear the world looks in this first total light. How purely form it is, without, for the moment, the shadow of meaning. . . . As the souls of the dead did, so have I, too, come back. I have returned.

These experiences, which changed her plans for the future, as well as her outlook on Voodoo, also show what may happen to those who try to fight rather than avoid these mechanistic processes by too strong an exercise of will-power. The emotion expended in the effort sometimes only hastens their breakdown. Maya Deren describes how she was caught in this way. Just before her possession, she

pert on the culture of the Songhay tribe, has recently made a remarkable documentary film showing Songhay migrants returning to the Ivory Coast from a visit to the Gold Coast. They are performing a dance learned from a Gold Coast cult-group who believe in spirit possession, and who help to arouse the necessary enthusiasm and suggestibility by drumming. One interesting feature of the film is that the devotees come to believe that they are possessed not by *loa* of ancient tradition, but by the personalities of important living beings. They even believe that the Governor General of the Gold Coast and senior officers of the West African Rifles make a spiritual entry into them and mime their gestures realistically; also, oddly enough, the spirit influences include a railway engine, conceived as a demon, since many Songhays become casual workers on the Gold Coast railway. In the film, the dancers are seen travelling onward, the next day, sober and obviously benefited by their abreactive experience.[62]

All such methods of implanting or fortifying beliefs may have somewhat similar results. When Maya Deren is discoursing on the spiritual values of Voodoo, she might well be compared to a patient trying to discuss, in a reasonable and restrained manner, a now successfully completed psychoanalysis:

> I would say that . . . it incorporates values with which I am in personal agreement, displays unorganizational, psychic and practical skill which I admire, and accomplishes results of which I approve. I would further say, that I believe that the principles which Ghede and other loa represent are real and true. . . . It was this kind of agreement with, and admi-

ration for, the principles and practice of Voodoun which was and is my conscious attitude towards it.[61]

A comparison between the methods already described and those used by some primitive tribes all over the world to initiate and condition adolescent boys into religious societies should also be mentioned, because the underlying physiological principles do appear to have certain similarities. In such cases, however, the new attitudes to be implanted will be more consistent with their previous experience and general tradition of culture than in some of the other instances given in this chapter. Gustaf Bolinder, in *Devilman's Jungle*,[63] describes how West African boys are taken away from their parents to an encampment in the woods, where all their clothes are removed and they are subjected to conditions of severe physical hardship. The procedure is suitably fear provoking. First, they are given a medicine which, they are told, will certainly kill them sooner or later if they ever reveal the secrets of the Society, or the details of the ceremonies they are about to undergo. Next comes the ritual bath. At dusk they are lined up and told:

> A life outside Poro is scarcely worth living. He who is not a member wanders about in the darkness. It is only through Poro that you realize what it is that you have to live for. He who wishes to become a member of Poro must say good-bye to life as he has lived it hitherto and be born afresh.

In an increasingly terrified state, they now see the secret society's most frightening mask approaching them, with:

. . . staring eyes and bushy eyebrows, huge jaws like a crocodile in which his teeth shine red with blood. He is bearded like an old man and he has horns and feathers on his head and a shapeless figure—a cloak of fibres that has no resemblance to anything human.

For the boys it is a real demon, but they are not allowed to utter a sound. They are laid side by side on the ground; then each in turn is seized by the demon's assistants and, almost unconscious with fright, lifted up and put between his jaws. They are then rescued and immediately given extremely painful ritual tattooing. The ceremony is accompanied by loud noises on wooden instruments:

> Gradually the half-conscious novices recover their senses. They feel convinced that the demon has made an end of them, but Poro has raised them to new life.

A few days after the tattoo scars have healed, the boys begin a prolonged training in the camp intended to make them useful members of the tribe and the society in which they are now adepts. Childhood habits are dispersed. They learn among other things, the correct attitude which they must in future adopt to their superiors, and increase their hardihood and fortitude by taking part in strenuous tests of endurance. Sex-training is given them, with education in primitive handicrafts, carpentry, fishing, and the like: all of which amounts to a new conditioning process as members of their tribe and secret society. Here again an overwhelming emotional stimulus carries the subject to the point of emotional collapse and increased suggestibility. And here again the fear-provoking stimulus is offset by a means of salvation—the benign Poro—to which the boy clings in his reconditioning process. Gustaf Bolinder also reports:

> Certain exercises are used to try and efface remnants of personal individuality or unorthodox ideas; these begin with monotonous movements of the body and conclude with mystical rites. The prime factor here is the dance, a dance anything but static; rather suggestive in its uniformity. . . . Round the tree the novices dance slowly with bowed heads. Now the booming wooden drums have taken up the accompaniment. Without a pause, slow and uniform, the dance continues hour after hour. In the end the novices are only semi-conscious treading mechanically in the same everlasting rhythm. They are no longer on earth—they have become merged in the unity of the mighty forest demon and feel spiritually uplifted.

Sir James Frazer in *The Golden Bough* [64] gives further examples of such initiation rites. He shows that some tribes in northern New Guinea, and many Australian tribes also, make circumcision an essential feature of the tribal initiation, and the initiation "is conceived by them as a process of being swallowed and disgorged by a mythical monster, whose voice is heard in the humming sound of the bull-roarer". (The bull-roarer, also used by the ancient Greeks and called the *rhombos,* is a wooden instrument which, when whirled around the head on a cord, makes a sound like a roaring bull or a rising gale.) Various terrifying ways of being swallowed are then described but the initiate is inevitably rescued. In one tribe:

. . . he has now to undergo the more painful and dangerous operation of circumcision. It follows immediately, and the cut made by the knife of the operator is explained to be a bite or scratch which the monster inflicted on the novice in spewing him out of his capacious jaw. While the operation is proceeding, a prodigious noise is made by the swinging of bull-roarers to represent the roar of the dreadful being who is in the act of swallowing the young men.

The same reconditioning process then takes place:

> After they have been circumcised, the lads must remain for some months in seclusion, shunning all contact with women and even the sight of them. They live in the long hut which represents the monster's belly. When at last the lads, now ranking as initiated men, are brought back with great pomp and ceremony to the village, they are received with sobs of joy by the women, as if the grave had given up its dead.

One interesting detail about the use of such methods is Frazer's statement that several tribes in New Guinea use the same word for the rhombos or bull-roarer as for the monster who is supposed to swallow the novices, and whose fearful roar is represented by its noise. A close association of ideas is established between the sound of the rhombos and the powerful ghost or ancestral spirit who swallows and disgorges the novice at his initiation. The rhombos or bull-roarer becomes, in fact, "his material representative on earth".

This use of the rhombos as a constant reminder of the power and presence of the god or ancestral spirit recalls Pavlov's discovery that most of the dogs which were nearly drowned in their cages during the Leningrad flood (see

Chapter 1, p. 17), and had their conditioned behaviour patterns broken up by it, became highly sensitized to the sight of that trickle of water under the laboratory door. He could get at them afterwards by merely emptying a bucket of water outside.

In highly civilized Christian countries today, a similar attempt is sometimes made to invest God's representative on earth with as much religiously-toned emotion as possible. But, in order to safeguard infants and young children against damnation, the rite of baptism, originally reserved for adults and a powerful ceremony indeed, is now carried out a few weeks or months after birth. Confirmation has, in general taken the place of baptism as an initiatory rite, and among Protestants still provides a strong emotional stimulus for boys and girls at the age of puberty, but in Latin countries the "First Communion" also tends to be taken too early for full emotional effect. It seems certain that such stimuli should be made emotionally disturbing to produce their desired effect—even severe enough sometimes to induce mystical experiences. Once a mystical experience is associated with the Cross, or some other religious emblem, it can be revived and confirmed by the emblem's subsequent appearance.

Intellectual indoctrination without emotional excitement is remarkably ineffective, as the empty pews of most English churches prove; the social pressure which once sent even the agnostic or lukewarm to Sunday matins having long been relaxed. And recently we found ourselves welcoming a high-powered American fundamentalist who had come to win back for the Churches the congregations that they had lost. What the force of religion could once be, even under civilized paganisms using effective methods, is shown by Frazer's account in *The Golden Bough* of the Syrian Astarte worship. The great festival of this goddess fell in early spring:

> While the flutes played, the drums beat, and the eunuch priests slashed themselves with knives, the religious excitement gradually spread like a wave among the crowd of onlookers, and many a one did that which he little thought to do when he came as a holiday spectator to the festival. For man after man, his veins throbbing with the music, his eyes fascinated by the sight of the streaming blood, flung his garments from him, leaped forth with a shout, and seizing one of the swords which stood ready for the purpose, castrated himself on the spot. . . . When the tumult of emotion had subsided and the man had come to himself again, the irrevocable sacrifice must often have been followed by passionate sorrow and life-long regret. This revulsion of natural feeling after the frenzies of a fanatical religion is powerfully depicted by Catullus in a celebrated poem.

It does seem that most powerful religious movements are attended by physiological phenomena which cause intellectual disgust and dismay in non-participants. Thus Fox's blameless "Friends", whose faith was based on non-violence, were given the sneering nickname of "Quakers" because they "shook and trembled before the Lord":

> Men, women and little children at their meetings are strangely wrought upon in their bodies, and brought to fall, foam at the mouth, roar and swell in their bellies.[52]

Fox himself reports in his *Journal*:

This Captain Drury, though he sometimes carried fairly, was an enemy to me and to Truth, and opposed it; and when professors came to me (while I was under his custody) and he was by, he would scoff at trembling, and call us Quakers, as the Independents and Presbyterians had nicknamed us before. But afterwards he once came to me and told me that, as he was lying on his bed to rest, in the day time, he fell atrembling, that his joints knocked together, and his body shook so that he could not get off the bed; he was so shaken that he had not strength left, and cried to the Lord. And he felt His power was upon him, and he tumbled off his bed, and cried to the Lord, and said he never would speak against the Quakers more, and such as trembled at the word of God.[65]

The Quakers later settled down to become rich and respectable, abandoning the means by which they had built up their early spiritual strength. It is the fate of new religious sects to lose the dynamism of their "enthusiastic" founders; later leaders may improve the organization, but the original conversion techniques are often tacitly repudiated. The wild militancy of General Booth's early Salvation Army is gone. The frantic scenes of the Welsh revival are forgotten in new and respectable chapels, where the *hwyl* (a Welsh preaching device for exciting the congregation to religious frenzy by breaking into a wild chant) is now rarely heard. The surprise that Dr. Billy Graham's success has caused in Great Britain, where all he has to compete with is religious addresses aimed at the congregation's intelligence rather than its emotions, shows how widespread is the general ignorance of matters discussed in this book.

Even in Christianity "the gift of tongues", sometimes only an incoherent babel, is still applauded by certain primitive sects as supposedly reproducing the experience of the Apostles at Pentecost, and great importance is placed in other religions too on the appearance of trance phenomena. This is shown by the attribution of divine wisdom to the Delphic Oracle in Classical Greece. It is shown in Tibet, where the national policy can still be decided by an oracle of the same sort. Harrer, in *Seven Years in Tibet*,[66] describes how his Tibetan friend Wandüla took him to an official consultation with the Oracle at the Nechung Monastery at Lhasa. A nineteen-year-old monk was the mouthpiece of the Oracle at that time, and Harrer remarks:

> It was always a curious experience to meet the State Oracle in ordinary life. I could never quite get accustomed to sitting at the same table with him and hearing him noisily gulping his noodle soup. When we met in the street, I used to take of my hat and he bowed and smiled in return. His face was that of a nice-looking young man, and bore no resemblance to the bloated, red-flecked, grimacing visage of the ecstatic medium.

Harrer gives details of what happened when the Oracle fell into a trance; and wondered whether drugs or any other means were used to induce it:

> The monk has to be able to dislodge his spirit from his body to enable the god of the temple to take possession of it and to speak through his mouth. . . . Hollow, eerie music greeted us at the gate of the temple. Inside the spectacle was ghastly. From every wall looked down hideous, grimacing faces, and the air was filled with stifling fumes of incense. The young

monk had just been led from his private quarters to the gloomy temple.

Here is Harrer's description of the actual possession:

> The trembling became more violent. The medium's heavily laden head wavered from side to side, and his eyes started from their sockets. His face was swollen and covered with patches of hectic red. . . . Now he started beating on his gleaming breastplate with a great thumb-ring, making a clatter which drowned the dull rolling of the drums. Then he gyrated on one foot, erect under the weight of the giant headdress, which just now two men could hardly carry. . . . The medium became calmer. Servants held him fast and a Cabinet Minister stepped before him and threw a scarf over his head. Then he began to ask questions carefully prepared by the Cabinet about the appointment of a governor, the discovery of a new Incarnation, matters involving war and peace. The Oracle was asked to decide on all these things.

Harrer goes on to say that he attended many consultations of the Oracle, but had "never been able to arrive even at an approximate explanation of the riddle".

Some persons can produce a state of trance and dissociation in themselves, or in others, with a decreasing need for strong and repeated emotional stresses, until it may become so much a conditioned pattern of brain activity that it occurs with only minor stresses and difficulties; for example, in the primitive religious context, at the renewed beat of a drum, or the screaming roar of the rhombos.

States of possession or trance have also been used by numerous religions to try to help the spectator, as well as the possessed person, to accept the relevant doctrine as true. If the trance is accompanied by a state of mental dissociation, the person experiencing it can be profoundly influenced in his subsequent thinking and behaviour. Even if the spectators remain unmoved and devoid of any emotional excitement, it may still help to persuade some of them of the truth of the belief professed, especially if they have been led to think that a trance means that the person concerned is now possessed by, or in communication with, a certain god. When the modern spiritualistic medium in her suburban house uses messages from dead relatives, or from the ghost of an Indian fakir, or from a childlike spirit called Forget-me-not, to help to create faith in spiritualism, the same mechanisms may be seen in operation as when the State Oracle of Tibet gyrates and clatters in the Nechung Monastery, or as when the drugged Pythoness of Delphi, her face distorted by Apollo's divine possession, raged on her tripod, pouring out a stream of confused prophecy which the priest in charge, if suitably paid, turned into hexameters for the visitant.

The proof of the pudding lies in the eating. Wesley changed the religious and social life of England for the better with the help of such methods in a modified and socially accepted form. In other hands and other countries they have been used for sinister purposes. But one can be thankful that there have always been scientifically curious people in all ages prepared to examine and report on the actual results obtained before condemning the use of such methods out of hand. Thomas Butts has this to report about Wesley's preaching as early as 1743:

As to persons crying out or being in fits, I shall not pretend to account exactly for that, but only make this observation: it is well known that most of them who have been so exercised were before of no religion at all, but they have since received a sense of pardon, have peace and joy in believing, and are now more holy and happy than ever they were before. And if this be so, no matter what remarks are made on their fits.[67]

The account given in the *Acts of the Apostles* (Chapter 2) of Peter's sermon at Pentecost also emphasizes the effectiveness of the religious methods discussed in this chapter. No less than three thousand converts are said to have been added that day to the very small group of apostles and other believers who remained faithful after Jesus's farewell on the Mount of Olives. The chapter begins:

And when the day of Pentecost was fully come, they were all with one accord in one place. And suddenly there came a sound from heaven as of a rushing mighty wind, and it filled all the house where they were sitting. And there appeared unto them cloven tongues like as of fire, and it sat upon each of them. And they were all filled with the Holy Ghost, and began to speak with other tongues, as the Spirit gave them utterance . . . (and) . . . every man heard them speak in his own language.

Peter then rises and begins to preach. He adds further tension to an audience already half-stupefied by the news of that strange Gift of Tongues. In a very powerful speech he announces that they are now watching what has long been foretold by the prophets. He quotes the Prophet Joel:

> And it shall come to pass in the last days, saith God . . . I
> will shew wonders in heaven above, and signs in the earth
> beneath; blood, and fire, and vapour of smoke: The sun
> shall be turned into darkness, and the moon into blood,
> before that great and notable day of the Lord come: And it
> shall come to pass, that whosoever shall call on the name of
> the Lord shall be saved.

Then he flings an emotional thunderbolt at his scared
and excited listeners. He tells them that Jesus of Nazareth
was "a man approved of God among you by miracles and
wonders and signs . . ." whom the chief priests had handed
over to the Romans to be "crucified and slain by wicked
hands". He makes them understand just who the man was
whom they had allowed the chief priests to hand over for
crucifixion to their Roman patrons, but whom God had
now raised up from the dead. By not making a mass protest, however busy they may have been on preparing for
the Passover, they have become, he insists, murderers in
the second degree:

> Therefore let all the house of Israel know assuredly, that
> God hath made that same Jesus, whom ye have crucified,
> both Lord and Christ.

Peter's audience had now come to believe that the "Gift
of Tongues" was a sign from God, God who, in accordance
with eschatological prophecy, had darkened the sun at the
Crucifixion and turned the moon to the colour of blood,
with a fearful dust-storm from Elam. Now they are assured that the victim was God's representative on earth

and they cannot escape the guilt of his death. It is therefore easy to understand how:

> . . . when they heard this, they were pricked in their heart, and said unto Peter and to the rest of the apostles, Men and brethren, what shall we do? Then Peter said unto them, Repent, and be baptized everyone of you in the name of Jesus Christ for the remission of sins, and ye shall receive the gift of the Holy Ghost. . . . And with many other words did he testify and exhort, saying, Save yourselves from this untoward generation. Then they that gladly received his word were baptized: and the same day there were added unto them about three thousand souls.

New beliefs and habits now seemed readily imposed on the converts:

> And they continued steadfastly in the apostles' doctrine and fellowship, and in breaking of bread, and in prayers. And fear came upon every soul: and many wonders and signs were done by the apostles. . . . And the Lord added to the church daily such as should be saved.

The case of Saul on the road to Damascus confirms our other finding: that anger may be no less powerful an emotion than fear in bringing about sudden conversion to beliefs which exactly contradict beliefs previously held. *Acts*, Chapter 9, tells:

> And Saul, yet breathing out threatenings and slaughter against the disciples of the Lord, went unto the high priest and desired of him letters to Damascus to the synagogues, that if he found any of this way, whether they were men or women, he might bring them bound unto Jerusalem. And

as he journeyed, he came near Damascus: and suddenly there shined round about him a light from heaven: And he fell to the earth, and heard a voice saying unto him, Saul, Saul, why persecutest thou me? And he said, Who art thou, Lord? And the Lord said, I am Jesus whom thou persecutest: it is hard for thee to kick against the pricks. And he trembling and astonished said, Lord what wilt thou have me to do?

A state of transmarginal inhibition seems to have followed his acute stage of nervous excitement. Total collapse, hallucinations and an increased state of suggestibility appear to have supervened. Other inhibitory hysterical manifestations are also reported:

And Saul arose from the earth; and when his eyes were opened, he saw no man: but they led him by the hand, and brought him into Damascus; And he was three days without sight, and neither did eat nor drink.

This period of physical debilitation by fasting, added to Saul's other stresses, may well have increased his anxiety and suggestibility. Only after three days did Brother Ananias come to relieve his nervous symptoms and his mental distress, at the same time implanting new beliefs:

And Ananias went his way, and entered into the house; and putting his hands on him said, Brother Saul, the Lord, even Jesus, that appeared unto thee in the way as thou camest, hath sent me, that thou mightest receive thy sight, and be filled with the Holy Ghost. And immediately there fell from his eyes as it had been scales: and he received sight forthwith, and arose, and was baptized. And when he had received meat, he was strengthened.

Then followed the necessary period of indoctrination imposed on Saul by the brethren at Damascus and of his full acceptance of all the new beliefs that they required of him:

> Then was Saul certain days with the disciples which were at Damascus. And straightway he preached Christ in the synagogues, that he is the son of God. But all that heard him were amazed, and said, Is not this he that destroyed them which called on this name in Jerusalem, and came hither for that intent, that he might bring them bound unto the chief priests?

At all events, the most striking and momentous individual conversion, and the most far-reaching mass conversion in the history of the early Church are both recorded in the *Acts* in terms consonant with modern physiological observations, and the authorship of the *Acts* is attributed to St. Luke who was himself a physician. It would therefore be foolish to underestimate the efficiency of such methods. Not only have they assisted in the emergence of Christianity as the leading religion of the Western world today; but they have been used, time and time again, to reinforce numerous other types of religious and political belief—which will be discussed in the rest of this book.

CHAPTER 6

Applications of Religious Techniques

Homer's epics are still being published in many languages nearly three thousand years after they were first composed. His readers throughout the centuries have been brought up in quite different social and religious environments, yet the psychological types, and the normal and abnormal behaviour patterns he describes in his heroes, are still easily recognized. Often his descriptions of mental conflicts make us feel that he is describing our own.

If our temperaments and modes of thought were so largely the result of environment, upbringing and the exercise of "free will" as some people think, the behaviour of characters in ancient literature could mean very little to us. Yet, as Ben Jonson[68] showed in his "Humour" comedies, there was no noticeable difference between the basic temperamental types of the Jacobean age and those described by Hippocrates some two thousand years before; and Jonson's plays still attract packed houses. Basic behaviour patterns in man are indeed more dependent on our inherited higher nervous systems than we sometimes care to admit. The personality can react only along limited lines to all environmental changes, and to a life full of stresses. If stress be severe enough, the most secure and stable personality can show symptoms of anxiety, hypochondria, depression, hysteria, suspiciousness, excitement, anger or aggressiveness, and the list is then almost complete.

Since, therefore, the same basic patterns of reaction to stress were all noted in the Classical era, if not for thousands and thousands of years previously, and since their equivalents can also be demonstrated in the behaviour of animals, they are most likely, it seems, to be physiologically determined. Moreover, physiological treatments can be shown to be most effective in ridding ordinary brains of previous patterns of behaviour and thought; and it has been pointed out repeatedly in this book that in abnormal persons and in the overmeticulous, particularly violent treatments may be needed if firmly fixed delusions and obsessional habits are really to be changed at all.

In 1902, William James in *The Varieties of Religious Experience* wrote about states of deep spiritual depression:

> But the deliverance must come in as strong a form as the complaint, if it is to take effect; and that seems the reason why the coarser religions, revivalistic, orgiastic, with blood and miracles and supernatural operations, may possibly never be displaced. Some constitutions need them too much.[56]

The cure for the most severe types of religious melancholia for which nothing could be done in James's day, has turned out to be even more drastic than he predicted. Melancholics, whom even orgiastic revivals leave cold and unimpressed, are now quickly benefited by simple convulsions, mechanically induced by passing an electric current through the brain.*

* John Wesley was, interestingly enough, a great believer in electrical

Wesley's preaching could stir up such a state of external or internal excitement in some types of people that brain inhibition finally supervened and they collapsed from emotional exhaustion. Voodoo dances, drums, and other similar methods producing feelings of conversion to, and possession by, gods, can also cause such states of brain excitement in suitable subjects. Many kinds of spiritual healers seem to use the same basic technique with differing interpretations added. In Tripoli, for instance, Alberto de Pirajno in *A Cure for Serpents* describes the treatment of a girl suffering from melancholia supposedly "caused by a dark and evil spirit". A large frog with henna-tinted legs was said to contain the *jinn* or spirit which gave the native healer his power to heal "without medicine by provoking curative convulsions in sick people". The method required the depressed person to dance to the point of frenzy for hours on end to beating drums and rhythmic singing, and

treatment though not given to the point of producing a convulsion. A Leyden jar that was used for this purpose can be seen in Wesley's museum, City Road, London. Starting in 1756, special clinics for this treatment were provided at Moorfields, Southwark, St. Paul's and the Seven Dials. Wesley writes in almost a modern vein:

> Hundreds, perhaps thousands, have received unspeakable good; and I have not known one man, woman, or child, who has received any hurt thereby; so that, when I hear any talk of the danger of being electrified (especially if they are medical men who talk so), I cannot but impute it to great want either of sense or honesty.

And he also said:

> We know it is a thousand medicines in one; in particular, that it is the most efficacious medicine in nervous disorders of every kind, which has ever yet been discovered.

Wesley is quoted in Tyerman's *Life of Wesley*. See note 55.

a mounting group excitement till "a stream of foam and sweat ran down from the corners of her mouth". With a "piercing shriek" the patient finally flung herself on the ground, was stripped of her clothes and was repeatedly plunged into water:

> Naked, the girl seemed to be made of ivory as she hung between the smoke-black arms of the negresses who carried her towards the tub. . . . When I saw the girl again, she was wrapped in a blanket and her expression was completely altered. . . . She smiled ecstatically and cast her eyes heavenwards . . . and smilingly received the congratulations of her friends, as they led her to the magician's feet. The *faqth* had not moved at all throughout the seance, except to take on his lap the frog with the henna-tinted legs.[69]

Electric convulsion therapy for depressed patients also seems to belong to this same physiological category; because here the patient's brain is excited electrically to the point of convulsion, and this convulsion continues until the brain becomes totally exhausted and a temporary stupor sets in. Is it then surprising to observe the astonishing effects that a series of electrically produced fits can have on melancholias seen in a *religious* setting, despite all the complicated philosophical and metaphysical theories that used to be put forward to account for them?

Most readers can cite the cases of relatives or friends who have suffered from mental depression, the symptoms of which—greatly exaggerated ideas of guilt and unworthiness—disappear suddenly and completely when the attack is over. A long period, for instance, of overwork, or an emotional shock, or a bereavement may make the patient start to torture himself with the remembrance of minor sins, and fill him with forebodings about the future. He has an urge to confess to all and sundry—a habit which fills him with retrospective embarrassment when he recovers—and may attempt to kill himself, even though believing that suicides are punished with eternal damnation—because he is convinced that this will be his fate in any case.

A main symptom of the illness is the patient's complete irresponsiveness to intellectual argument or spiritual consolation. Whether the surroundings be pleasant or unpleasant, the feelings of guilt persist until the depression lifts; sometimes the attacks are periodic and separated by interludes of normal behaviour and even elation; sometimes they are chronic and last for years. William James had this to say about religious melancholias:

> . . . but were we disposed to open the chapter of really insane melancholia . . . it would be a worse story still—desperation absolute and complete, the whole universe coagulating about the sufferer into a material of overwhelming horror . . . and no other conception or sensation able to live for a moment in its presence. . . . Here is the real core of the religious problem: *Help! Help! No prophet can claim to bring a final message unless he says things which will have a sound of reality in the ears of victims such as these.*[70]

And now the introduction of a simple physiological method—electrical shock treatment—has meant that numerous sufferers from this condition, for whom the saintliest or most understanding priest could do nothing, are cured in three or four weeks' time, instead of dying, as they sometimes did, from exhaustion brought on by a continuous obsession of remorse and guilt. No psychotherapy at all may be needed to relieve an attack, and the treatment seems just as effective now it is given to an anaesthetized and deeply unconscious patient who feels nothing, though he still has to have a complete "cerebral fit" for a good result to be obtained. It is also important to note in other types of nervous illness, such as anxiety states or obsessional neuroses, that this same powerful treatment can make patients worse rather than better. This again suggests that different patterns of abnormal brain behaviour may often need different methods of handling.

Revivalists have long been aware how dangerous it is to use fear-provoking preaching on depressive patients; though useful as a first phase in the conversion of many ordinary persons, mention of hellfire may aggravate the religious melancholic to the point of suicide. He is no longer open to group suggestibility; being perhaps already too deeply inhibited to respond to dancing, shouting, drumming, group singing, or even the handling of poisonous snakes. Formerly, revivalists could only tell these unresponsive melancholics to wait until God's favour returned and the attack of depression lifted of its own accord; now it is possible to recommend electric shock treatment. If this advice is followed, the patient may become once more amenable to group suggestion, and at the next revival meeting regain his feelings of spiritual possession, so that the enormous weight of guilt created by brooding on a trivial peccadillo will fall from his back like Christian's load in *The Pilgrim's Progress*.

Dr. Denis Hill, describing the epileptic fit itself, writes:

> An epileptic seizure can be compared to a civil riot in the life of a population. Preceding it and leading to it have been either one serious or many less serious failures in the organism's techniques for meeting difficulties, ridding itself of tensions, accommodating to harmful agencies within itself. Like a riot, the seizure alters the total situation for the organism. We need not pursue the analogy further, but it is a commonplace that the tension, irritability and personality disorder which often precedes a seizure is usually relieved by it.[71]

The relief of tension that comes after such fits in certain patients can be most dramatic. It was once thought that the epileptic patient was a fundamentally different person from the normal; but the method of inducing fits electrically shows that every human being is potentially an epileptic. If the brain is sufficiently excited by means of a nicely calculated electric current, an epileptic fit will occur, just as a course of Voodoo drumming, or enough orgiastic dancing, will lead on to hysterical excitement and collapse in exhaustion. We also know that certain drugs, such as mescaline or lysergic acid, can produce mystical states: mescal—a cactaceous plant—having long been in use at certain Mexican tribal ceremonies to give participants the complete certainty that a god is indeed possessing them.

Aldous Huxley gives a very interesting and reasoned account of his own experiences while taking mescaline—an alkaloid extract of mescal;[72] he expresses surprise at the similarity of the mystical phenomena he underwent and those reported in accounts of Christian and Indian religious mysticism. Yet the brain possesses only a limited number of thought patterns it can produce under such physiological and chemical stresses; and prolonged unremitting mysticism can in some instances, be almost indistinguishable from schizophrenia.

Cases of schizophrenia sometimes give the doctor an opportunity to examine conditions somewhat analogous to the ecstatic states reported by the medieval saints, or moderns who have taken mescaline and similar intoxicants. The subject may see the outside world through a distorting mirror and becomes intensely preoccupied with his own subjective experiences; and it has been claimed that some of the greatest contributions to art, religion and philosophy have been made by visionaries in whom some, at least, of the symptoms of schizophrenia have been present. But it is not a happy fate to be a schizophrenic; he may feel himself at the mercy of uncontrollable impulses or sinister influences. Voices talk to him day or night, some good, some evil; mostly evil. It is very rare indeed for a patient to experience delusions and hallucinations of a constantly pleasant type; hell on earth may be his fate for thirty years or more, unless proper treatment can be given at an early stage.

Schizophrenia was once attributed to God's vengeance for sin, or to possession by the devil; and, more recently in psychological speculation, to a subconsciously motivated withdrawal from reality on the individual's part, an attempt to evade life's problems. But it is also known that purely psychological treatment helps only some patients with this sickness, which still fills the beds of mental hospitals with more young adults than any other mental illness.

The theory that schizophrenia was mainly due to a subconsciously motivated withdrawal from reality was rudely shattered for many therapists some years ago when insulin shock therapy was first employed. In this treatment, as has been mentioned in Chapter 3, a temporary lowering of the blood sugar under large doses of insulin produces periods of mental confusion and excitement, leading on to a deep coma. A series of daily comas is given. The schizophrenic will then often emerge from his mystical world of delusion and terror, apparently delighted at being well again and able to resume the daily tasks of normal living. He also becomes more open to persuasion and the correction of any delusional ideas acquired during his illness. Insulin shock therapy has proved to be one of the most effective treatments of cases of early schizophrenia; but it must be administered as soon as possible and is no certain cure. Although something like two out of every three patients can be helped in the first few weeks or months by insulin—combined, if necessary, with the tranquillizing drugs, electrical shock treatment and psychotherapy—yet if they are neglected for as long as two years, or perhaps given psychotherapy alone, their chances of recovery with insulin may then become much smaller.[73] And when all else fails and the delusions have become so firmly fixed as not to be dispersable by any form of shock, drug therapy or talk, there is still recourse to the newer forms of the brain operation of leucotomy (see Chapter 4).

Schizophrenia and depressive melancholia have been discussed to show that the human mind, when religiously sick (as well as when religiously well), can still be profoundly influenced by physiological means, and by the inducement of nervous excitement, leading on to a state of increased suggestibility and in the end to mental confusion and collapse, when recently acquired morbid symptoms may disperse; and that, when even the more drastic forms of this treatment fail, an operation on the brain will often loosen the hold of abnormal religious beliefs which no amount of religious persuasion (whether intellectual or emotional) can overcome, and restore patients to peace and happiness and a life of service to their fellow men, which so many of them enjoyed before their illness.

The enormous potentialities of the technique of physiological group-excitation, as demonstrated, for instance, by Wesley and many others, are admitted by Catholic theologians, such as the late Monsignor Ronald Knox. His book *Enthusiasm*,[52] a study of religious sects who have used such methods and thereby scandalized orthodox believers of their time, both Catholic and Protestants, emphasizes the variety and range of religious viewpoints that can be firmly implanted in many minds under excitatory stress. He has a great deal to say about Wesley, but is less concerned with understanding the mechanics of the process than with the fundamental philosophy influencing these various heterodox movements:

> How to explain these phenomena—Camisard child prophecy, or Jansenist convulsions, or Methodist swoonings, or Irvingite glossolaly—is a question that need not detain us. What is important is that they are all part of a definite type of spirituality, one which cannot be happy unless it is seeing results. Heart-work, Wesley called it; the emotions must be stirred to their depths, at frequent intervals, by unaccountable feelings of compunction, joy, peace and so on, or how could you be certain that the Divine touch was working on your soul?

Knox, himself a Catholic convert from Protestantism, pays an unwilling tribute to the extreme effectiveness of these methods:

> If I have dealt at some length with this single side of Wesley's character—I mean his preoccupation with strange psychological disturbances, now commonly minimized—it is because I think he, and the other prophets of the Evangelical movement, have succeeded in imposing upon English Christianity a pattern of their own. They have succeeded in identifying religion with a real or supposed experience . . . for better or worse, the England which weathered the excitements and disappointments of the early nineteenth century was committed to a religion of experience, you did not base your hopes on this or that doctrinal calculation; you *knew*. For that reason the average Englishman was, and is, singularly unaffected by reasonings which would attempt to rob him of his theological certainties, whatever they may be.

The technique of group excitation has many spectacular forms in the United States, to which numerous persecuted sects have fled in times of religious intolerance. Monsignor Knox's quotations show how closely the behaviour of some American congregations resembles that once noted by Wesley in the British Isles:

> . . . trembling, weeping and swooning away, till every appearance of life was gone, and the extremities of the body assumed the coldness of a corpse. At one meeting not less than a thousand persons fell to the ground apparently without sense or motion.

Numbers of people, he shows with quotations, could even be persuaded by revivalists to believe that behaving like certain kinds of animals was a sign of possession by God:

> When attacked by the jerks, the victims of enthusiasm sometimes leaped like frogs and exhibited every grotesque and hideous contortion of the face and limbs. The barks consisted in getting down on all fours, growling, snapping the teeth, and barking like dogs. . . . These last (who barked like dogs) were particularly gifted in prophecies, trances, dreams, rhapsodies, visions of angels, of heaven, and of the holy city.

In 1859, however, a Protestant priest, the Rev. George Salmon,[74] later Provost of Trinity College, Dublin, had warned the Catholic writers, and especially the Jesuits of his day, that they could not afford to be too critical of the excitatory methods used by other sects:

> And the person, perhaps, who best understood the art of exciting religious emotion, and who reduced it to a regular system, was the founder of the order of Jesuits. Any person who knows anything of the system of spiritual exercises which he invented, how the disciples in their retreats, assemble together in a darkened chapel, have their feelings worked up by ejaculations gradually lengthening into powerful descriptions, first, of the punishment due to sin, of the torments of hell and purgatory, then of the love of God, of the sufferings of the Saviour, the tenderness of the Virgin; how the emotion heightens as the leader of the meditation proceeds, and spreads by sympathetic contagion from one to the other:—anyone who knows anything of this must be aware that the Roman Catholic Church has nothing to learn from anything which the most enthusiastic sects of Protes-

tants have invented. The most violent and extensive religious excitement that history recalls took place in one of the darkest periods of the Church's history. I mean that which led to the Crusades; when millions of Christians believing what they exclaimed—"it is the will of God"—deserted their homes only to perish in heaps in foreign land.

Salmon rubs in this point most forcibly, by adding:

> Who shall say that that movement (the Crusades) was all superstition and fanaticism; for it was participated in by the best and most devout of the time. . . . But, yet, the result proved how much that great movement was brought about by merely human causes. For we cannot believe that God seduced those great multitudes with false promises, and led them out to perish miserably in a distant land. We see then that religious excitement may exist without religious knowledge.

P. F. Kirby in his *The Grand Tour in Italy* points out that a hundred years earlier, Smollett had also commented on the way Catholics emphasized the frightening and more gruesome aspects of their religious history to rouse the emotions:

> The palace of the Escurial in Spain is laid out in the form of a gridiron, because the convent was built in consequence of a vow to St. Laurence, who was broiled to death like a barbecued pig. What a pity it is that the labours of painting should have been so much employed on the shocking subjects of martyrology. Besides numberless pictures of the flagellation, crucifixion, and descent from the cross, we have Judith with the head of Holofernes, Herodias with the head of John the Baptist, Jael assassinating Sisera in his sleep, Pe-

ter writhing on the cross, Stephen battered with stones, Batholomew flayed alive, and a hundred other pictures equally frightful, which can only serve to fill the mind with gloomy ideas, and encourage a spirit of religious fanaticism.[75]

Salmon also felt that far deeper research was needed to explain the phenomena then appearing at the Great Revival in Northern Ireland. He observes:

We have still much to learn as to the laws according to which the mind and the body act on one another, and according to which one mind acts on another; but it is certain that a great part of this mutual action *can* be reduced to general laws, and that the more we know of such laws the greater our power to benefit others will be.

He also correctly compared the more remarkable Revival symptoms with hysterical ones, and with the phenomena of hypnosis—which was then already being practised and discussed in Great Britain. Salmon warns his readers against the dangers and risks of using such methods, but is honest enough to write:

. . . I desire to add, that the testimony that I have received leaves me no room to doubt that the Revival movement in the North has been attended by the suppression of drunkenness and profanity; by general reformation of moral character; by increased interest in everything pertaining to religion; by increased attendance at public worship, and at the holy communion. That this work will be permanent in every case it would be too much to expect—that it will be so in very many, I hope and believe.

In a postscript, some of the phenomena seen in this great Revival, and generally admitted to have had, on the whole, most beneficial results, are detailed:

> Strong men burst into tears; women fainted, and went off in hysterics. The piercing shrieks of those who called aloud for mercy, and the mental agony from which they suffered, were, perhaps, the most affecting that you could imagine. The penitents flung themselves on the floor, tore their hair, entreated all around to pray for them, and seemed to have the most intense conviction of their lost state in the sight of God.

He goes on to say that:

> The physical affections are of two kinds. (1) The patient either becomes deeply affected by the appeals which he or she may have heard, and bursts into the loudest and wildest exclamations of sorrow, and continues praying and pleading with God for mercy, sometimes for hours; or (2) falls down completely insensible, and continues in this state for different periods varying from about one hour to two days.

The results of continuing this excitement to the point of collapse are also noted:

> During continuance of the state (2), the person affected remains perfectly tranquil, apparently unconscious of everything going on around; the hands occasionally clasped, as in prayer, the lips moving, and sometimes the eyes streaming with tears; the pulse generally regular, and without any indications of fever . . . and the persons who have recovered from it represent it as the time of their "conversion". There is a most remarkable expression in their countenances, a

perfect radiance of joy, which I have never seen on any other occasion. I would be able to single out the persons who have gone through this state by the expression of their features.

In *The Epidemics of the Middle Ages,* J. F. C. Hecker[76] describes the hysterical dancing mania which occurred in Europe in the fourteenth century:

> The effects of the Black Death had not yet subsided, and the graves of millions of its victims were scarcely closed, when a strange delusion arose in Germany, which took possession of the minds of men, and, in spite of the divinity of our nature, hurried away body and soul into the magic circle of hellish superstition. . . . It was called the Dance of St. John or of St. Vitus, on account of the Bacchantic leaps by which it was characterized, and which gave to those affected, whilst performing their wild dance, and screaming and foaming with fury, all the appearance of persons possessed.

He describes how:

> [The dancers] exhibited to the public both in the streets and in the churches the following strange spectacle. They formed circles hand in hand, and appearing to have lost all control over their senses, continued dancing regardless of the bystanders, for hours together, in wild delirium, until at length they fell to the ground in a state of exhaustion. . . . While dancing they neither saw nor heard, being insensible to external impressions through the senses, but were haunted by visions. . . . Others, during the paroxysm, saw the heavens open and the Saviour enthroned with the Virgin Mary, according as the religious notions of the age were strangely and variously reflected in their imaginations.

The disease soon spread from Germany to Belgium. Many priests tried to disperse the symptoms by means of exorcism, attributing the disease to diabolic possession, despite the religious character of the ideas held by many of the victims. The streets of Metz were said to have been filled at one time with eleven hundred dancers.

St. Vitus was made the patron saint of those afflicted with the dancing mania, just as St. Martin of Tours guards smallpox cases, and St. Denis of France the syphilitics. St. John was also connected with this special type of dancing, not as its patron saint but because the festival of St. John's Day had taken over the pre-Christian midsummer festival, which had always been associated with orgiastic dancing. Hecker, in fact, thinks it likely that it was the wild revels of St. John's Day at Aix-la-Chapelle in A.D. 1374 which inaugurated the epidemic. Nevertheless, nearly a hundred children had been seized by the same symptoms at Erfurt in 1237 and among the many peculiar explanations then offered for the outbreak was the ineffectuality of baptism by unchaste priests.

Until the beginning of the sixteenth century, when the dancing mania became the subject of medical interest by Paracelsus and others, the Church alone was considered capable of treating it. It is fascinating to see Hecker anticipating modern findings in recording that the most reliable cure found was to keep the patient dancing on until the point of total exhaustion and collapse was reached:

> Roaring and foaming as they were, the bystanders could only succeed in restraining them by placing benches and chairs in their way, so that, by the high leaps they were thus

tempted to take, their strength might be exhausted. As soon as this was the case, they fell as it were lifeless to the ground, and, by very slow degrees, again recovered their strength. . . . The cure effected by these stormy attacks was in many cases so perfect that some patients returned to the factory or the plough as if nothing had happened.

No general diagnosis of the disease can be attempted: some patients probably suffered from the more ordinary forms of mental disorder, some from induced hysteria, and the symptoms in others suggest poisoning by ergot, a black "smut" to which rye was liable and which found its way into bread.[77] The Black Death would also have created widespread nervous depression. But what concerns us here is that the most effective treatment found was to carry such states of abnormal excitement to terminal exhaustion, after which the symptoms would disperse of themselves:

> On this account the magistrates hired musicians for the purpose of carrying the St. Vitus's dancers so much the quicker through the attacks, and directed that athletic men should be sent among them in order to complete the exhaustion, which had been often observed to produce a good effect.

Matthioli (1565) is also quoted by Hecker as observing:

> Care was taken to continue the music until exhaustion was produced; for it was better to pay a few extra musicians who might relieve each other than to permit the patient in the midst of the curative exercise to relapse into so deplorable a state of suffering.

Much the same mania appeared in the seventeenth century in Italy, where the nervous symptoms were attributed to the bite of the tarantula spider, and a special dance called the Tarantella was played to ensure the patient's cure. Hecker quotes G. Baglivi's report in 1710 that this belief was still so strongly held that he had seen patients suffering from malignant fevers forced to dance to music, for fear that the symptoms were due to the bite of the tarantula. One of these died on the spot, two others very shortly afterwards.

The Catholic Church regarded the Black Death as a punishment for the general wickedness of Christendom and used the threat of its return as a means of bringing the people to a state of submission and true repentance. With their assent, the Brotherhood of Flagellants, also called the Brethren of the Cross, began to arrange special meetings where sins could be publicly confessed and supplications offered to God for the aversion of plague. The Flagellant bands became well organized and, though starting as a working-class and peasant movement, came to be controlled by the wealthier classes. Their methods for working up group excitement were most effective: they rang bells, sang psalms, and scourged themselves until blood flowed in torrents. Their leaders found it convenient to organize a persecution of the Jews not only on the old charge of crucifying Christ, but on the new and equally inept charge of spreading plague by poisoning the wells. Just as Hitler's conversion of the German masses to the Nazi faith was helped by meetings where rhythmic chanting, torchlight processions, and the like, could arouse them to states of hysterical suggestibility even before he rose to speak, so it was with the

Flagellants, who anticipated his anti-Semitic fury. In Mainz alone, twelve thousand Jews were killed or committed suicide; the arrival of a procession of Flagellants would often be the signal for a massacre.

Hecker, who wrote over a century ago, seems to have had a far clearer insight into the physiological mechanisms of such group reactions than some modern theorists. He had grasped the importance of what psychologists now call "transference"; and in a special chapter entitled "Sympathy" stressed the existence in all such movements of an increased state of suggestibility and the presence of an instinct, which:

> . . . connects individuals with the general body, which embraces with equal force, reason and folly, good and evil, and diminishes the praise of virtue as well as the criminality of vice.

He goes on to point out the similarity between this and the first efforts of the infant mind:

> . . . which are in great measure based on imitation. . . . To this instinct of imitation when it exists in its highest degree, is also united a loss of all power over the will, which occurs as soon as the impression on the senses has become firmly established, producing a condition like that of small animals when they are fascinated by the look of a serpent.

After thus anticipating Pavlov's comparison of hypnotic phenomena in human beings and animals, Hecker claims that his findings:

. . . place the self-independence of the greater portion of mankind in a very doubtful light, and account for their union into a social whole. Still more nearly allied to morbid sympathy . . . is the diffusion of violent excitements, especially those of a religious or political character, which have so powerfully agitated nations of ancient and modern times, and which may, after an incipient compliance, pass into a total loss of will-power and an actual disease of the mind.

From a study of these epidemics, Hecker had come to understand pretty well some of the basic mechanics behind what we now call "brain-washing" and "thought control". He had also grown aware that his studies were leading him into very dangerous ground, and found it necessary to soft-pedal his findings:

Far be it from us to attempt to awaken all the various tones of this chord, whose vibrations reveal the profound secrets which lie hidden in the innermost recesses of the soul. We might well want powers adequate to so vast an undertaking. Our business here is only with that morbid sympathy, by the aid of which the dancing-mania of the middle ages grew into a real epidemic.

To illustrate his thesis that the tendency to "sympathy" and "imitation" increases under induced excitement, Hecker describes what happened at a cotton workshop in Lancashire, in 1787. A woman worker put a mouse down the neck of a companion who had a dread of mice; the fit which she immediately threw continued with violent convulsions for twenty-four hours. On the next day three other women had fits, and by the fourth no less than twenty-four people had been affected; among these was a male factory worker so exhausted by restraining the hysterical women that he had caught the illness himself; and two children both about ten years old. The disease spread to neighbouring factories, because of the fear aroused by a theory that the illness was due to some sort of cotton poisoning. The treatment prescribed sounds surprisingly modern:

> Dr. St. Clare had taken with him a portable electrical machine, and by electric shocks the patients were universally relieved without exception.

As for after-treatment, as soon as the patients and their fellow workers had been reassured that the complaint was merely nervous and not an occupational disease, like "lead" among painters, the hysteria ended. And:

> To dissipate their apprehensions still further, the best effects were obtained by causing them to take a cheerful glass and join in a dance. On Tuesday, the 20th, they danced, and the next day were all at work, except two or three, who were much weakened by their fits.

Hecker also mentions a much severer religious epidemic, caused by group suggestion, in 1814, at Redruth, Cornwall, where there was a Methodist Chapel:

> [A man] cried out with a loud voice: "What shall I do to be saved?". . . Some other members of the congregation, following his example, cried out in the same form of words, and seemed shortly to suffer the most excruciating bodily pain.

The scene caught the popular attention, and some of those who came to the chapel out of curiosity caught the hysterical infection. The chapel remained open for some days and nights, whereupon the symptoms spread to other Methodist chapels in the neighbouring towns of Camborne, Helston, Truro, Penryn and Falmouth, besides several villages in the region:

> Those who were attacked betrayed the greatest anguish, and fell into convulsions; others cried out, like persons possessed, that the Almighty would straight away pour out His wrath upon them, that the wailings of tormented spirits rang in their ears, and that they saw Hell open to receive them.

The conversion of Cornwall from a traditionally Catholic county to a predominantly Nonconformist one can be explained, in part, by the skill of its revivalists, for we read:

> The clergy when, in the course of their sermons, they perceived that persons were thus seized, earnestly exhorted them to confess their sins, and zealously endeavoured to convince them that they were by nature enemies to Christ; that the anger of God had therefore fallen upon them; and that if death should surprise them in the midst of their sins, the eternal torments of hell would be their portion. The over-excited congregation upon this, repeated their words, which naturally must have increased the fury of their convulsive attacks. When the discourse had produced its full effect, the preacher changed the subject; reminded those who were suffering of the power of the Saviour, as well as of the grace of God, and represented to them in glowing colours the joys of heaven. Upon this a remarkable reaction sooner or later took place. Those who were in convulsions felt them-

selves raised from their lowest depths of misery and despair to the most exalted bliss, and triumphantly shouted out that their bonds were loosed, their sins were forgiven, and that they were translated to the wonderful freedom of the children of God.

Reports on this particular Cornish revival mention practically every symptom occurring in the combat neuroses of World War II (see Chapter 3); they even show that the lower extremities were affected later by comparison with the rest of the body—as happened to our Blitz and Normandy patients, and as was also noted in the dogs which Pavlov subjected to the severest stresses.

The increase in suggestibility, often brought about by such methods, comes out clearly in the Rev. Jonathan Edwards' account of the 1735 revival that he initiated at Northampton, Massachusetts. Wesley may, in fact, have read Edwards' account before starting his own campaign four years later. Edwards incidentally admitted that even ideas of suicide could be implanted and transferred from person to person in an overwrought congregation. One of Edward's parishioners, overcome by religious melancholia, had attempted suicide; and another later succeeded in cutting his throat (which was one of the gravest sins imaginable at the time):

> The news of this extraordinary event affected the minds of the people here, and struck them as it were with astonishment. After this, multitudes in this and other towns seemed to have it strongly suggested to them, and pressed upon them, to do as this person had done, and many that seemed to be under no melancholy, some pious persons that had no spe-

cial darkness, or doubts about the goodness of their state, nor were under any special trouble or concern of mind about anything spiritual or temporal, yet had it urged upon them, as if somebody had spoken to them, "Cut your own throat, now is a good opportunity! Now! Now!" So that they were obliged to fight with all their might to resist it, and yet no reason suggested to them why they should do it.[78]

The religious practices of Rasputin, the Orthodox Russian monk whose hypnotic influence over the last Czarina helped to precipitate the March Revolution, are also enlightening in view of the methods under discussion. Prince Youssoupoff who, in 1916, felt it his patriotic duty to assassinate Rasputin, describes them as follows:

He [Rasputin] came under the influence of a priest who awakened the mystic in him; but his conversion lacked sincerity. Owing to his brutal, sensual nature he was soon drawn to the sect of Flagellants, or *Khlystys*. They claimed to be inspired with the Word and to incarnate Christ. They attained this heavenly communion by the most bestial practices, a monstrous combination of the Christian religion with pagan rites and primitive superstitions. The faithful used to assemble by night in a hut or in a forest clearing, lit by hundreds of tapers. The purpose of these *radenyi*, or ceremonies, was to create a religious ecstasy, an erotic frenzy. After invocations and hymns, the faithful formed a ring and began to sway in rhythm, and then to whirl round and round, spinning faster and faster. As a state of dizziness was essential for the "divine flux", the master of ceremonies flogged any dancer whose vigour abated. The *radenyi* ended in a horrible orgy, everyone rolling on the ground in ecstasy, or in convulsions. They preached that he who is possessed by the "Spirit" belongs not to himself but to the "Spirit" who controls him and is responsible for all his actions and for any sins he may commit.[79]

G. R. Taylor[80] suggests that it may have been as much because of the early Christians' use of the dance and "because they were seized with the Spirit, that the Persians called them 'tarsa' or 'shakers'". He also points out that a continuous line of descent can be traced from the Johannine Christians through the medieval dancers and the post-medieval Shakers and Quakers, down to the shaking and dancing sects of the nineteenth and twentieth centuries; and this dancing "is actually the mechanism through which theolepsy is brought about". The words of an incantatory dance in honour of the Gnostic Ogdoad are even ascribed to Christ in an early Egyptian papyrus.[45]

The highest common factor in some of the changes obtained by the early Methodists, the Holy Rollers, the Jansenists, the modern psychotherapists, and those psychiatrists who rely on insulin, electric shocks, leucotomy and the like, is probably to be found in brain physiology rather than psychology; especially when the implantation and disruption of behaviour patterns and presumably of thought seems also influenced in animals by analogous disturbances of brain function. This is by no means an original view; but the present doctrine of presumed progress discourages many people from thinking that the intelligence can be overborne by artificially induced brain disturbances when new beliefs are promulgated.

William James wrote, in 1903 in *The Varieties of Religious Experience*:[56]

In the end we fall back on the hackneyed symbolism of a mechanical equilibrium. A mind is a system of ideas, each with the excitement it arouses, and with tendencies impulsive and inhibitive, which mutually check or reinforce one another. . . a new perception, a sudden emotional shock, or an occasion which lays bare the organic alteration, will make the whole fabric fall together; and then the centre of gravity sinks into an attitude more stable, for the new ideas that reach the centre in the rearrangement seem now to be locked there, and the new structure remains permanent.

James's researches had also led him to conclude that:

Emotional occasions, especially violent ones, are extremely potent in precipitating mental rearrangements. The sudden and explosive ways in which love, jealousy, guilt, fear, remorse or anger can seize upon one are known to everybody. Hope, happiness, security, resolve, emotions characteristic of conversion, can be equally explosive. And emotions that come in this explosive way seldom leave things as they found them.

And he quotes Professor Leuba's conclusion:[81]

The ground of the specific assurance in religious dogmas is then an affective [emotional] experience. The objects of faith may even be preposterous; the affective stream will float them along, and invest them with unshakable certitude. The more startling the affective experience, the less explicable it seems, the easier it is to make it the carrier of unsubstantiated notions.

John Wesley, though attributing to the hand of God the thousands of conversions he induced all over England, in the most unlikely people, nevertheless speculated about possible additional physiological factors:

> How easy it is to suppose that strong, lively and sudden apprehension of the hideousness of sin and the wrath of God, and the bitter pains of eternal death, should affect the body as well as the soul, suspending the present laws of vital union and interrupting or disturbing the ordinary circulation and putting nature out of its course.[36]

It was by thus observing scientifically the results achieved by different types of preaching that Wesley was helped to make even Great Britain, which is so notoriously resistant to change, transform some of its traditional religious and political behaviour patterns.

It is most unlikely that Dr. Billy Graham will have the same sort of success as Wesley, if only because he does not attempt to consolidate his gains by such an efficient follow-up system (see Chapter 10). Those who attend his meetings are impressed by the care with which he avoids the mention of hell—one of Wesley's powerful conversion weapons. One of the most important occasions in English religious history may prove to have been when a workman is said to have rushed jubilantly out of a church where Dean Farrar was preaching, and shouted: "Good news, mates, old Farrar says there's no 'ell!"[45] This could have been about the year 1878 when Farrar published his book *Eternal Hope,* containing the five sermons he had preached in Westminster Abbey critical of eternal punishment.[82] But Dr. Graham is aware that the fear of hell is not yet completely laid; and, should he use the familiar revivalist technique: "The salvation 'plane is due to leave Harringay airport at 3.30 sharp. . . . Which of you sinners will be there waiting at the barrier to catch it?" He would probably not describe the flames, the brimstone, and the devil's pitchfork, but content himself with an impressive: "You had better hurry, folks. Or else . . ." The "or else" seems to be effective enough in many cases. The reader will also realize how important the hydrogen bomb may become to the future success of certain kinds of religious evangelism. Already we read of Dr. Graham warning his fellow countrymen:[83]

> The greatest sin of America is our disregard of God . . . God may allow Russia to destroy America. . . . When I see a beautiful city such as New York, I also have a vision of crumbling buildings and dust. I keep having the feeling that God will allow something to fall on us in a way I don't anticipate unless we return to him.

And like many evangelists before him, Dr. Graham believes that he is the agent of this all-destroying God because of the many sudden conversions he obtains by the use of these methods:

> I'm no great intellectual, and there are thousands of men who are better preachers than I am. You can't explain me if you leave out the supernatural. I am but a tool of God.

CHAPTER 7

Brain-Washing in Religion and Politics

The evidence marshalled in Chapters 5 and 6 shows how various types of belief can be implanted in many people, after brain function has been sufficiently disturbed by accidentally or deliberately induced fear, anger or excitement. Of the results caused by such disturbances, the most common one is temporarily impaired judgment and heightened suggestibility. Its various group manifestations are sometimes classed under the heading of "herd instinct", and appear most spectacularly in wartime, during severe epidemics, and in all similar periods of common danger, which increase anxiety and so individual and mass suggestibility.

Another result of over-stimulation can be the occurrence of the "equivalent", "paradoxical" and "ultra-paradoxical" phases of abnormal brain activity, discussed in previous chapters, which reverses the subject's normal patterns of behaviour. If a complete sudden collapse can be produced by prolonging or intensifying emotional stress, the brain slate may be wiped clean temporarily of its more recently implanted patterns of behaviour, perhaps allowing others to be substituted for them more easily.

In fact, what happens to animals when subjected to stress also seems to happen to some human beings: if, that is to say, psychological interpretations of their behaviour are temporarily laid aside, and attention concentrated on the purely physiological phenomena, the mechanical principles involved will often be found similar.

The techniques of political and religious indoctrination are often so similar that in primitive communities, or in more civilized theocratic states such as the ancient Jewish, they are actually identical. Thus a study of the better recorded methods of religious indoctrination will yield results that are, *ceteris paribus,* equally applicable to the political field. Yet some of the most obvious similarities are often ignored because either the religious approach (as in Western Europe and the United States today) or the political (as in Eastern Europe and China) is accorded official respect at the other's expense.

The same broad differentiation of belief separates Communists and capitalistic Democrats politically as separates Catholics and Protestants religiously. Much the same minor functional disagreements have in the past embittered the relations of Stalinists and Trotskyists; Methodists, Primitive Methodists and Calvinistic Methodists. Political leaders have been as ready to use mass shootings and the gas-chamber to support their beliefs as were religious leaders in the past to use fire and sword. Neither Catholics nor Protestants can claim to have a cleaner record than their opponents. There was little to choose, for savagery, between the Protestants and Catholics in the German religious wars; Catholic massacres of the Protestant Huguenots in France were no less fanatic than the massacre of Irish Catholics by Cromwell's Protestants. Moreover, both Catholics and Protestants have carried the sword of God with equal vigour against the heathen overseas, and against members of the pre-Christian witch cult of Europe; always acting in the firm conviction that they were inspired by the highest and noblest motives. The most kindly, generous and humane of men have in fact been conditioned, throughout history, to commit acts which appear horrifying in retrospect to those who have been differently conditioned. Many otherwise sensible people cling to strange and cruel views merely because these have been firmly implanted in their brains at an early age, and they can no more be disabused of them by argument than could the generation that still insisted on the flatness of the earth, though it had been circumnavigated on several occasions. To alter fundamental points of view, one does not necessarily have to disrupt them by Voodoo drumming or religious revivals. There are other less crude and less spectacular methods which can be very effective.

* * *

At this point the reader will perhaps forgive a recapitulation of first physiological principles:

With their variety of temperaments, it was found that breakdown or dramatic change in patterns of behaviour in animals could be caused not only by increasing the strength of the stimulus applied, but in three other important ways.

1. One could prolong the time between the giving of a preliminary signal and the giving or withholding of food or an unexpected electric shock; the prolongation of a state of tension and anxiety was found to be very disturbing. The result was "protective inhibition", which might rapidly become "transmarginal", with chaotic effects on brain function.

2. One could alter behaviour patterns by confusing the brain if positive and negative food-conditioning signals followed one another rapidly and were not followed by the expected food or shock. Most animals seemed able to adjust, within limits, to what they expected; but experienced more difficulty in coping with the unforeseen.

3. If all these means failed to produce alteration or breakdown one could resort to physical debilitation, fevers, etc., which might be effective when the same stimuli are later repeated.

* * *

In the conversion and brain-washing techniques presently to be discussed all these physiological mechanisms also come into action, either singly or in combination, and it is not surprising to see how little the methods of conversion or eliciting confessions used by the Spanish Inquisition in the sixteenth and seventeenth centuries differ from those that have been used by Communists behind the Iron Curtain. It is, nevertheless, likely that the Communists attained a greater technical perfection, from a better understanding of the basic physiological principles learned on animals, and by checking empirical findings against these. On the other hand, the use of physical violence in the eliciting of statements and confessions is officially banned by law in Russia, as in the United States and the United Kingdom. Accused persons are also in general given ample opportunity to learn that what they say may be given in evidence in their subsequent trials.

Brain-washers use a technique of conversion which does not depend only on the heightening of group suggestibility, but also on the fomenting in an individual of anxiety, of a sense of real or imaginary guilt, and of a conflict of loyalties, strong and prolonged enough to bring about the desired collapse. In Jonathan Edwards' revival at Northampton mentioned above (see p. 145) it has already been reported that group suggestibility was increased to a point where the attempted suicide of one depressed parishioner, and the actual suicide of another, affected their neighbours so deeply that, forgetting their newly-found joy and certainty of eternal salvation, many of them found themselves obsessed with what they recognized as a diabolical temptation to follow suit. Anyone who wishes to investigate the technique of brain-washing and eliciting confessions as practised behind the Iron Curtain (and on this side of it, too, in certain police stations where the spirit of the law is flouted) would do well to start with a study of eighteenth-century American revivalism from the 1730's onwards. The physiological mechanics seem the same, and the beliefs and behaviour patterns implanted, especially among the puritans of New England, have not been surpassed for rigidity and intolerance even in Stalinist times in the U.S.S.R. We are not here concerned with the truth or falsity of their fundamentalist and Calvinist beliefs; this book is concerned only with the physiology of conversion and thought control.

Edwards[82] believed that the world might well:

> . . . be converted into a great lake or liquid globe of fire, in which the wicked shall be overwhelmed (and) . . . their heads, their eyes, their tongues, their hands, their feet, their loins and their vitals shall for ever be full of a glowing, melting

fire, enough to melt the very rocks and elements. Also they shall be full of the most quick and lively sense to feel the torments, not for ten millions of ages, but for ever and ever, without any end at all. . . .

He also said that the eternally damned would be:

> . . . tormented also in the presence of the glorified saints. Hereby the saints will be made more sensible how great their salvation is. The view of the misery of the damned will double the ardour of the love and gratitude of the saints in heaven.

In an account of the Northampton Revival,[78] he states that, before it started:

> . . . licentiousness, for some years, greatly prevailed among the youth of the town: many of them were very much addicted to night-walking, and frequenting the tavern, and lewd practices. In which some, by their example, exceedingly corrupted others . . . but. . . in the April following, 1734, there happened a very sudden and awful death of a young man, in the bloom of his youth. . . . This was followed by another death of a young married woman, who had been considerably exercised in mind about the salvation of her soul, before she was ill, and was in great distress in the beginning of her illness.

These deaths, it seems, made Edwards' parishioners more than normally susceptible to his preaching about hellfire; for, in a short time:

> There was scarcely a single person in the town, either young or old, that was left unconcerned about the great things of the eternal world. Those that were wont to be vainest and

loosest, and those that had been most disposed to think and speak slightly of vital and experimental religion, were now generally subjected to the great awakenings.

Edwards goes on to describe the "awakening", so helpful in religious or political conversion:

> Persons are first awakened with a sense of their miserable condition by nature; the danger they are in of perishing eternally; and that it is of great importance to them that they speedily escape and get into a better state. Those that before were secure and senseless, are made sensible how much they were in the way to ruin in their former courses.

He also recognizes important differences in temperamental types which have to be considered during the "softening-up" phase, prior to conversion:

> There is a very great variety as to the degree of fear and trouble that persons are exercised with, before they obtain any comfortable evidence of pardon and acceptance with God. Some are, from the beginning, carried on with abundantly more encouragement and hope than others: some have had ten times less trouble of mind than others, in whom yet the issue seems to be the same: some have had such a sense of the displeasure of God, and the great danger they were in of damnation, that they could not sleep at night; and many have said, that when they have laid down, the thoughts of sleeping in such a condition have been frightful to them, and they have scarcely been free from terror while they have been asleep, and that they have awakened with fear, heaviness, and distress still abiding on their spirits. . . . The awful apprehensions persons have had of their misery, have for the most part been increasing, the nearer they have

approached to deliverance though they often pass through
many changes and alterations in the frame and circumstances
of their minds: sometimes they think themselves wholly
senseless, and fear that the Spirit of God has left them, and
that they are given up to judicial hardness; yet they appear
very deeply exercised about that fear, and are in great ear-
nest to obtain convictions again.

Edwards[78] made a practice of inducing guilt and acute
apprehension as the first step towards the conversion of
normal persons, and insisted that the tension must be increased until the sinner broke down and made complete
submission to the will of God; yet his parishioners seem to
have realized that to do so in the case of a sinner already
suffering from religious melancholia might force him to
the horrid crime of suicide:

> Another thing that some ministers have been greatly blamed
> for, and I think unjustly, is speaking *terror* to those who are
> already under great terrors, instead of comforting them. . . .
> To blame a minister for thus declaring the truth to those
> who are under awakening, and not immediately adminis-
> tering comfort to them, is like blaming a surgeon, because,
> when he has begun to thrust in his lance, whereby he has
> already put his patient to great pain, and he shrinks and
> cries out with anguish, he is so cruel that he will not stay his
> hand, but goes on to thrust it in further till he comes to the
> core of the wound.

So occasional cases of suicide and insanity had to be put
to the debit side of his conversion ledger; but while preaching of the terrors of hellfire and eternal damnation he al-

ways bore in mind that an escape route, consisting of the main belief to be implanted, should be left open:

> Indeed, something besides terror is to be preached to those whose consciences are awakened. They are to be told that there is a Saviour provided, who is excellent and glorious; who has shed his precious blood for sinners, and is every way sufficient to save them; who stands ready to receive them, if they will heartily embrace him; for this is also the truth as well as that they now are in an infinitely dreadful condition. . . . Sinners, at the same time that they are told how miserable their case is, should be earnestly invited to come and accept of a Saviour, and yield their hearts to him, with all the winning, encouraging arguments that the gospel affords.

Edwards found that some of his converts might have to endure mental conflicts and torture for days, weeks or months before they broke down, accepted the Calvinistic terms for salvation preached by him, and so achieved deliverance. He noted also that:

> Those that, while under legal convictions, have had the greatest terrors, have not always obtained the greatest light and comfort; nor have they always light most suddenly communicated; but yet, I think, the time of conversion has generally been most sensible in such persons. Oftentimes, the first sensible change after the extremity of terrors, is a calmness, and then the light gradually comes in; small glimpses at first . . . and there is felt inwardly, perhaps, some disposition to praise God; and, after a little while, the light comes in more clearly and powerfully. But yet, I think, more frequently, great terrors have been followed with more sudden and great light, and comfort; when the sinner seems to be, as it were,

subdued and brought to a calm, from a kind of tumult of mind. . . .

This terminal calm of the sudden conversion state is equally well described by William James in his *Varieties of Religious Experience.*[56] The more obdurate sinners, that is to say those of a temperamental type least open to suggestion, will have lost considerable weight under their protracted agonies of mind, before both the final submission and sanctification. Their case recalls that of the "strong" dogs which Pavlov had to debilitate before he could break down their behaviour patterns. All the physiological mechanisms exploited by Pavlov in his animal experiments, short of glandular change by castration, seem, in fact, to have been exploited by Edwards or his successors in their Calvinist missionary campaigns.

The lasting success of these methods is illustrated by the reactions of Harriet Beecher Stowe, author of *Uncle Tom's Cabin,* a hundred years later, when the spirit of Jonathan Edwards still ruled her community:

> Her first serious theological ordeal occurred at the age of eleven, when her older sister Catherine lost in a shipwreck the man she was going to marry and she could not be certain he was saved. Lyman Beecher (her father) was not reassuring. Catherine worked on the case and finally found a journal. Oh, horror! Her sweetheart had never repented: he was doomed to an eternity of torment. Catherine fell into despair, and Harriet shared her anguish, but both of them, from this moment, began seriously to question the fundamental Calvinist doctrine that God chooses only a few for grace and consigns the rest to damnation, without either

the saved's or the sinful's being able to influence the out-
come. . . . In 1840 she got to the point of refuting Jonathan
Edwards' words (in writing) . . . and by 1857 she had gone
as far as to deny Original Sin.[84]

In 1835, Charles G. Finney, who had been making mass
conversions in the State of New York, published a frank
and detailed handbook on the subject, *Lectures on Revivals
of Religion.*[85] Everything, he recommends, must be put to
potential converts in simple black and white; they should
be sent home, for instance, to read for themselves the following hymn by Dr. Watts:

> My thoughts on awful subjects roll,
>   Damnation and the dead:
> What horrors seize the guilty soul,
>   Upon a dying bed!

> Lingering about these mortal shores,
>   She makes a long delay,
> Till like a flood, with rapid force,
>   Death sweeps the wretch away.

> Then, swift and dreadful, she descends
>   Down to the fiery coast,
> Amongst the abominable fiends—
>   Herself a frightened ghost.

> There endless crowds of sinners lie,
>   And darkness makes their chains;
> Tortured with keen despair they cry,
>   Yet wait for fiercer pains.

> Not all their anguish and their blood

> For their past guilt atones,
> Nor the compassion of a God
> Shall hearken to their groans.

But a concluding verse gives the terrified reader his escape route, and he is congratulated on not having died in his sins before taking it:

> Amazing grace, that kept my breath,
> Nor did my soul remove,
> Till I had learn'd my Saviour's death,
> And well insured his love.

Finney also wrote:

> Look, as it were, through a telescope that will bring it up near to you; look into hell, and hear them groan; then turn the glass upwards and look at heaven, and see the saints there, in their white robes, with their harps in their hands, and hear them sing the song of redeeming love; and ask yourself—Is it possible that I shall prevail with God to elevate the sinner there?

Those who agree with Dean Farrar on the theological improbability of eternal punishment (p. 149) may find this less frightening than it was to most of Finney's hearers. But one has only to change the threat of eternal fire to one of hard labour for life in an Arctic prison camp, and the efficacy of the method in either a political or a religious context should be obvious.

In brain-washing and the eliciting of confessions, the physiological importance of inducing a sense of guilt and conflict can hardly be over-emphasized. The prisoner may be bombarded with accusations and continually cross-examined until anxiety confuses him and he contradicts himself on some small point. This is then used as a stick to beat him with; presently his brain ceases to function normally and he collapses. In a subsequent highly suggestible state, with old thought patterns inhibited, he will readily sign and deliver the desired confession.

Finney insisted that the revivalist should never relax the mental pressure on a prospective convert:

> One of the ways in which people give false comfort to distressed sinners is by asking them: "What have you done? You are not so bad." . . . When the truth is, they have been a great deal worse than they think they have. No sinner ever had an idea that his sins were greater than they are. No sinner ever had an adequate idea of how great a sinner he is. It is not probable that any man could live under the full sight of his sins. God has, in mercy, spared all his creatures on earth that worst of sights, a naked human heart. The sinner's guilt is much more deep and damning than he thinks, and his danger is much greater than he thinks it is; and if he could see them as they are probably he would not live one moment.

Once the sense of guilt has been implanted, Finney knew that, to clinch the matter, no concessions of any sort could be made:

> An anxious sinner is often willing to do anything else but the very thing which God requires him to do. He is willing to go to the ends of the earth, or to pay his money, or to endure suffering, or anything but full and instantaneous submission to God. Now, if you will compromise the mat-

ter with him, and tell him of something else which he may do, and yet evade *that point,* he will be very much comforted.

He had also found that:

> Protracted seasons of conviction are generally owing to defective instruction. Wherever clear and faithful instructions are given to sinners, there you will generally find the convictions are *deep* and *pungent,* but short. . . . Where sinners are deceived by false views, they may be kept along for weeks, and perhaps months, and sometimes for years, in a languishing state, and at last, perhaps, be crowded into the kingdom and saved. But where the truth is made perfectly clear to the sinner's mind, if he does not soon submit, his case is hopeless. . . . So far as I have had opportunity to observe, these conversions which were most sudden have commonly turned out to be the best Christians. . . . There is not a case of protracted conviction recorded in the whole Bible. All the conversions recorded there, are sudden conversions.

Considering the stresses that Finney's method would produce on the brains of his listeners, once he had made them accept any part of his faith in the reality of hellfire, his final conclusions are probably justified:

> Afraid of sudden conversions! Some of the best Christians of my acquaintance were convicted and converted in the space of a few minutes . . . and have been shining lights in the church ever since, and have generally manifested the same decision of character in religion, that they did when they first came out and took a stand on the Lord's side.

He is said to have been responsible for many thousands of such conversions.

Contemporary opinions on Finney's methods by a number of religious leaders were published by William B. Sprague in a book called *Lectures on Revivals of Religion.*[86] A fear was expressed that people who won a sense of salvation from such a type of evangelism tended to become critical of the more staid and intellectual type of worship. Unless great care were exercised, the converts would try to dominate the preacher because of the strength of their own new convictions. The Rev. Edward D. Griffin, President of Williams College, Williamstown, Massachusetts, for instance, reports:

> Among other excesses, when the awakened were called out into the aisle, some women found themselves converted, and in the midst of a crowded assembly, and with a loud voice, began to pray for their husbands. And this was taken by men hitherto deemed sober—perhaps *too* sober—as proof of the extraordinary descent of the Holy Spirit. Such disorders, and worse than these, will infallibly spread themselves all abroad, if ministers and distinguished members of the church did not combine in earnest to check present measures. . . . Such excesses . . . lay stumbling blocks before the blind over which millions will fall into hell.

On the other hand, the Rev. Noah Porter, pastor of a Congregational Church in Farmington, Connecticut, comes out strongly in favour of revivals. He summarized his findings as follows:

> It thus appears that, by these gracious visitations, during a period of thirty-seven years, four hundred and sixty persons

have been added to this church. Within the same period, the whole number added beside, only a little exceeds three hundred, and of these more than one hundred have come from other churches. . . . In these few short seasons, God has done far more for us than during all the protracted months and years that have intervened; and, indeed, it has seemed to be chiefly in these that the church has so far renewed her strength, as to hold forth her testimony with any degree of success in the intervals.

His contribution concludes with this important observation:

But if experience and observation have taught me anything, it is, that there is a way of discussing these subjects most logically in the pulpit, which does little good. . . (listeners must) be made to feel they are their own destroyers, that fallen, dependent and lost as they are, salvation is most freely and sincerely offered to them, and that if they perish, the blame must for ever rest upon themselves.

A final quotation from Finney, very relevant to our problem:

Take pains to learn the state of his mind—what he is thinking of, how he feels, and what he feels most deeply upon— and then press that thoroughly; and do not divert his mind by talking about anything else. Do not fear to press that point, for fear of driving him to distraction. Some people fear to press a point to which the mind is tremblingly alive, lest they should injure the mind. . . . You should clear up the point, throw the light of truth all around it, and bring the soul to yield, and then the mind is at rest.

No better mechanical method could be described for keeping the brain in the necessary state of persistent tension and excitement until suggestibility is increased and final submission occurs. All methods, whether noisy or grimly silent, aim for this point, a point which horse-trainers also have in mind when breaking a colt—when the subject acquires the "paradoxical" feeling that the new "service is perfect freedom". This feeling, which Christians claim as unique to their own faith, was expressed in these words by Marcus Apuleius's hero Lucius when converted to the worship of Isis.[87]

Finney's advice that the revivalist preacher should find the point on which "the mind is tremblingly alive", stresses again the importance of the reported observation that every dog (and therefore probably every man) has a weakness or sensitivity of the brain which can be exploited once it is discovered. Orwell in his novel *Nineteen-Eighty-Four* [88] tells how the hero, while being indoctrinated, is found to have an overwhelming fear of rats, the relic of a fright in early childhood. This knowledge is used by his interrogator to procure his final submission, and to convert his hatred of "Big Brother" into an uncritical love. Whether or not Orwell was introducing fact into fiction, the method described is physiologically convincing. A study of the techniques of modern political brain-washing and the eliciting of confessions shows that the interrogators are always in search of topics on which the victim is sensitive; they play on these until they force him to confess or believe whatever is desired. If nothing can be found in his past life to arouse feelings of anxiety or guilt, then suitable situations or interpretations of situations have to be invented to create them—as some psychiatrists did during World War II, to cause states of excitement and collapse in their patients during drug abreactive treatment. (See Chapter 3.)

Finney had first to persuade an ordinary decent American citizen that he had been leading a sinful life, and was certainly doomed to hell fire, before persuading him to accept a particular brand of religious salvation. Specialists in political conversion likewise make ordinary people confess to having led lives of pluto-democratic error, or acted like Fascist beasts, and, by way of atonement, gladly accept whatever severe penalty is imposed on them, death included.

Edwards and Finney were carrying to extremes methods that have been found effective from time immemorial by many religious sects, and are starting to be copied increasingly by certain political faiths. For instance, many persons over the centuries have remained fascinated by the tremendous strength, and endurance both in behaviour and belief shown by the highly trained Jesuit priest. Somerset Maugham in his book *Don Fernando* says this about their founder St. Ignatius's famous book *Spiritual Exercises,* used by Jesuits as their training manual:

> When you look at the exercises as a whole you cannot but observe how marvellously they are devised to effect their object. . . . It is said that the result of the first week is to reduce the neophyte to utter prostration. Contrition saddens, shame and fear harrow him. Not only is he terrified by the frightful pictures on which his mind has dwelt, he has been weakened by lack of food and exhausted by want of sleep. He has been brought to such despair that he does not know where to fly for relief. Then a new ideal is set

before him, the ideal of Christ; and to this, his will broken, he is led to sacrifice himself with a joyful heart. . . . The *Spiritual Exercises* are the most wonderful method that has ever been devised to gain control over that vagabond, unstable and wilful thing, the soul of man.[89]

Those who have followed our arguments so far will not be surprised, as Maugham was, to find that:

> Considering that their effect has been achieved through a constant and ruthless appeal to terror and shame it is surprising to observe that the last contemplation of all is a contemplation of love.

Somerset Maugham also discusses an old Spanish edition of the *Spiritual Exercises* in which the editor, Father Raymon Garcia, S.J., tried to help the neophyte by describing for him in considerable detail the subject-matter of some of his meditations. Talking about the meditations on hell, for instance, Somerset Maugham writes:

> With the eyes of his fancy the penitent must see the terrible flames and the souls enclosed as it were in bodies of fire. "Look," he [Father Raymon] cries, "look at the unhappy creatures writhing in the burning flames, their hair standing on end, their eyes starting out of their heads, their aspect horrible, biting their hands, and with sweats and anguish of death and a thousand times worse than death. . . . And what," asks Father Raymon, "shall we say of the thirst and hunger that torments them?" Much. Raging is the thirst caused by the heat and the ceaseless wailing. . . . The damned live plunged in this, like fish in water, or rather (better, says my author) penetrated as by a red-hot coal, the flames en-

tering their throats, veins, muscles, bones, entrails and all their vitals.

The lesson of the meditation was also brought home to the exercitant by Father Raymon in the following grim reminder:

> What do you say to this, my soul? If in your soft bed it is so painful to you to pass a long night of sleeplessness and pain, waiting eagerly for the relief of dawn, what will you feel in that eternal night upon which the dawn never breaks, during which you will never have an instant of refreshment, during which you will never see a ray of hope?

Somerset Maugham finds the *Spiritual Exercises* a book that cannot be read without awe:

> For it must be remembered that it was the efficacious instrument that enabled the Society of Jesus for centuries to maintain its ascendancy. Four hundred commentaries have been written on it. . . Leo XIII said of it: "Here is the sustenance that I desired for my soul."

All such methods can be used to help bring about some of man's noblest patterns of living. But we must also realize how they can be used to destroy them.

Political Conversion and Brain-Washing

In a special appendix to his *The Devils of Loudun* Aldous Huxley has emphasized the strength of these methods under discussion:

No man, however highly civilized, can listen for very long to African drumming, or Indian chanting, or Welsh hymn singing, and retain intact his critical and self-conscious personality. It would be interesting to take a group of the most eminent philosophers from the best universities, shut them up in a hot room with Moroccan dervishes or Haitian Voodooists and measure, with a stop-watch, the strength of their psychological resistance to the effects of rhythmic sound. Would the Logical Positivists be able to hold out longer than the Subjective Idealists? Would the Marxists prove tougher than the Thomists or the Vedantists? What a fascinating, what a fruitful field for experiment! Meanwhile, all we can safely predict is that, if exposed long enough to the tom-toms and the singing, every one of our philosophers would end by capering and howling with the savages.

He also says:

> . . . new and previously undreamed-of devices for exciting mobs have been invented. There is the radio, which has enormously extended the range of the demagogue's raucous yelling. There is the loud-speaker, amplifying and indefinitely reduplicating the heady music of class hatred and militant nationalism. There is the camera (of which it was once naively said that "it cannot lie") and its offspring, the movies and television. . . . Assemble a mob of men and women previously conditioned by a daily reading of newspapers; treat them to amplified band music, bright lights, and the oratory of a demagogue who (as demagogues always are) is simultaneously the exploiter and the victim of herd intoxication, and in next to no time you can reduce them to a state of almost mindless subhumanity. Never before have so few been in a position to make fools, maniacs, or criminals of so many.[90]

Despite the success of such assaults on the emotions, Western democracies underestimate their political importance; perhaps because the results similarly obtained in religious fields may be solely attributed to spiritual forces, rather than, in part at least, to their physiological effects on the subject. It is still considered a mystery how Hitler persuaded many intelligent people in Germany to regard him as little short of a god; yet Hitler never concealed his method, which included deliberately producing such phenomena by organized excitement and mass hypnotism, and even boasted how easy it was to impose "the lie of genius" on his victims.

The strength of the Mau Mau rebellion was underestimated by the Kenya authorities who did not realize that Jomo Kenyatta, the originator, never appealed primarily to the intellect of his followers; instead he deliberately used an emotional religious technique for political purposes. In 1953, the strength of the Mau Mau methods was such that at Nairobi, it was reported, the police-hut housing prisoners condemned to death on the following day, rang with songs and hilarity;[45] a phenomenon that must have puzzled many, as the enthusiastic Hallelujahs in Newgate Gaol in Wesley's day must equally have done (see p. 244). Mau Mau swearing-in ceremonies were designed deliberately to arouse emotional horror and excitement in the participants—so much so, that they cannot even be reported in detail, because the English laws relating to obscenity prevent this.[91]

The ineffectiveness of crude beating-up methods on subjects who have probably undergone such thorough politico-religious conversion is suggested by the following report. Two European police officers were each sentenced to eighteen months hard labour on charges of causing grievous bodily harm to a Kikuyu prisoner, Kamau Kichina, who died in custody. A chief inspector was fined £25 and a former district officer was fined £10 on a lesser charge of causing actual bodily harm:

> The magistrate, Mr. A. C. Harrison, said that the medical witness, Dr. Brown, had considered the most likely cause of death to be the injuries sustained by Kamau together with exposure: "Throughout Kamau's captivity no effort was spared to force him to admit his guilt. He was flogged, kicked, handcuffed with his arms between his legs and fastened behind his neck, denied food for a period, and was left out at least two nights tied to a pole in a shed, not surrounded by walls, with only a roof overhead, and wearing merely a blanket to keep out the cold." Although a day or two before his death he was no longer able to stand or walk properly, no medical attention was obtained or even sought for him. He was never brought before a magistrate in a proper manner and received no trial whatsoever—a right of all British subjects. The magistrate said that one disturbing factor was the possibility that Kamau might have been innocent in fact as well as in law. In spite of his treatment he died without admitting any guilt.[92]

The Chinese Communists spread their gospel by similar methods. They had had the sense to avoid a purely intellectual approach, and to arouse political anger by continually reporting and emphasizing the United States' hostile attitudes towards the New China. But if the hostile attitude of the United States, as opposed to the more conciliatory tone of Britain at that particular time, had not provided the Communists with an excuse for stirring up intense anger and hatred in the Chinese population, they would have had to invent another external enemy, to keep alive the fear and hatred which Chiang Kai-shek had excited before they defeated him. The Americans made things easy by continuing to support Chiang.

Not only were anger and fear about external enemies aroused, as a means of making the masses suggestible, but even stronger emotions were provoked against supposed internal enemies, such as rich landowners, bankers and merchants. Every endeavour was made to arouse intense guilt and anxiety in as many non-Communists as possible. Even small shopkeepers were made to feel that they had been reactionary capitalists and grievous sinners against the new Communist State. Orgies of group confession about political deviation were encouraged. The denouncing of parents and relatives by their children—as under Hitler—added to the desired atmosphere of insecurity and anxiety; since almost everybody has some incident in his past of which he is ashamed. But except where it was judged necessary to excite the mob by spectacular executions—as in France during the Terror—the escape route from real or imaginary sins was usually provided: even the worst sinners, once they had expressed true repentance, could in theory work their passage back to social acceptance, though perhaps only after many years of slave labour. The use of such methods makes it easier to understand reports like the following about an interview with a thirty-five-year-old American woman, shortly after she was released from a Peking prison. She had been there for more than four years and declared that:

. . . the Chinese had been "absolutely justified" in arresting her for her "acts inimical to the Chinese people". She said that she had been chained and handcuffed at intervals for several months until 1953. "I was handcuffed and had ankle chains," she stated. "I did not consider this as torture. They use chains to make you think seriously about things. It could be described as a form of punishment for intellectual dishonesty. The main thing about a Communist prison is that it is a place of hope." . . . To further questions she replied: "I am not worthy of being a Communist. To be one is a terribly exacting thing.". . . [She said] she had not been indoctrinated, but "underwent rehabilitation", read many books and made regular studies. Her confession to the Chinese was made voluntarily.[93]

The mental condition of some Americans now being allowed to return to the U.S.A., after indoctrination in Chinese prisons, shows how vulnerable even people of high intelligence may be to such situations; though it is not yet known how long the effects of conversion last once the victims are back in their old environment.

A woman writer, Han Suyin, in *A Many Splendoured Thing*,[94] describes the methods used in Communist China soon after the Civil War had ended:

Three months after liberation of the town the drums were still beating. Sometimes from the grounds of the Technical College, or from the Mission School at the East Gate; often from the soldiers' camp outside the South Wall. When I left they were beating. They beat today still as through the main street the open lorries roll slow, bringing the enemies of the people to swift death, while the crowds hiss and roar and thunder hatred and applause, and the cheer-leaders raise their high-pitched voices in the shriek of slogans, and fire-crackers are let off as for a festival, and the dancers, the dancers dance, dance, dance.

I wonder, Sen, whether Master Confucius heard this five-beat harmony and deemed it a fit measure to regulate the emotions of mankind? I wonder whether eight hundred years before that gentle Jew, the Christ, was born, our ancestors held their Spring Festival and their Fertility Rites to this dancing and this beat? It is from deep within our people, this bewitchment of drum and body. I feel it surge up from my belly, where all true feeling lies; strong and compelling as love, as if the marrow of my bones had heard it millions of days before this day.

Han Suyin also writes:

For Man would always strive to conquer the world, to establish the will of man in the name of his God. With banners and shouting, legions and crosses, eagles and suns, with slogans and with blood. Feet in the dust, head among the stars. Old gods with new, wet paint upon their faces.

And she emphasizes:

To the Communist, each individual was a fortress to be taken by spiritual struggle alone. That the struggle involved sleepless nights and physical strain was added proof of spiritual superiority. They were out to conquer souls and the bodies would follow.

Fear of continued civil war, or foreign intervention, or both, convinced the Chinese Communist leaders that they must use shock tactics to convert the masses. A more intellectual approach might have resulted in a more stable type of conversion, but it would have taken dangerously long, and been consummated only with the gradual dying off of those brought up in the old ways of thought, and the growing up of the children educated in the new. To make a new China overnight, emotional disruption was essential; and so effective were the methods used, that thousands killed themselves in despair, a sense of guilt artificially implanted in them being so strong that they felt unworthy to accept the proffered Communist salvation; leaving the more resilient millions to dance, dance, dance for joy at their liberation from millenniary bondage—until they learned to tremble at the periodic visits of the Household Police who now keep a dossier on the history and activities of every household.

The American magazine *Time* has recently been insisting that the "non-Communist world, which had not been able to prevent this vast upheaval, at least had a duty to understand it". Some of the further details[95] of the methods that have been used in China should now be easily understood by readers who have followed the argument of this book:

> What gave the Chinese terror speed and weight was tested techniques borrowed from the Soviet Union at a time when Stalin was at the top of his power. But the Chinese system differs in one important respect from the Russian. . . . Mao's terror gets the utmost publicity. . . . Hundreds of mass trials, often involving thousands of blood-yelling participants, (are) carried out in the big cities, usually at a popular sports ground, in which the victims are publicly denigrated, then publicly shot. There is an official phrase for this peculiarly

Chinese variation of the Communist terror: "Campaign for the suppression of counter-revolutionaries *with fanfare.*"

Lo Jui-ching, the inventor of this pat phrase, has become the police chief and chief "working terrorist" of Communist China. He is said to have realized in 1949 that the new resistance to the Communist regimentation "lay not in the rifles of a few thousand guerillas, but in millions of hearts". He repeatedly advised the Chinese that: "two ways are open to all counter-revolutionaries: the way of death for those who resist, and the way of life for those who confess. . . . To confess is better than not to confess." In October, 1949, Lo launched two successive campaigns:

> The "Five-Anti" (sometimes called the "Five Vices") campaign was ostensibly waged against bribery, tax evasion, cheating in contracts, theft of state property and theft of state economic secrets. Under its cover, business men and industrialists were pressured with endless "struggle meetings" (brain-washing) . . . hundreds of thousands committed suicide. At one time in Shanghai, the Bund on the Whangpoo River was roped off, the roofs of tall buildings were guarded to prevent suicides, and residents developed the habit of avoiding walking on the pavement near skyscrapers for fear that suicides might land on them from the rooftops . . .

Some who did confess were still shot but others were given the opportunity of working for their political salvation in labour camps:

> In the background of the terrorist picture there are the forced labor camps. . . . According to the Communist theory, all

the forced labor workers are "voluntary", and the cadres supervising the slave labor always use high-sounding, almost loving words, to describe their charges. Those who die of exposure and overwork are eulogized as "dead heroes".

Time finally records:

> Something of deep significance to China, to Asia, and all the world, occurred in the last six months of 1955. The crescendo of terror in 1951, and the skillfully timed and carefully calculated applications of terror since, had their cumulative effects. One of the most enduring and resilient of peoples apparently gave up hope. . . . Plans which were to have been accomplished in ten or fifteen years were cut to five years. . . . "The socialist revolution, in the main," said Mao, "could be completed on a national scale within about three years more."

Richard L. Walker in *China Under Communism*[96] gives a detailed account of the individual and small group methods used in training active Communist workers to serve as a "transmission belt" between the Party and the masses. They must express the Party point of view wherever they may be sent. Walker finds that these methods originate in "the training techniques developed by the Communist party of the Soviet Union being applied everywhere in the Communist orbit today—from Roumania and East Germany to the jungles of Malaya and the battle-scarred towns of North Korea". He goes on to say:

> Pavlov held that man integrates impressions from his environment into his reflexes. This seemed to fit ideally with the Communist conviction of economic environmental de-

termination. Thus, by an extension of Pavlov's theories, when they prevailed over those of voluntarism in the U.S.S.R., Soviet psychologists have held that, given the proper conditioning, the human being could be turned into the ideal new Soviet man. Pavlovian psychology holds that the human physique cannot resist the conditioning, and Soviet scientists have since been attempting to perfect Pavlovian techniques so that any focus of resistance in the individual can be overcome.

This special training course usually lasts from nine to twelve months, and the same general programme is everywhere used, though with variations that allow for the intellectual level of the trainee. The details given by Walker neatly bear out the physiological principles outlined in this book. He describes the six factors present throughout the period of training. First, the training takes place in a special area or camp, which almost completely severs all ties with the trainees' families and former friends; and facilitates the breakup of old behaviour patterns:

> A second constant factor is fatigue. Students are subjected to a schedule which maintains physical and mental fatigue throughout the training. There is no opportunity for relaxation or reflection, they are occupied with memorizing great amounts of theoretical material and are expected to employ the new terminology with facility. Coupled with the fatigue is a third constant: tension. . . . Uncertainty is a fourth factor throughout the process. . . . Trainees who conspicuously fail to comprehend the camp pattern in the first few weeks disappear overnight, and there is usually a well-sown rumour concerning their fate. . . . A fifth constant factor is the use

of vicious language. . . . The final factor is the seriousness attached to the whole process. Humour is forbidden.

There are always small discussion groups of ten or twelve trainees, who keep together throughout the course (see Wesley's class meetings, p. 249). These groups always contain an "informer", though the members usually have the greatest difficulty in identifying him. The small groups then combine in larger group meetings to hear lectures and report confessions made to them by individual members. An important part of the training technique is the writing of autobiographies and diaries, which are discussed both by the small and the larger groups.

Walker quotes a former trainee as explaining:

> A straight narration of your past life was not enough. For every action you described, you had to give its motive in detail. Your awakened criticism had to be apparent in every sentence. You had to say why you smoked, why you drank, why you had had social connections with certain people— why? why? why?

Such detailed confessions then became public property, and they could be used by directors in finding a "sore spot" to work upon. (Sore spots, it has been shown (see p. 167) used to be sought out and exploited by revivalists of the eighteenth and nineteenth centuries in an attempt to bring about rapid religious conversions.)

As a means of inducing increased fatigue, the trainees are encouraged to volunteer for extra work and study and make others in their group follow their example. An important part of the process is the stimulation of fear and doubt. Shall he tell all to his group? If so, will it then be used against him? The trainee has to wrestle silently and alone with all these anxieties and conflicts, until he finally breaks down and decides to confess all; and this is the beginning of his end as an individual.

The first phase of the conversion process is called "the phase of physical control" and lasts about two months. Novices are allotted all sorts of routine physical tasks, often of a demeaning nature. And, as might be expected:

> During this period of physical exhaustion, training themes are designed to instil a maximum of disillusionment in the mind of the trainee. He is disillusioned with his past; he is disillusioned with his training. . . . It is during this time that the pattern for the next stage is established. The small groups meet once a day for at least two hours for purposes of "study". Initial study is devoted to analysis of each trainee's background, his ideas, his family, past friends, ideals, and so on. This gives the leader and the secretly planted cadre an opportunity to become intimately acquainted with each member of their group and to note weak spots for later exploitation. Criticism and self-criticism play an important role; there is competition to determine which recruit can be most successful in uncovering the mistakes of his past.

After two months of "physical control" a second phase of more intense indoctrination begins. Physical work is now reduced, and the number of small and large group meetings greatly increased. Care is taken that for six and sometimes seven nights a week the trainee shall go to bed mentally and physically completely exhausted:

During this period the intense strain becomes obvious to all, yet there is no escape. Tension mounts within discussion sessions; tempers are short in living quarters, social competition is keen in all activities.

During this phase the promising candidates are gradually sorted from the unpromising. Those who react in an undesirable way to the stresses imposed are weeded out and sent elsewhere—"many are never heard of again". Finally, as might again be expected, the remainder reach a third stage of "crisis" and breakdown. This occurs after about six months' training:

> The crisis usually starts with hysteria and sobbing at night, which go on during the small group meeting the next day and are immediately discussed. . . . The crisis usually comes at about the same time for all the members of a small group. Apparently the breakdown of one of the members launches a chain reaction. . . . In some cases, of course, it is much more evident than in others. The cynics and those with a sense of humour seem to survive best; those with strong emotions or deep religious or other convictions frequently break first.

According to Walker, one former trainee claimed that a fifth of the trainees broke down completely and some ended as "babbling maniacs". It is usually during this acute crisis and breakdown that what the Chinese aptly call "tail-cutting" takes place:

> The "tails" are ties with the old society, such as family, friends, old values, and so forth.

With this total disruption of old behaviour patterns, the new ones become much more firmly implanted, as in cases of sudden religious conversion:

> Up to the period of crisis, most of the Communist jargon was relatively meaningless. It was just a new language to be memorized, played with, and rearranged in patterns. Now he begins to find that it does have some pertinence to his problem. . . . In place of his feeling of guilt he is now fired with the conviction that he must publicize his newly found security and help others find peace of mind through service to the Organization. . . . It takes at least another four months of intense work to consolidate the hold on the now willing mind. Some rewards are given for enthusiasm and in appreciation of the conversion of the trainee.

These now highly trained and "dedicated" missionaries go out to organize discussion and confession groups of various types all over China. Each profession and trade has its specialized group, and the same training techniques are used in them, though on a less intense scale. Walker points out: "The methods of mutual spying and attitudes engendered in cadre-training have no limits. They penetrate into the innermost privacy of the home and family. In the China of Mao Tse-tung every action is political."

In fact, the Chinese experiments on mass excitation and in breaking down and reconditioning the minds of small-group members are seen to be based on the same physiological principles as may govern, not only various types of religious conversion, but some individual and group psychotherapeutic treatments: tension may be produced in each case; fear, anxiety and conflict are stimulated, and the director aims at a point where his subjects will start to become uncertain of themselves, where suggestibility will be increased, and where old behaviour patterns will be disrupted. When this stage of "tail-cutting" is reached, new patterns and beliefs are likely to assume a wholly new force and significance. The long history of religious conversion provided numerous examples of people picking up the Bible and suddenly finding new meaning aflame in old familiar texts. So also the converted Communist, at the tail-cutting stage, suddenly finds a surprising illumination in Party slogans which have hitherto left him cold, and the patient on the couch similarly ceases to fight his psychotherapist and is at last granted a novel and fascinating "insight" into his own mental condition. But in studying the effects produced on brain function by the stress-techniques, of whatever discipline, it must be remembered that when clumsily handled they may lead to an increase in contrasuggestibility rather than suggestibility. Each discipline has its casualties and defeats when applied to unsuitable temperamental types. The high proportion of "transmission belt" failures reported to Walker—one in every five a complete nervous wreck, many more liquidated—may reflect on the excessive standardization of the training method used; but this at least ensures more mental and spiritual uniformity of the survivors—for what that is worth.

One of the methods of consolidating the ground won by such methods of political or religious conversion is still the maintenance of further controlled fear and tension. The Chinese Communists know, perhaps from a study of Catholic missionary methods, that everybody, at one time or another, has what can be branded as "evil thoughts"; and that, if the doctrine can be accepted that thought is as wicked in its way as action, they have the whip-hand over the people. In political democracies it is a general rule that anyone can *think* what evil he likes, so long as he does not carry the thought into anti-social action. But the Gospel text of *Matthew* v. 28, which makes mental adultery as reprehensible as physical adultery, has justified some Christian sects in applying the same rule to all the Commandments. The anxiety and guilt thus induced in the faithful can keep them in a continuous state of physiological tension, and makes them dependent on their religious advisers for daily guidance. But whereas the penitent troubled by lecherous thoughts for his neighbour's wife, or murderous thoughts for his neighbour, feels safe enough in the confessional, because the priest is bound by the most sacred bonds not to reveal these confidences to another, a Communist reign of terror is a different matter. Many Chinese plagued with deviationist thoughts will think twenty times before confessing them to the local group leader, despite invitations to do so; and will be in constant fear of talking in their sleep or giving themselves away in public by some slip of the tongue. This ensures that they will take excessive care to do the right thing politically, even if they cannot think it. The Household Police are a most constant reminder of their danger.

Such anxiety is self-perpetuating. Even the most conformist members of a dictator state are bound to suffer from recurrent anxiety, or feelings of guilt; since, with the frequent modifications of the party line and such palace revolutions as make it necessary for the people to anathematize former leaders, they will often automatically think wrong thoughts. And the penalty for wrong thinking is not hellfire in the life to come, but economic and social disaster in the present one. This tense atmosphere allows dictators to exploit revivalist methods with even greater effect than the church leaders who first refined them.

In the London *Times* an article on "Moulding Minds for the New China"[97] also emphasizes the similarities between some religious practices and the new Communism. Its Special Correspondent writes:

> Communists deny that Marxism is a religion, yet anyone listening to the shy and rather halting old man's account of how the authorities dealt with him was bound to think of religious zealots wrestling for the soul of a sinner—and getting the man himself to win the fight. He had been the owner of a modest drug store and chemist shop . . . he saw which way things were going and he went along to the authorities to present them with his concern. Instead of thanking him for his generous and forward-looking offer, they catechized him pretty severely, told him that they were not at all satisfied that his offer was made of his own spontaneous will without ulterior motives, and sent him back to think it quietly over by himself. They would not interfere, they said; they wanted only willing and convinced volunteers. Back he went at the end of the month; back he was sent again to search his heart. Then, when he naturally pressed his offer still more fervently with each delay, and when they finally agreed that his own motives were pure, they reminded him of his shareholders. Were they all of one heart and voice? He had to call a meeting of the group, and only then— when they were all clamouring to be allowed to tread the

new way—only then did the State agree to take over the concern from them, promising them a share in the profits.

The Times correspondent goes on to say that he did not know how much to admire and how much to be appalled at the methods used by the authorities:

> It was a glimpse into the process of "moral regeneration" or "brain-washing" about which so much is heard in China. It cannot be left out in any attempt to understand the forces at work. . . . Nothing is more striking than the skill and patience with which party members all down the line work on people's minds. Supported by all the social pressures, they spend hours, days and weeks in striving for conversion and willing co-operation wherever possible. And they get results, whether in public confession or private avowals. Where Russia set out to shape lives first and foremost, China is embarked on the task of shaping minds as well. It is something much more formidable. . . . About the stability of the régime and its determination to lead the country to new strength, there can be no doubt at all.

Aldous Huxley has commented on these matters in general terms:

> True, crowd-delirium evoked by members of the opposition and in the name of heretical principles, has everywhere been denounced by those in power. But crowd-delirium aroused by government agents, crowd-delirium in the name of orthodoxy, is an entirely different matter. In all cases where it can be made to serve the interests of men controlling church and state, downward self-transcendence by means of herd intoxication is treated as something legitimate, and even highly desirable. Pilgrimages and political rallies,

corybantic revivals and patriotic parades—these things are ethically right so long as they are *our* pilgrimages, *our* rallies, *our* revivals and *our* parades. . . . When crowd-delirium is exploited for the benefit of governments and orthodox churches, the exploiters are always very careful not to allow the intoxication to go too far.

Controlled religious and political ceremonies are welcomed, however, by those in authority, since they provide:

> . . . opportunities for planting suggestions in minds which have momentarily ceased to be capable of reason or free will.[90]

Although there will generally be dissenters uninfluenced by any particular method used, the mechanics of indoctrinating large and small groups of people can be relatively simple, and that is why they should be better understood by all those who may be subjected to them. The historical accuracy or logical coherence of the belief implanted can sometimes be unrelated to the amount of success achieved if only the disruptive human emotions of fear and anger are invoked, and kept going long enough, to increase suggestibility and to allow the other mechanisms discussed in this book to come into play.

A British publication by the Ministry of Defence describes how the Chinese Communists, by using rough and ready methods, often poorly adapted to the British mind, contrived to indoctrinate quite a number of the British junior N.C.O.s and private soldiers who were prisoners in Korea. In most cases the indoctrination was incomplete or only temporary; but forty soldiers became firmer converts. The officers and all senior non-commissioned officers, who were kept separated from the rest are, officially, said to have remained almost completely unaffected. Physical violence also seems to have been used—as it was against "the drunken private of the Buffs" in Sir Francis Hastings Doyle's famous poem, who refused to *kow-tow* when captured by the Chinese of an earlier age and died in the best soldierly tradition. Yet if it had not been for the language difficulty, and the relatively unskilled techniques that the Chinese seemed to have used on this occasion, more soldiers would almost certainly have been won over. And despite the British Government's White Paper on the subject, it seems very difficult to believe that the holding of a senior non-commissioned or officer rank in the British Army renders one so immune to methods which can result in at least the temporary breakdown of a Cardinal Mindszenty.

CHAPTER 8

Brain-Washing in Ancient Times

An Account written by Robert Graves

It seemed important to find out whether, since basic behaviour patterns do not seem to change in human beings, Greek physicians or priests had anticipated any of the findings in this book—unaffected as they were by the "other-worldliness" of Christianity and bound to a more mechanistic view of nature. I passed on this problem to Robert Graves and explained to him the mechanistic principles that seemed important. It soon became obvious that many anticipations of modern methods existed. The following is his account of some of those, which he kindly supplied me.

* * *

The Greeks consulted oracles for some particular and urgent reasons when they needed advice or psychological treatment; just as nowadays one might visit a psychiatrist, a fortuneteller, or a Roman Catholic priest. And just as the Freudian and Jungian therapists now claim to explain physical symptoms in terms of subconscious conflict, interpreting their patients' symbolic dreams during prolonged treatment on the couch, so the Greek priests would interpret the dreams of the troubled visitants to their temples, and also account in theological terms for hysterical and convulsive symptoms. Writers of the Hippocratic medical school, with its headquarters at Cos, were no less critical of these priestly psychiatrists than modern neurologists are apt to be of some present-day psychosomatic theorists:[98]

> If the patient imitates a goat, if he roars or is convulsed in the right side, they say the Mother of the Gods is the cause. . . . If he foams at the mouth and kicks, the cause is assigned to the Aries. If the symptoms are fears and terrors at night, delirium, jumping out of bed and rushing out of doors, they are described as attacks of Hecate, or assaults of the spirits of the dead.

The dreams and trances seem often to have been deliberately induced under suggestion; and Marcus Apuleius's account in *The Golden Ass* of the visions he experienced in the Temple of Isis after his spectacular conversion, make the technique quite clear. He writes:

> Not long after, would you believe it, I was granted yet another vision in which my instructions were to undergo a third initiation. I was surprised and perplexed, not being able to make head or tail of the order. I had already been twice initiated, so what mystery still remained undisclosed? "Surely," I thought, "the priests have failed me. Either they have given me a false revelation, or else they have held something back." I confess that I even began to suspect them of cheating me. But while I was still puzzling over the question and nearly driven mad by worry, a kindly god whose name I did not know explained the case to me in a dream. . . .[87]

The modern psychotherapist, I gather, often experiences the same early difficulty in holding his patient's faith; and must constantly hark back to his original ideas of the ailment until at last the patient obligingly dreams what he is required to dream—and this is offered as proof positive that the diagnosis is sound.

The ancient Greeks also used religious dancing as a cure for nervous diseases. Their Corybantic rites consisted of dancing in an abandoned manner to flutes and drums until the performers collapsed in exhaustion. The Corybantes not only induced trances and feelings of divine possession, but also claimed to cure them. And Aristotle later observed that before morbid affections could be expelled, they might first have to be artificially stimulated; which is, again I gather, what was found with drug abreaction in the recent war.

Those young Greeks who became initiates at the Mysteries—whether the Eleusinian, Samothracian, Corinthian or Mithraic—underwent a more formal type of religious indoctrination than visitants to the oracles. What happened on these secret occasions can, unfortunately, be recovered only in outline from occasional hints and indiscretions of initiates mostly those who later became converted to Christianity—but here is a brief summary of events at the Eleusinian Mysteries, based on trustworthy authorities, including J. E. Harrison's *Prolegomena to the Study of Greek Religion,*[99] and Victor Magnion's *Les Mystères d'Eleusis.*[100] The Lesser Mysteries, sacred to Persephone or Dionysus, took place in the spring and were a preparation for the Greater. The candidate's condition and record had to be carefully scrutinized by the priests, from whom he could expect no more than cold disdain. They made him first symbolically surrender his fortune to the temple, and then undergo a protracted probation of abstinence and silence. Finally he drank a soporific draught and went to sleep in a hut made of branches, on a bed spread with leaves and flowers. Sweet music awakened him, and after plucking a fruit from the Tree of Life, and making a formal choice between a right road and a wrong, he was instructed in secret philosophical doctrine purified by fire and water, and at last admitted into the sacred choir.

He now possessed the password for admission at a much later date to the Greater (and more ancient) Mysteries, sacred to Demeter, for which he willingly submitted to a far more severe probation. He fasted from flesh, garlic, beans, crabs, eggs and certain kinds of fish; kept sexually chaste; preserved complete silence, drank only sacred water; bathed in the sea; took purges. The coming initiation ceremony would represent death and rebirth. On admittance into the temple, he was stripped of all his garments, and presently appeared before a judge, who sentenced him to die. Execution having been formally carried out, a mystagogue led him down a slope into a dark grotto representing the Underworld, where he heard the cries of the damned and met horrible phantoms, including wild beasts, serpents, and lecherous Empusae. Unseen hands daubed him with filth, and he could not escape because Furies with brazen whips threatened him from behind. Presently he was instructed to bathe in a pool and wash himself clean, before approaching another tribunal.

Being sentenced to chastisement, he was struck on the head, caught by the hair, thrown down, and beaten soundly by demons; but dared not defend himself. When he seemed sufficiently humbled in spirit, the mystagogue moralized on these sufferings and gave him a draught of Lethe water to make him forget the past. Next, apparently, he entered a magical circle and went tediously round and round, until he managed to escape—but only by a ritual of rebirth from the Goddess herself—and was given a new name. He mounted into a bright, delectable place, put on clean garments, partook of milk and honey, and joined the band of illuminates. Finally he assisted at the climax of the Mysteries—a sacred sexless marriage in the dark between himself and the chief hierophant and the priestess of Demeter; watched an ear of grain being reaped in silence; and heard the birth of the sacred child announced.

Professor George Thomson observes that "several Greek writers describe in detail the emotional effects of mystical initiation, and the uniformity of the symptoms shows that they were recognized as normal. They consisted of shuddering, trembling, sweating, mental confusion, distress, consternation, and joy mixed with alarm and agitation."[98]

At Lobadeia, however, the local rites of Demeter had been taken over by the oracular priests of Trophonius; and since the visitants were not sworn to absolute secrecy, as at Eleusis, Corinth and elsewhere, two or three circumstantial accounts of the proceedings survive. From the account of Pausanias, who wrote about A.D. 174, and had himself visited the Oracle of Trophonius, it is seen how carefully the mystagogue disturbed the brain activity of initiates before trying to indoctrinate them. Pausanias's account[101] is as follows:

The Oracle of Trophonius is a chasm in the earth, not a natural chasm but built in careful masonry. The shape is like that of a pot for baking bread. There is no passage leading down to the bottom; but when a man goes to Trophonius, they bring him a narrow and light ladder. When he has descended, he sees a hole between the ground and the masonry. So he lays himself on his back on the ground, and holding in his hand barley-cakes kneaded with honey, he thrusts his feet first into the hole and follows himself, endeavouring to get his knees through the hole. When they are through, the rest of his body is immediately dragged after them and shoots in, just as a man might be caught and dragged down by the swirl of a mighty and rapid river.

Pausanias adds that the method of illumination varied with the visitant: some were given auditory, some visual stimuli, but they all returned through the same aperture, feet foremost:

They say that none of those who went down died, except one of Demetrius's bodyguard . . .

The after-treatment is also described:

When a man has come up from Trophonius the priests take him in hand again, and set him on what is called the "chair of Memory", which stands not far from the shrine; and, being seated there, he is questioned by them as to all he saw and heard. On being informed, they hand him over to his friends, who carry him, still overpowered with fear and quite unconscious of himself and his surroundings, to the buildings where he lodged before, in preparation for this event, namely the House of Good Fortune and the Good Demon. Afterwards, however, he will have all his wits as before, and the power of laughter will come back to him. I write not from hearsay: I have myself consulted Trophonius, and have seen others who have done so.

We can imagine from this account the acute fear and excitement aroused in the victim as he suddenly "shoots in, just as a man might be caught and dragged by the swirl of a mighty and rapid river". It is important to note that, after his experience in the Oracle, the visitant is described as being returned to his friends still "overpowered with fear and quite unconscious of himself and his surroundings".

Plutarch[102] has left a convincing account of what happened inside Trophonius's chasm to help to make the victim more vulnerable:

> He [Timarchus] being eager to know—for he was a fine youth, and a beginner in philosophy—what Socrates's Daemon might be, acquainting none but Cebes and me with his design, went down to Trophonius's cave, and performed all the ceremonies that were requisite to gain an oracle. There he stayed two nights and one day, so that his friends despaired of his return and lamented him as lost; but the next morning he came out with a cheerful countenance, and told us many wonderful things he had seen and heard . . . As soon as he entered, a thick darkness surrounded him; then, after he had prayed, he lay a long while upon the ground, but was not certain whether awake or in a dream, only he imagined that a smart stroke fell upon his head, and that through the parted sutures of his skull his soul fled out . . .

It is difficult to know whether the effects he then describes were all real or partly hallucinatory:

Looking up he saw no earth, but certain islands shining with a gentle fire, which interchanged colours according to the different variation of the light, innumerable and very large, unequal but all round ... When he looked downward there appeared a vast chasm. ... Thence a thousand howlings and bellowings of beasts, cries of children, groans of men and women, and all sorts of terrible noises reached his ears; but faintly as being far off and rising through the vast hollow; and this terrified him exceedingly. A little while after, an invisible thing spoke thus to him: "Timarchus, what dost thou desire to understand?" And he replied: "Everything; for what is there that is not wonderful and surprising?"

Several paragraphs are then devoted to the philosophical indoctrination received by Timarchus when he had been put into a suitable mental state of preparedness by the methods described above. For instance:

Every soul hath some portion of reason; a man cannot be a man without it; but as much of each soul as is mixed with flesh and appetite is changed, and through pain or pleasure becomes irrational. There are four divisions of all things; the first is of life; the second of motion; the third of generation; and the fourth of corruption. The first is coupled to the second by a unit, in the substance visible; the second to the third by understanding, in the Sun; and the third to the fourth by nature, in the Moon ...

These four divisions suggest that the priests belonged to the Orphic disciples. And again:

The purer part of the soul is not drawn down into the body, but swims above, and touches the extremest part of the man's head; it is like a cord to hold up and direct the subsiding part of the soul, as long as it proves obedient and is not overcome by the appetites of the flesh.

These revelations seemed of crucial importance to the listener, in the bewildered mental state produced partly by being hit over the head; but remind me of some of the theories about egos, ids, archetypal myths, and dianetic pre-natal dreams given in treatment by various schools of modern doctrinaire psychotherapy.

Plutarch goes on:

> The voice continuing no longer, Timarchus (as he said) turned about to discover who it was that spoke; but a violent pain, as if his skull had been pressed together, seized his head, so that he lost all sense and understanding; but in a little while recovering, he found himself in the entrance of the cave, where he first lay down.

This account confirms Pausanias's statement that whoever decided to approach the Oracle of Trophonius, had first of all to lodge for a stated number of days in a building sacred to the Good Demon and Good Fortune. During his sojourn there he was expected to observe certain rules of purity, and in particular refrain from warm baths, presumably because they would relax tension. He came to the oracle clad in an linen tunic, girt with ribbons, and shod with the boots of the country. Before going down to the oracle, he talked to the priests and after his return was made to write down what he had seen or heard, doubtless to assist in its firmer implantation.

This technique often, it seems, had lasting effects on the mental state of the person undergoing it, since a Greek proverb is quoted by several writers, to the effect that "He must have come from Trophonius's Oracle". It was applied to anyone who seemed particularly grave or solemn, and meant that the fright given the visitant had made him unable to laugh again. The after-treatment at the House of Good Fortune and the Good Demon may have been intended to discredit this proverb.

Another Greek proverb, taken over by the Romans, was applied to anyone who talked or acted so strangely that he might be suspected of mental derangement: "He ought to visit Anticyra!"—this being generally acknowledged as the most hopeful place in the world for a cure. Anticyra, a small Phocian town built on a rocky isthmus, three miles in circumference, which juts into the Corinthian Gulf near Mount Parnassus, had originally borne the Cretan name Cyparissos. Stephanus of Byzantium, the lexicographer, reports (under *Anticyra*) that Heracles was treated there for homicidal mania, which suggests the curative establishment was a very ancient one. No autobiographical account survives of the treatment given; but it can be deduced from various sources. Phocis in general belonged to Apollo, God of Medicine, but his twin-sister Artemis, who also had healing powers and was said to specialize in dangerous drugs, owned the one temple of note at Anticyra, where she figured on the city coins with torch and hound. (She was called "Dictynnaean Artemis", which establishes the Cretan connection.) The torch and her famous antique black image show her to have been an Earth-goddess with Underworld affiliations, and therefore a suitable patroness of the curative centre. The temple stood under a cliff at some distance inland from the city.

The reason given by Strabo[103] for Anticyra's fame is that both varieties of the sovereign specific against insanity, namely the bellebore, grows particularly well here and were mixed by the local druggists with another uncommon local shrub, named sesamoides, which made its action safer and more effective. But this cannot be the whole truth; for, unless there were psychotherapists at work who were not able to leave that city, it would have been unnecessary for a Roman senator to ask special leave from the Emperor Caligula to complete his cure there:[104] he could have brought a supply of drugs and physicians back to Rome with him, and Anticyra was a bleak, barren and depressing place where nobody would stay unless obliged. Since "hellebore" means "the food of Helle" (another goddess of the same type as Dictynnaean Artemis), and since a famous gold charm called *helleborus*, with hellebore flowers on it, was worn only by women, it seems probable that the priestesses of Artemis were the local psychotherapists.

According to Dioscorides[105] both varieties of hellebore, the white and the black, grew best at Anticyra. Though "white" hellebore closely resembles the black, except for the colour of the root, Dioscorides, Pausanias[106] and Pliny[107] agree that the white was a vomitory, and the black (also called "melampodium", in honour of the hero Melampus who cured the three homicidally insane daughters of Proteus) was a strong purgative. Pliny says the black hellebore inspired immense religious awe, even more than the white, and was gathered with careful ceremony. The sesamoides which the druggists of Anticyra mixed with the white hellebore also acted as a strong purgative. But it was not merely the debilitating powers of black and white hellebores, and sesamoides—taken fasting, in bean-porridge, and after the administration of other emetics!—which were counted on for the cure; Pliny reports that both hellebores are narcotics. The treatment evidently included a form of drug-abreaction combined with strong suggestion. The fear inspired by the gloomy place and the poisonous drug with its "alarming symptoms"[108] would be increased by debilitation—even wine was banned—and in the "unnatural drowsiness" which supervened after taking hellebore, the priestesses doubtless used Underworld ritual to help disperse the patient's symptoms. Resemblances to some modern methods are obvious.

Dioscorides, Pliny, and Pausanias claim that delirium, insanity, paralysis, and melancholia (among other diseases) were cured here, but the treatment was so rigorous that no woman, child or timorous man was advised to undergo it. It is known that in obstinate cases the cure was protracted; the senator who asked permission to stay at Anticyra had been there for some time. Caligula sent him a sword as a command to commit suicide, saying: "If you have been taking hellebore so long without success, you had better try the blood-letting cure."

CHAPTER 9

The Eliciting of Confessions

Much the same basic methods of eliciting confessions are used by police forces in many parts of the world today; but the Communist Russian technique under Stalin seems to have been the most efficient. This was inherited in a crude form from the Czarist police; and whether the Czarists borrowed it from the Catholic Inquisitors, or whether it developed spontaneously in Russia because of the similarity between religious and political intolerance, is a nice historical point. At any rate, while a study of Protestant revivalism throws the strongest light on the procedure of inspiring mass guilt, it is to the history of the Catholic Inquisition that one should turn for information on the techniques of forcing confessions from the individual deviationist. The Russian Communists may merely have used physiological researches to perfect already established techniques.

To elicit confessions, one must try to create feelings of anxiety and guilt, and induce states of mental conflict if these are not already present. Even if the accused person is genuinely guilty, the normal functioning of his brain must be disturbed so that judgment becomes impaired. If possible he must be made to feel a preference for punishment—especially if combined with a hope of salvation when it is over—rather than a continuation of the mental tension already present, or now being induced by the examiner. Whenever guilty persons make "voluntary" confessions to the police against their better interests, thus earning sentences of imprisonment or death, and the evidence suggests that physical violence has not been used, it is interesting to enquire whether one or more of the four physiological methods have been used which were also found by Pavlov to succeed in breaking down the resistance of animals (see p. 9).

The following questions may be asked:

1. Have the police examiners deliberately stirred up anxiety? Have they increased the strength of any exciting stimulus applied to the brain?

2. Have they prolonged tension to a point where the brain becomes exhausted and "transmarginally inhibited"? Then a "protective inhibition", starting to become "transmarginal", could bring about temporary disturbance of normal judgment and greatly increased suggestibility.

3. Was the suspect's brain bombarded with such a variety of stimuli in the form of ever-changing attitudes and questions by the examiners that he became confused and incriminated himself, perhaps falsely?

4. Were measures taken to produce an added physical debilitation and mental exhaustion, which finally caused a breakdown of normal brain function and resistance—even when (1), (2) and (3) used alone failed to have any effect?

Once breakdown under questioning begins, the normal brain may exhibit changes similar to those obtained by group excitation, because group and individual methods of exciting and exhausting the brain tend to have the same basic end effects on its function. Either there is an increase in suggestibility, which might allow a police examiner to persuade even an innocent person of his guilt; or the "paradoxical" and "ultraparadoxical" phases of cortical activity may supervene and make him completely reverse his former beliefs and patterns of behaviour, so that he feels a desire to make confessions which are the opposite of his normal nature and judgment.

In some phases of cross-examination under stress, prisoners may feel a desire to confess coming on and then receding again. At this stage they will observe that things are "getting very peculiar"; from one minute to the next they may be holding quite different attitudes and opinions, because of the fluctuations of brain function being induced. Sooner or later, however, the new attitude is likely to dominate and they will confess. Every attempt is then made to stabilize the change and prevent a reversion to former ways of thinking when the emotional pressure is relaxed.

There should be no mystery made about the details of these police techniques. They are in the public domain. Alexander Weissberg's *Conspiracy of Silence*[109] should be made an adult textbook in all free countries, to teach us what can happen to the independent-minded under a dictatorship, and what may happen, to a lesser degree, even in democracies not eternally on guard to preserve their civil rights. Weissberg, a German Communist, survived the Stalinist purge which took place in Russia shortly before World War II and sent millions of people either to execution or to long periods of forced labour. After spending three years in Russian prisons, and being forced to sign confessions which he later withdrew, Weissberg was repatriated to Germany under the Russo-German Treaty of

1939. The account of his experiences is detailed and, when read in conjunction with similar autobiographic reports from other hands, bears the stamp of authenticity.

Stypulkowski's book *Invitation to Moscow*[110] tells how he successfully avoided making a confession despite over one hundred and thirty periods of interrogation, some of which lasted for many hours; however, his confession was needed in a hurry because a Polish trial was being rapidly staged for propaganda purposes, and the examiners had to desist before the required point of exhaustion could be reached. Stypulkowski was acquitted and sent back to Poland, but subsequently escaped to Western Europe, where he wrote the book.[110] Koestler's autobiography discusses the brain-washing techniques described to him by Communist friends with special sources of information; and Orwell's novel *Nineteen-Eighty-Four,*[88] written in 1949, also seems to be based on factual accounts filtering from Eastern into Western Europe. Substantially the same methods appear to have been used in such Russian satellite states as Bulgaria, Roumania, Poland and Hungary. We have already mentioned the Ministry of Defence's exposé of the methods used by the Chinese on British prisoners of war in Korea, and the United States Government has recently published theirs.[2] More recently, Krushchev[111] in his indictment of Stalin gave some further general information on the means of eliciting confessions used during the Stalin régime, and even more recently still, Drs. L. E. Hinkle and H. G. Wolff have published a full and detailed account of the methods used in Russia and China from information which was collected and studied by them while working as consultants to the United States Department of Defense.[112]

Once the basic principles are properly understood, many local variations of technique become more explicable, and people who are unfortunate enough to become victims of police cross-examination in many countries may have a useful insight into methods which can be legally used against them, and learn how they can best avoid the final phase of the process where normal judgment is undermined.

Granted that the right pressure is applied in the right way and for long enough, ordinary prisoners have little chance of staving off collapse, only the exceptional or mentally ill person is likely to resist over very long periods. Ordinary people, let me repeat, are the way they are simply because they are sensitive to and influenced by what is going on around them; it is the lunatic who can be so impervious to suggestion. Dr. Roy Swank (see Chapter 2, p. 25) found that if kept *long enough* in front-line fighting, without any intermission, *all* United States active fighting personnel, except some of the insane, eventually broke down; and this fits in with our own views during the same war. Yet even greater nervous tension, because it is more persistent, can be aroused in a prison cell or police station by skilled interrogation than in a fox-hole by enemy snipers or machine-gunners.

To return to the actual methods that were used behind the Iron Curtain under Stalin: every effort was made to stir up anxiety, to implant guilt, to confuse the victim, to create a state in which he does not know what is going to happen to him from one minute to the next. His diet was restricted to ensure loss of weight and debilitation; because physiological stimuli, which may fail when body-weight is at its normal figure of, say, 140 lb., tend to produce rapid breakdown when body-weight has dropped to about 90 lb. Every effort was also made to disrupt normal behaviour patterns. To begin with, the victim might be called from his work for questioning by the police, and then be ordered to resume it again and attend a further examination a few days later. Several such examinations might take place before his eventual arrest.

An immediate element of anxiety is produced by the warning that it is a criminal offence to tell anybody—his friends, his relatives, or even his wife—that he is under examination by the police. Being thus cut off from all advice which he would ordinarily expect from those near and dear to him, he finds his tension and anxiety redoubled. If the temptation becomes so overwhelming that he makes a confidant of someone, this immediately lays him open to a long term of imprisonment for the crime, even if he has committed no other. Further anxiety that his error may come to light will harass him during the cross-examination and may hasten the breakdown. Tension may be increased in numerous other ways, such as letting him hear the firing-squads at work, or keying him up for a trial which is constantly postponed.

The prisoner who is told: "We know everything; you will be wise to confess!" is put in a quandary if he has nothing in fact to confess. While being questioned before his arrest, Weissberg reports:[109]

> I went over the events of the last ten years in my mind. I considered everyone with whom I had been in personal contact, or with whom I had corresponded. And in the end I found nothing at all which could reasonably offer grounds

for suspicion . . . . Suddenly a long-forgotten incident which had taken place in 1933 came to my mind and what calmness I had left was utterly destroyed. My God! I thought, that must be it!

It was a small incident completely unconcerned with the alleged crime for which he was wanted; yet he went through torments wondering whether or not to confess it. How guilt and anxiety can be artificially created is shown by the instructions he was given before his arrest:

> Go home again and come back the day after tomorrow. In the meantime think over the whole of your life. Then come back here and tell me when you first got into touch with the enemy and what ideas caused you to go over to his side. If you freely confess and show us that you want to be a loyal Soviet supporter again, we'll do all we can to help you.

Arrest would generally take place at dead of night, which increases fear still further. Once in his prison cell, the prisoner is virtually cut off from all contact with the outside world, and it may be as long as a fortnight before he is even given any hint as to what the charge is against him. These are further means of prolonging his tension so that, long before questioning starts, his thinking may have begun to get distorted. He will have been foraging in his mind for all possible reasons why he has been imprisoned, and perhaps finding every answer but the right one. He may even begin to believe in his speculations as though they were facts.

The ordinary prisoner in Russia had certain rights even when things were at their worst. Physical violence was supposedly forbidden, and if he felt that his interrogation was not being conducted fairly, he had the right of appeal to a higher official than his police examiner. However, Khrushchev[111] now admits what Weissberg also had reported earlier, namely, that starting in 1937 "physical pressure" amounting to torture had been used on certain political prisoners. "Thus Stalin had sanctioned in the name of the Central Committee of the All Union Communist Party (Bolsheviks) the most brutal violation of socialist legality. . . ." The Russian examiner was like his British counterpart, also officially forbidden to accept confessions which he did not believe correct. This regulation is of very great importance to a proper understanding of the whole process because, as in other countries as well, confessions can be made which, though largely false, come to be believed by both the examiner and the prisoner. This is because the examiner first suggests to the prisoner that he is guilty of a crime, and tries to convince him, if he is not already convinced that this is so. Even if the prisoner is innocent, the long tension to which he has been subjected may well have already frightened him into suggestibility, and if he is an unstable type he may then accept the examiner's view of his guilt. If the examination is pressed, he may even begin, as it were, to play back an old record—confessing to crimes suggested by the police in earlier cross-examinations. The police, forgetting that the incidents were originally their own guesswork, are deceived: the prisoner has now "spontaneously" confessed what they have been suspecting all along. It is not usually realized that fatigue and anxiety induce suggestibility in the examiner as well as the prisoner—the task of eliciting confessions is a very difficult

and trying one—and that they can delude each other into
a belief in the genuineness of the confessed crime. It is
now reported, however, that under the new régime a change
in regulations was made in Russia, in 1955, so that a
prisoner's own confession is no longer acceptable as evidence of his guilt.[113]

In British, as in United States law, no man can be compelled to make any statement, or answer any question, that
will incriminate him. Yet every year large numbers of anxious and sometimes temporarily distraught people, after
being carefully warned that what they confess may be used
in evidence, can also be made to confess their major and
minor crimes to the British police, who are almost certainly the best and fairest police force in the world today.
A very strict code of Judges' Rules has to be observed at
police stations; no violence of any sort can be threatened,
or promises made, and yet newspapers continue to report
long and detailed statements of guilt that are constantly
being given and signed by such people, often putting their
actions in the blackest possible light. Later they may calm
down, return to a more normal state of brain activity, and
ask to withdraw these statements. It is then, of course, too
late. Pavlov's experiments on animals may help to show
why this so often happens. For judges, the police, and prison
doctors have long been well aware of the paradoxical finding that by far the most detailed and truthful confessions
may be made by a suspect *just after* he has been formally
charged with murder or some other serious crime. Suspects, whether they have been arrested soon after the com-
mission of the alleged crime, or whether only after frequent
interrogations and a long period of suspense, are likely to

be put into a highly anxious and emotional state when formally charged and to find the power of their brain temporarily disorganized. This is the precise point when a state of increased suggestibility, or the "paradoxical" or "ultra-paradoxical" phase of reaction to stress, is most likely to occur; when, in fact, such persons may be most easily persuaded to make statements which not only increase their chances of conviction, but even sometimes incriminate them unjustly. Then a prisoner often spends the entire period before his trial, and during it, trying to understand how he came to sign so damaging a "voluntary" statement as he has given to the police, and trying to explain or extricate himself from its implications.

Members of the United States police forces have no compunction about writing practical textbooks on the subject of how to elicit police confessions. Mr. Clarence D. Lee, for instance, in the *Instrumental Detection of Deception*,[114] explains the use of the lie detector. Mr. Lee knows it can be sometimes a most unreliable instrument and is one which cannot be safely used in a court of law,* but it can be wonderfully effective for scaring the inexperienced and ignorant who are guilty into making confessions:

> The instrument and the test procedure have a very strong psychological effect upon a guilty subject in inducing him to confess. Sight of the pens swinging to every heart-beat and breath may well shatter his morale. Showing him the recorded results, with a brief explanation of the significance

---

* A false but strongly positive response was given, for instance, by a suspect watching a girl sunbathing in the nude through the police-station window.

of the different indices of deception, often will produce immediate results. Or pointing out the similarities between the reactions accompanying the single lie in a control test and (his) reactions to relevant questions in the formal test is likewise helpful. . . . As a means of inducing confession, any procedure of this type is permissible *after* the examiner is convinced of the subject's guilt through the prescribed methods of testing.

Mr. Lee adds that sixty to eighty per cent of those shown as guilty by the test eventually confess; but that the percentage of confessions obtained depends on the examiner's:

> . . . confidence in himself and the method employed, his persuasiveness, perseverance, and a sympathetic attitude towards the suspect. By one means or another the examiner should impart to the subject the idea that he is certain of his guilt, as any indication of doubt on the examiner's part may defeat his purpose.

Even if a test is negative, the examiner can still pretend to believe it positive, to help win a confession. Mr. Lee also confirms what we have found in so many other instances, namely that:

> . . . those most susceptible to an appeal to the emotions are the easiest to induce to confess. In this group are the so-called accidental offenders, such as the hit-and-run offender, those who kill in the heat of passion, juveniles and first offenders, as well as the sex-offenders—those in whom the sex instinct is perverted, the homosexuals, rapists and rape-murderers, sadists and masochists.

Those who cannot be made to confess with the lie detector are the "career" criminals—who have probably learned by experience the danger of co-operating in any form of police questioning or examination and so refuse to answer any questions at all:

> This type of offender presents the only really difficult problem in the matter of obtaining confessions.

Mr. Lee's advice to examiners who find it difficult to elicit confessions in certain cases is that, once anxiety has been aroused (and suggestibility perhaps heightened):

> . . . the examiner must lose no time in bringing to bear his best strategy before the suspect has fully recovered from the mental trauma resulting from the test. The psychological advantages are all held by the examiner, while the subject is in an exposed position.

Interesting details of the techniques used are given:

> Where a sympathetic approach is indicated, it is well to play on the self-justification that is usually in the mind of the criminal for his misdeeds. Suggest that there was a good reason for his having committed the deed, that he has too much intelligence to have done it without rhyme or reason. In the case of sex crimes, explain that sex hunger is one of the strongest instincts motivating our lives. In case of theft, suggest that the subject may have been hungry, or deprived of the necessities of life; or in homicide, that the victim had done him a great wrong and probably had it coming to him. Be friendly and sympathetic and encourage him to write out or relate the whole story—to clean up and start afresh.

Mr. Lee considers these methods ethical and necessary for the protection of the law-abiding citizen in a country as plagued by crime as the United States; he points out that:

> Before punishment can be meted out, the accused must be convicted by due processes of law, and one of the most effective means of insuring conviction is confession by the accused.

Those interested in comparing recognized Western methods of eliciting confessions with those that have been used behind the Iron Curtain will find a bibliography in Mr. Lee's most revealing book. Mr. Lee quotes a most enlightening statement by a former Deputy Commissioner of the New York Police Department, published in the *Police Magazine* as early as 1925:

> My usual method is to take down the prisoner's statement when he is first brought in in just the form he is willing to make it. The next day, when we have gathered additional information, we question him again, pointing our questions from the light of this information. We then analyse the discrepancies between his first statement and the second one. Then we examine him the next day and again analyse the discrepancies and draw the net closer around him if the facts assembled point more surely to his guilt. We get him to talk again and again, day after day; and at last, if he is guilty or has a guilty knowledge of the crime, he is bound to break down and come out with the whole story. In the case of a suave, adroit, well-educated criminal who is able to present smooth answers to almost any questioning we keep at him until we discover this weak spot. His first story he tells glibly.

In fact, he is glib on each and every occasion following. But the discrepancy begins to appear more and more clearly each time. Go at him again and he'll break. Of course, if he's telling the truth he will tell the same story each time. But if he is lying he will slip up at some time. The liar can't remember everything. He's bound to forget something he said before. There was never such a thing as the "third degree". You simply get a man into a mental corner, provided he is really guilty, and then he will wilt every time, that is, if you get a wedge in as a start. It's pretty hard to get a confession unless you have some little clue to start with on your line of questioning. *But having found that weak spot, the discrepancies in the man's story begin to widen until finally he becomes so confused and befuddled that he sees the game is up. All his defences have been beaten down. He's cornered, trapped. That's when he bursts into tears. The torture comes from his own mind, not from outside.* [115]

The only thing to add is that in such a technique, it is known that truth and falsehood can get hopelessly confused in the minds of both the suspect and the examiner, and that if what he calls a "weak spot" is not present, the police examiner determined to get a confession can create it by suggestion.

The eliciting of what turn out later to be false confessions, believed genuinely by the examiners and suspects alike recalls a similar phenomenon in a psychotherapist's consulting-room, when he begins by believing and conveying to his patient, for instance, that certain childhood traumata have caused his symptoms. After hours of thought and anxiety, on and off the couch, due to reliving early fears and guilty feelings concerned with sex, the patient may come up with detailed and complicated accounts of emotional damning done him on this or that occasion. If the therapist is one of those who believe in birth traumata and asks about it, the patient may even begin to remember and to relive this in detail.[116] The therapist may now be convinced that his particular theory of birth trauma is correct; yet, what has probably happened is what may also happen in police examinations: the patient has merely given back, in all good faith, what has been originally implied or suggested. Yet both the patient and the doctor can genuinely come to believe in such happenings by using such methods of investigation; and we must also remember that all present Freudian theories, about the sexual content of the human subconscious mind have only been arrived at by the use of similar methods. Falsehoods can come to be believed equally with new important truths.

Freud, in the early stages of his work, found that almost all hysterical women coming to him for treatment gave him a history of sexual interference, often of a perverted kind, or of incest, by their fathers. This was almost certainly due to his being so interested in this particular line of enquiry, that he unknowingly implanted the ideas in his patients' minds, and then got them given back to him; the emotional stresses of the treatment making him and his patients reciprocally suggestible.

Ernest Jones, in his recent book on Freud,[117] says about this most interesting episode:

> But up to the spring of 1897 he [Freud] still held firmly to his conviction of the reality of these childhood traumas. . . . At that time doubts began to creep in. . . . Then, quite sud-

denly, he decided to confide to him [Fleiss] . . . the awful truth that most—not all—of the seductions in childhood which his patients had revealed, and about which he had built up his whole theory of hysteria, had never occurred.

Freud himself wrote:

> . . . the result at first was hopeless bewilderment. Analysis had led by the right paths back to these sexual traumas, and yet they were not true. Reality was lost from under one's feet. At that time I would gladly have given up the whole thing [psychoanalysis]. . . . Perhaps I persevered only because I had no choice and could not then begin again at anything else.[117]

The danger of the therapist as well as the patient being "brain-washed" is seen in Ernest Jones's book, in which he says: "Freud's passion to get at the truth with the maximum of certainty was, I again suggest, the deepest and strongest motive of his nature." Yet Jones had observed that:

> With a patient he [Freud] was treating before the war whose life history I knew most intimately, I would come across instance after instance where he was believing statements [during psychoanalysis] which I knew to be certainly untrue and also, incidentally, refusing to believe things that were as certainly true. Joan Riviere has (also) related an extraordinary example of this combination of credulity and persistence.

Even the most conscientious police examiner is liable to make the same mistakes as the equally conscientious Freud, and in the Russian purges, where emotional tension must have risen far higher than it usually does in the atmosphere of an English police station, or on a psychotherapeutic couch, the examiner and the prisoner must often have built up between them complete delusional systems. For the prisoner may be completely innocent, but the police examiner is required to continue the examination until he has dragged the truth out of him, which means that he must himself come to believe what has been confessed.

Major A. Farrar-Hockley gives an apt description of the techniques by which ideas can be implanted without the use of strong, direct and obvious suggestion.[118] He learned these as a result of his experiences as a British prisoner of war in Korea. The same principles obviously apply in some psychotherapeutic disciplines and in police examinations where strong direct suggestion is also denied:

> The Chinese are past masters at this technique. They wouldn't tell me what they really wanted. Whenever we got near to something substantial, they would immediately come back to it from another angle and we'd go all round it, but I'd never find out what it was. And then they would go away and leave me thinking. I believe if the interrogator went on long enough with someone who is in a very weak state, and then sprang the idea suddenly on him, the chap would seize on it and become obsessed by it. He would begin to say, "Well, by Jove, I wonder whether in fact it's all really true, and this is what I was thinking in the first place." Every time they went away I spent hours saying, "Now was it that? No, it couldn't have been that. I wonder if it was so and so?" And that's what they were trying to do. They were trying to get me to a state when the idea would suddenly

come Bingo, and I would begin to wonder whether I'd thought of it or they had.

As regards the means of bringing one to a point of confessing to some imaginary crime spontaneously, he also says:

> Now another method is to gradually suggest something by talking round it and getting a little nearer each time and just giving a fragment so that you build up the idea in your own mind, and eventually you say something (this presupposes you are in a pretty weak state of mind, which I wasn't at the time, at least I don't think I was). And then you say something and they say, "But you said this, you produced this, we didn't," and you begin to say after a time, "My God, I did produce it—where did I get it from?"

Here the resemblance between brain-washing and some modern methods of psychotherapy is obvious.

Of the many thousands of suspected witches burned in Europe, only a small proportion seem to have been actually connected with the cult; but that did not prevent the rest from giving the most detailed confessions of infanticides, and overlooking, and other abominable practices. *Malleus Maleficarum*[119] first published in the fifteenth century, which both Catholic and Protestant judges conducting witch trials used as a guide, describes contemporary beliefs about the power of witchcraft, and lays down the best way of extorting confessions. Johann Wier's protest against witch trials, *De Praestigiis Daemonum* published in 1583, aroused the fury of the clergy. But it did not prevent many thousands more of mistaken burnings and hangings, after trials conducted by the most conscientious and honest of examiners. Under the English Commonwealth alone nearly four thousand alleged witches were said to have been hanged.[120]

In Hutchinson's eighteenth-century *Essay on Witchcraft*[120] reference is made to Matthew Hopkins, the official witch-finder for the associated Eastern Counties in the years 1644-46. He had got no less than sixty reputed witches hanged in his own county of Essex within twelve months, and considered himself to be an authority on "special marks"—moles, scorbutic spots, or warts—which he regarded as supplementary teats used by old women to suckle imps. A few courageous clergy protested against the witch-finders; among them Gaul, rector of Stoughton in Huntingdonshire.

Gaul,[120] in a pamphlet of protest, listed the twelve usual signs of witchcraft "too much made use of at that time." He wrote as follows:

> To all these I cannot but add one at large which I have lately learnt, partly from some communications I had with one of the witch-finders (as they call them), partly from the confession (which I heard) of a suspected and a committed witch, so handled as she said, and partly as the country people talk of it. Having taken the suspected witch, she is placed in the middle of a room upon a stool or table, cross-legged, or in some other uneasy posture; to which, if she submits not, she is then bound with cords; there she is watched, and kept without meat, or sleep, for the space of four and twenty hours. (For they say that within that time they shall see her imp come and suck.) A little hole is likewise made in the door, for the imps to come in at; and lest it should come in some less discernible shape, they that watch are taught to be

ever and anon sweeping the room, and if they see any spiders or flies, to kill them. And if they cannot kill them, then they may be sure they are her imps.

Hutchinson comments:

It was very requisite that these witch-finders should take care to go to no towns, but where they might do what they would, without being controlled by sticklers; but if the times had not been as they were, they would have found few towns where they might be suffered to use the trial of the stool, which was as bad as most tortures. Do but imagine a poor old creature under all the weakness and infirmities of old age, set like a fool in the middle of a room, with a rabble of ten towns round about her house; then her legs tied cross, that all the weight of her body might rest upon her seat. By that means, after some hours, the circulation of the blood would be much stopped, her sitting would be as painful as the wooden horse. Then must she continue in pain four and twenty hours, without either sleep or meat; and since this was their ungodly way of trial, what wonder was it, if when they were weary of their lives, they confessed any tales that would please them, and many times they knew not what; and for a proof that the extorted confessions were mere dreams and inventions to free themselves from torture, I will add some of the particulars that they confessed. Elizabeth Clark, an old beggar with only one leg, they said had an imp called *Vinegar Tom;* another called *Sack and Sugar;* and another that she said she would fight up to the knees in blood before she would lose it. She said the devil came to her two or three times a week, and lay with her like a man; and that he was so very like a man, that she was forced to rise and let him in when he knocked at the door, and she felt him warm. Ellen Clark fed her imp. Goodw.

Proceedings of the Royal Society of Medicine

A revival meeting conducted by a snake-handling sect in one of the states of the South. Rhythmic beating, hand clapping, music and dancing heighten the excitement.

Then poisonous snakes are taken out of their box. Tension mounts further as the snakes are handled by believers.

These photos were taken with the consent of the pastor responsible for the meetings. Other similar photographs appeared in the local newspapers at the time.

Proceedings of the Royal Society of Medicine

An example of the powerful group
arousal and abreaction released during
these snake-handling services.

These two photographs show that transmarginal inhibition now seems to be setting in after prolonged excitement and dancing. This may help to increase suggestibility and disrupt previous conditioning.

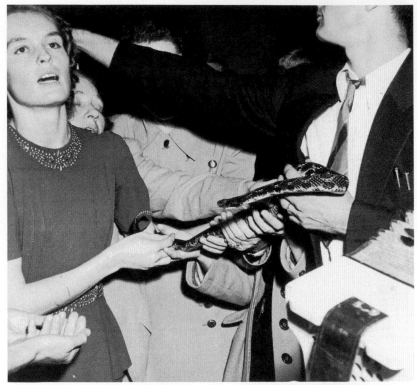

Proceedings of the Royal Society of Medicine

A snake is passed to a girl who handles it in a state of tension and ecstasy. The climax is near.

Terminal exhaustion
later supervenes.

States of acute
excitement leading on
to the final phase of
total collapse are
purposely worked for
in potential converts
during religious snake
handling. All the
phenomena are
explained as the work
of the Holy Ghost.

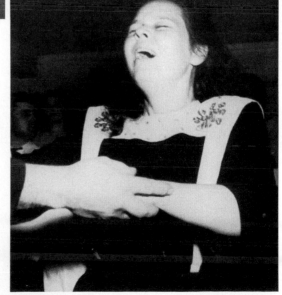

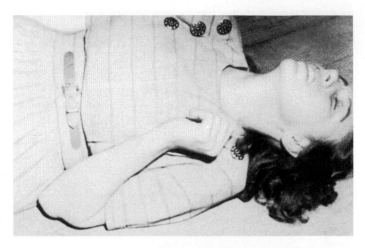

The final phase of total collapse.

Making use of the state of increased suggestibility
that occurs with such techniques.

A near-hypnotic state may
also be produced.

London Express News & Feature Service

Similar effects being produced in a
nonreligious setting in Great Britain by
the use of rhythmic drumming and
dancing in the craze for "Rock and Roll."

Hagtree kept her imp with oatmeal a year and a half and then lost it. Susan Cock's imp worried sheep, Joyce Boans's imp killed lambs, and Ann West's imps sucked of one another.

In witchcraft trials great importance was placed on obtaining these confessions as evidence of guilt, even though torture might have to be used to extract them. A letter has survived, showing how suspects were made to invent the evidence against themselves, just as in some of the treason trials behind the Iron Curtain in Stalin's time. On July 24th, 1528, Burgomaster Johannes Junius wrote and smuggled the following to his daughter from the witch prison in Bamberg:

> Many hundred thousand good-nights, dearly beloved daughter Veronica. Innocent have I come to prison, innocent have I been tortured, innocent must I die. For whoever comes into the witch prison must become a witch or be tortured until he invents something out of his head and—God pity him, bethinks him of something. I will tell you how it has gone with me . . . the executioner . . . put the thumbscrews on me, so that the blood ran out at the nails and everywhere, so that for four weeks I could not use my hands as you can see from the writing. . . . Thereafter they first stripped me, bound my hands behind me, and drew me up in the torture. Then I thought Heaven and Earth were at an end; eight times did they draw me up and let me fall again, so that I suffered terrible agony. The executioner said: "Sir, I beg you for God's sake confess something, whether it be true or not, for you cannot endure the torture which you will be put to, and even if you bear it at all, yet you will not escape".

Burgomaster Junius asked for a day to think again, invented a story of a witch meeting and, under threat of further torture, named various people as being present; he also admitted to other crimes. The letter goes on:

> Now, dear child, here you have all my confession, for which I must die. And they are sheer lies and made-up things, so help me God. For all this I was forced to say through fear of the torture which was threatened beyond what I had already endured. For they never leave off with the torture till one confesses something; be he never so good, he must be a witch. Nobody escapes. . .

On the margin of his letter the burgomaster had also written:

> Dear child, six have confessed against me at once: the Chancellor, his son . . . all false, through compulsion, as they have told me, and begged my forgiveness in God's name before they were executed. [121]

Weissberg[109] writes that, when asked about the millions of confessions elicited during the great Russian purges in which he was involved, he points to the witch-hunting mania in Europe; there was, he feels, as much smoke raised by as little fire on both occasions.

Even in Great Britain today false confessions are sometimes elicited quite unknowingly despite the acknowledged integrity of the British police, especially when evidence is being collected by them which may result in a suspect's prosecution, trial for murder and his subsequent hanging. A good recent example of this almost certainly happened in the case of Timothy Evans. His trial is bound to become a medico-legal classic as it involved the hanging of a probably innocent man, because wrong third and fourth confessions were elicited from him and then quite genuinely believed in by the police. Evans was tried and hanged for murder in 1950 after the dead bodies of his wife and child had been found hidden in the house in London in which the family rented rooms.

In 1953, another tenant of rooms in the same house discovered human remains hidden behind the wall. A subsequent police search of the house and garden uncovered the remains of the bodies of six women, all of whom had been murdered. A man named Christie was tried and convicted for murder, and confessed to the killing of all six. Christie had been a friend and co-tenant of the Evans family at the time of the murder of Mrs. Evans and her child. Information is available for a study of this case in a White Paper published by H.M. Government[122] as well as in a book: *The Man on Your Conscience,*[123] and a special publication by the *Spectator* written by Lord Altrincham and Ian Gilmour: *The Case of Timothy Evans.*[124]

Evans was so mentally backward and illiterate that he was unable to read or write, and had already been in the hands of the police for forty-eight hours, without any legal aid, before he made his third and fourth full confessions to the murder of his wife and child, on which he was hanged. He had previously given himself up to the police and made two previous confessions of disposing of the body of his wife, but not to murdering her. Very few persons still believe that Evans did murder his wife despite his detailed confession to having done so. This particular murder was almost certainly one of a whole series of identical murders later found to have been committed by Christie in the same house. There is now also very grave doubt that Evans even murdered his child, to which he also finally confessed.

The complete transcript of this now famous trial was not made available for ordinary public reading and detailed study till just recently.[125] But those sections of it published in this White Paper show the various emotional stresses which Evans's defective brain must have had to endure before his final confessions were made. These could certainly have brought into play all the various alterations in brain function and consequent behaviour that have been discussed in this book.

First of all, Evans had a long period of panic and anxiety after finding his wife dead in his and Christie's house, and this resulted in his subsequent flight to Wales. There we have the first two confessions to the Welsh police, not of having murdered his wife but of having disposed of her body. These confessions were followed by a train journey back to London in custody of the police. There he met a new Chief Inspector who was to take over the case. On arrival, Evans claimed he learnt for the very first time that his child, of whom he was so fond, had now been found murdered, as well as his wife, in the same-house. Having no time to recover from this blow, he was then, he said, shown some of the clothing of both his dead wife and child: a length of rope, a green tablecloth and a blanket, all of which were said to connect him as the suspected but unconfessed murderer of both his wife and child. He also said he was informed of the manner in which both bodies had been found by the police concealed in the house, and told that he was considered responsible for both deaths.

He then made a general and later a detailed confession to both murders.

Mr. Scott Henderson, Q.C., in the White Paper, gave as his opinion that the police did not provide Evans with the important details of the two murders to which he later confessed. But in re-examining all the evidence now available, Altrincham and Gilmour give their reasons for saying that:

> . . . there can be no reasonable doubt that Evans, before he confessed, was told or shown by the police all the details which Mr. Scott Henderson considers so incriminating. In particular, it is clear from the evidence of Inspector Black that Evans did not mention the tie with which his wife was strangled, until he was shown it by the police . . . We are satisfied that the Notting Hill "confession" was false . . .

If Evans's long fourth statement is read, it will be seen how possible it is that at least some of the details, describing how he murdered his wife and child, could have included matters inadvertently, and even quite unknowingly, suggested and implanted in his mind by his police examination and questioning. The police at that time had every reason to believe that Evans had committed both these murders in the way he finally confessed to doing, and Christie became their chief prosecution witness. It does seem possible that some of their own beliefs were given back to them again in the form of a confession once fatigue and an increase of suggestibility had occurred in Evans. We also happen to know how mentally disturbed Evans was at the time he made his final confession, because in the Government White Paper we read of his fears that "the police will take me downstairs and start knocking me about," if a full confession were not made. Actually this could never happen to a man due to appear on a murder charge in a British court, if only because expert defence lawyers would bring the matter up in court to show that the confession was made under duress. The following extract of his trial in the White Paper gives an informative picture of the state of Evans's mind at the time of these confessions and how, according to him, they were obtained.

Q. On the 2nd December in the afternoon did Mr. Black bring you up from Wales to Paddington?—*A.* Yes, Sir.

Q. When you arrived at Paddington were you met by Chief Inspector Jennings, as you now know him?—*A.* Yes, Sir.

Q. Did you go to Notting Hill Police Station?—*A.* Yes, Sir.

Q. What happened when you got there?—*A.* He told me about my wife and baby being dead, Sir.

Mr. Justice Lewis: I cannot hear what he says.

Mr. Macolm Morris: Now you will speak up; this is most important, and it is most important that you should speak without any unnecessary questions being asked. Just tell your own story. He told you that your wife and baby?—*A.* Had been found dead, Sir.

Q. Did he say where?—*A.* Yes, Sir, No. 10, Rillington Place in the washhouse, and he said he had good reason to believe that I knew something about it.

Q. Did he say how it appeared they had died?—*A.* Yes, Sir, by strangulation.

Q. Did he say with what?—*A.* Well, a rope, Sir, my wife, and my daughter had been strangled with a necktie.

Q. Was anything shown to you at the same time?—*A.* Yes, Sir, the clothing of my wife and my daughter.

Q. Was there also a green tablecloth and blanket?—*A.* Yes, Sir.

Q. And a length of rope?—*A.* Yes, Sir.

Q. I do not want to ask the same question twice, but before he told you had you any idea that anything had happened to your daughter?—*A.* No, Sir, no idea at all.

Q. One other question I should have asked you; did he tell you when he said the bodies had been found in the washhouse whether they had been concealed or not?—*A.* Yes, Sir; he told me they had been concealed by timber.

Q. Having told you that and shown you those garments and said that he had reason to believe you knew something about their death, did he say that he had reason to believe you were responsible for causing their deaths?—*A.* Yes, Sir.

Q. What did you say?—*A.* I just replied "Yes, Sir."

Mr. Justice Lewis: What?—*A.* I said "Yes."

Mr. Malcolm Morris: Why?—*A.* Well, when I found out about my daughter being dead I was upset and I did not care what happened to me then.

Q. Were you very fond of her?—*A.* Yes, Sir.

Q. Did you then make the statement which the Chief Inspector took down in his notebook?—*A.* Yes, Sir.

Q. Before we go to that, was there any other reason why you said Yes, as well as the fact that you gave up everything when you heard that your daughter was dead?—*A.* Well, Sir, I was frightened at the time.

Q. Why were you frightened, or what were you frightened of?—*A.* Well, I thought if I did not make a statement the police would take me downstairs and start knocking me about.

Mr. Justice Lewis: Thought what?—*A.* That the police would take me downstairs and start knocking me about if I did not make a statement.

Mr. Malcolm Morris: You really believed that, did you?—*A.* Yes, Sir.

Q. Did you then make this statement saying that your wife was incurring one debt after another, "I could not stand it

any longer so I strangled her with a piece of rope"?—*A.*
Yes, Sir.

Q. And later that you had strangled your baby on the Thursday evening with your tie?—*A.* Yes, Sir.

Q. Had you in fact got any rope in your flat?—*A.* No, Sir.

Q. Is it your tie which is Exhibit 3 in this case?—*A.* No, Sir.

Q. Had you ever seen it before you were shown it by the Chief
Inspector?—*A.* No, Sir.

Evans did everything possible at his trial to deny the content of his previous confession and he blamed Christie for
both murders. But it was now too late. Some further indications of the exhausted and suggestible state of Evans—
showing that it may not always be the guilty that can be
influenced by such means—are seen from his cross-
examination by the prosecuting Counsel, before he was
found guilty and hanged:

Q. Is it true that on five different occasions at different places
and to different persons you have confessed to the murder
of your wife, and to the murder of your wife and child?—
A. I have confessed it, Sir, but it is not true.

Q. Is it right you have confessed it five times in different places
and to different persons?—*A.* Yes, it is

Q. Are you saying on each of these occasions you were upset?—*A.* The biggest part of them, Sir.

And later we read:

Q. Later you signed a written statement in some greater detail,
did not you, Exhibit 8, saying of your wife she was incurring one debt after another. "I could not stand it any longer,
so I strangled her with a piece of rope and took her down
to the flat below the same night whilst the old man was in
hospital, waited till the Christies downstairs had gone to

bed, and then I took her to the washhouse after midnight. This was on the 8th November." Did you say that?—A. I did say that.

Q. Then you go on to say: "On Thursday evening after I came home from work I strangled my baby in our bedroom with my tie, and later that night I took her down into the washhouse after the Christies had gone to bed." Did you say that?—A. Yes, Sir.

Q. Why?—A. Well, as I said before, Sir, I was upset and I did not know what I was saying.

Q. Still upset?—A. Yes, Sir.

Q. Hour after hour, day after day?—A. I did not know my daughter was dead till Det. Inspector Jennings told me about it.

Q. I see; that is your defence, that you pleaded guilty, that is what it comes to, or confessed to the murder of your wife and child because you were upset at learning that your daughter was dead?—A. Yes, Sir, because I had nothing else to live for.

Over three years later, we now find Mr. Scott Henderson, Q.C. trying to solve the disputed problem of Evans's innocence or guilt (after the discovery of so many other similar murders done by Christie in the same house) and trying to elicit a further new confession from Christie two days before he was due to be hanged. Christie, however, had a long history of repeated hysterical illnesses dating back to World War I. And so, not unexpectedly, we see in the White Paper that he ended his life perhaps more hysterically suggestible and confused than even Evans had ever been. For Christie, too, had by now totally collapsed and reached the point where he seemed prepared to admit almost anything put to him strongly enough by Mr. Henderson, just as he had confessed to so many things put to him by the police, his Counsel and various doctors before and during his own trial. For instance, in the White Paper he is reported as saying to Mr. Scott Henderson:

> The same thing occurred with the Police at the beginning. When they asked me about certain things I did not know what on earth they were talking about. I begged of Inspector Griffin to tell me something to draw my mind on some lines. Then he told me that some bodies had been found, and I did not even know then about the case until he said: "You must have been responsible for it, because they were found in the kitchen in an alcove," and so he said: "There is no doubt about it that you have done it." So I turned round and said: "Well, if that is the case I must have done it," but I did not know whether I had or I had not. From what he said it was very obvious that I must have done it.

Later we also read:

Q. Does the same apply to Mrs. Evans? Can you remember whether or not you had anything to do with her death?—

A. Well, I am not sure. If somebody came up to me—this is what I was going to mention previously—and told me that there is definite proof that I had something to do with one of them or both of them, I should accept it as being right, that I must have done it, but I want to know the truth about it as much as you do.

Q. Short of your being satisfied that there is definite proof that you must have done it, are you prepared to say that you did do it?—

A. I was only informed yesterday that there is no such proof.

Q. So that if there is no proof that you had anything to do with Mrs. Evans's death, are you prepared to say that you were responsible?—

A. Well, I cannot say that I was or I was not.

Q. You are not prepared to say one way or the other?—

A. I cannot say one way or the other. It is not a case of whether I am prepared to or not. I just cannot unless I was telling some lie or other about it. It is still fogged, but if someone said: "Well, it is obvious you did, and there is enough proof about it," then I accept that I did.

The cases of these two men have been quoted at length because they are well documented and show how mistakes may be possible when confessions are elicited, despite the very greatest pains being taken by all concerned to avoid such things happening. They are much more likely to occur when the examiner starts with very strong beliefs, which are then given back to him in subsequent confessions; but a person confessing sometimes succeeds in brain-washing the examiner because of the very strength and fixity of his own true or false beliefs.

* * *

We have already described some of the means used in some other countries for bringing about a state of suggestibility in prisoners about to be cross-examined. In Russia, the prisoner was generally deprived of normal sleep; he was interrogated at night and not allowed to doze off during the day. The bright light continually burning in his cell, and the order that he must keep his hands and face outside the blankets if he lay down, were, theoretically, precautions against attempted escape or suicide, but in reality were also designed to prevent him from relaxing in warmth and darkness. Stypulkowski[110] describes the journey to the examination room:

> This journey itself was menacing. Everything contributed to make it so; the hands bent to the back, the gloomy behaviour of the silent guard, the dark, empty corridors, the wire netting on the staircase, the rhythm of the movements, and the echo of smacking lips. It stimulated imagination as to what would happen to me in a few minutes' time. Where were they taking me, and what for? The staging played an important part in the methods of inquest which were applied to me. It remained suggestive until the last day, although, after many migrations of this kind, I knew, like a well broken horse, where I should have to turn my face to the wall, and whether the guards gripped my right or left arm.

A prisoner's past life is also gone over in the greatest detail to find out any particular incident to which he is particularly sensitive. Having found a sore spot, the examiners act in the spirit of Finney's advice to keep touching on any experience which is "tremblingly alive" in the prisoner's mind. Meanwhile, the prisoner loses weight, becomes physically debilitated, and more nervous every hour. His mind is confused; the effort of trying to remember what he has said at previous interrogations and thus to make the story hang together becomes increasingly arduous. Sometimes he is made to fill in long questionnaires, the purpose of which is to fatigue him further, rather than exact any new information of value. When his memory about his answers in previous questionnaires begins to fail him, the difficulty of keeping to the same story makes him more anxious than ever. Finally, unless some accident brings the examination to a premature end, his brain will be too disorganized to respond normally; it can become "transmarginally inhibited", vulnerable to suggestions, "paradoxical" and "ultra-paradoxical" phases may supervene, and the fortress finally surrenders unconditionally.

Many other types of stress can be used to bring on abnormal states of brain activity. A person can be made to hold his water indefinitely while sitting on a chair; or bright lights can be shone in his eyes during the long interrogation. Thus we read of a West Berlin journalist captured and made to confess in an East German prison in the following manner:

> The torture consisted of treatment which prevented him from sleeping for ten days. Sleep was forbidden during the day. At night, lying under a bright electric light in his cell, he was awakened every fifteen minutes. Fifteen minutes after "lights out" he would be awakened by pounding on his cell door, fifteen minutes later there would be shrill whistling, and next the electric light would be connected to an automatic device alternating a dim red light with a fierce white light from a powerful bulb. . . . This was repeated night after night for ten nights until [he] collapsed with shivering fits and hallucinations. After this softening-up process he was considered fit for interrogation, which took place almost nightly for six to seven hours at a time over a period of three months and another period of two months. Interrogation was endlessly prolonged because the interrogator deliberately put down the opposite of what the prisoner said and then laboriously started a new and corrected deposition.[126]

All these methods stimulate and exhaust the brain and so hasten the onset of "protective brain inhibition", and thus of suggestibility to the examiner's continuous reiteration, hour after hour, of the same charge. A further means of altering a prisoner's normal conditioning, especially one who has hitherto been a person of authority or consequence, is to make him wear old and ill-fitting prison clothes, with trousers which he must support with his own hands, and to leave him unshaven—the excuse being that he might have money or poison concealed in his clothes, and that he might try to commit suicide with a belt or braces. He is then addressed by his cell number, and forced to give the prison authorities their full title whenever approached by them. Such sudden social degradation can prove most effective.

For the phlegmatic and unyielding, many extra stresses are found that may still keep within the law against the use of torture or physical violence. One is solitary confinement in the early stages of the examination; then when the prisoner shows signs of abnormality but is still not suggestible enough to confess what is expected of him, he is put into a cell with two or three other prisoners. These are stool-pigeons, under instructions to sympathise with him, identify themselves with his problems, and persuade him if possible to confess his crime, accept his punishment and get things over. The stool-pigeons are usually prisoners who have broken down under the same treatment and become genuinely convinced of the need for "co-operation" with the examiner. The influence they exert is that of the tamed elephant on the newly captured one; of the trained circus dog on the restive newcomer; of the now sure convert on a person still struggling with his religious problems.

Then there is the old trick, as old at least as the Spanish Inquisition, of confronting an obstinate prisoner with the real or pretended confession of some associate charged with the same crime. "It is all up now, you had better come clean." He is then gently chided for his misguided loyalty to his friends and family and assured that, even though confession is no longer necessary, because his guilt has been established by the evidence of others, it will be better for him to make a formal statement of repentance. This will secure him a more merciful sentence, and hasten his return as a respected and self-respecting member of the community. As in religious conversions, the strength of this method lies in the offer of an escape route from the tortures of hell to future salvation.

Weissberg[109] gives a harrowing account of the less subtle means used by Russians during the Stalinist terror for eliciting confessions:

> He (Shalit) hated the prisoners because they resisted him and were not prepared to admit at once what he wanted them to admit. . . . He was capable of bawling exactly the same question for six hours on end without the slightest variation and without showing any signs of fatigue. . . . He repeated exactly the same question in exactly the same loud voice and with exactly the same gestures hundreds—no, I really believe thousands—of times. . . . I often asked myself whether Shalit was utterly stupid. Couldn't he think of anything different to say? . . . Gradually I came to the conclusion he wasn't stupid. . . . All he could do was to try and exhaust his prisoners physically, and he used this technique

with more determination and iron logic than any other examiner I have ever met. From the G.P.U. point of view he was right.

This Shalit was a member of what was called the "Conveyor" system, an "endless moving band", in which an accused "was kept under continuous interrogation day and night until he broke down":

> As the examiners were regularly relieved it could go on indefinitely. . . . Some prisoners had even held out under torture but I only knew one man who managed to resist the "Conveyor".

He describes the sort of feelings produced in a person undergoing the ordeal:

> I can hold out another night, and another night, and another night, he might think. But what then? What's the good of it? They have all the time in the world. At some point or other I must physically collapse.

Weissberg describes the later stages of the "Conveyor" when used on himself:

> My eyes were two balls of pain in a head that felt as though it would split open but for the iron band being drawn tighter and tighter around it. For four hours Shalit repeated his favourite question. . . . When Weissband relieved him at eight o'clock in the morning, I was almost unconscious. . . . I was not taken down for my food until nine o'clock. Lavatory, wash and the meal had to be over in ten minutes. Then I was taken back to the "Conveyor".

After over one hundred and forty hours, Weissberg reports:

> Red rings whirled before my eyes and my brain no longer
> functioned. The room began to swim. The pain was worse
> than ever before and seemed to extend over my whole
> body. . . . But I managed to hold out till Weissband relieved
> Shalit in the evening.

Finally he recalls:

> It was midnight on the seventh day of my "Conveyor". I
> had fought till I dropped but now I was beaten. There was
> nothing left for me but capitulation and "confession".

However, Weissberg subsequently withdrew this confession and had to have another period on the "Conveyor"
till he made another confession, also withdrawn later.

At any sign of weakening or switch-over, the examiner
may drop his role of prosecuting counsel and assume that
of the prisoner's friend, sympathetically advising confession. As the examiner told Stypulkowski:

> I am sorry for you. I see how tired you are. I am happy to
> inform you, on behalf of the authorities, that the Soviet
> Government has no wish you should lose your life, or spend
> thirty years rotting in some labour camp in Siberia. On the
> contrary, the Soviet Government wants you to live and work
> as a free man.

The examiner then adopted the religious evangelist's traditional role:

> You must decide today which path your future is to take.
> You could be a Cabinet Minister, one of the leaders of the

new world-order, and work for your country; the alternative is to depend on Anglo-Saxon protection, rot in prison and await the result.

Stypulkowski pays his tribute to the persuasive power of this appeal:

The dawn was breaking when I had to repel this attack, the strongest delivered so far.

The last grim phase of the prisoner's breakdown and unconditional surrender is described only too well:

Recalling the things he was supposed to do, he hastens to explain them to his examiner, but confuses true facts with those suggested to him by the latter. In his determination to confess all, he talks about things that never happened, repeats gossip he once heard. It is still not enough for the examiner, so the prisoner tries to remember something more—just to prove conclusively he does not intend to conceal anything. The prisoner still relies on his intelligence, his critical powers and his character to guide him and restrict his depositions to harmless statements of fact. But here he is wrong. He does not realize that during the few weeks of questioning his faculties have diminished, his power to reason has become corrupted . . . he is a completely changed man.

F. Beck and W. Godin, whose book *Russian Purge* is also based on their personal experiences of interrogation and imprisonment in the Soviet Purge of 1936-39, emphasize that once the suspect decided to confess:

The method of interrogation, proudly referred to by the officials of the N.K.V.D. as the Yeshov method, consisted of making it the arrested man's primary task to build up the whole case against himself. . . . The grotesque result of this was that the accused strained every nerve to convince their examining magistrates that their invented "legends" were true and represented the most serious crimes possible. . . . If they were rejected, it only meant a continuation of the interrogation until the "legend" was altered or replaced by a new one involving a sufficiently serious political crime.[127]

As in the examination of witches and in the uncritical use of some psychotherapeutic techniques, confessions obtained were "occasionally distinguished by a high degree of creative imagination." They report a worker in an educational supplies factory, for instance, who "maintained that he belonged to an organization whose object was the construction of artificial volcanoes to blow the entire Soviet Union sky high." Such confessions can even be believed, I repeat, by an examiner who gets himself too emotionally involved and fatigued in obtaining them.

Stypulkowski also records the physical changes deliberately produced to hasten final collapse:

I only realized this fully when I was confronted with [one of] my friends at the end of the [two months'] interrogation. . . . I could hardly recognize him. His eyes were restless and wild, sunk deep in his skull. His skin was yellow and wrinkled and covered thickly with sweat. The face of this skeleton was spotted. His body was incessantly shaking. . . . His voice was uncertain and spasmodic: "You have changed a little," I said. . . . "You too," he answered, trying to smile. I had not seen myself in a mirror.

One of the more horrible consequences of these ruthless interrogations, as described by victims, is that they suddenly begin to feel affection for the examiner who has been treating them so harshly—a warning sign that the "paradoxical" and "ultra-paradoxical" phases of abnormal brain activity may have been reached: they are near to "breaking point" and will soon confess. Then the more obdurate the alleged criminal, the more lasting the indoctrination may be after he has finally been broken down and made to confess: he will sometimes be eager to sacrifice many years of his future life in rehabilitating himself after his disgrace.

The Inquisitors of the Holy Office made use of much the same basic methods.[128] Suspected heretics were also called for preliminary examination and forbidden to tell their relatives that they were being questioned. Once in prison, they faced the constant threat of being burned alive, which could be avoided only by a full confession; yet, since this had to be a sincere confession, they had to believe themselves genuinely guilty of crimes suggested by the Inquisitors or conveniently invented by their own overwrought imagination. Confessed penitents were privileged to be strangled before being burned; or even spared, deprived of all their possessions, and made to perform lifelong penance. They were also required to inform on their own families; and the withholding of any relevant information about even a parent's guilt was equally punishable with the stake. The instruments of torture to induce confession were always ready, but seem to have been rarely used;*[129] the threat

---

* The following is a description of the threat of torture made to Joan of Arc by the Inquisitors, but not carried out. She was, however, burned alive later:

of torture being, as a rule, sufficient to cause breakdown. Every effort was made to obtain the desired confessions without physical violence, because it might later be claimed that the heretic had confessed only under duress—for it is still a widely-held but physiologically untenable dogma that no ill-treatment that leaves a man with a whole skin, the use of his limbs, and unimpaired senses, can be construed as duress.

The importance of working on the heretic until he broke down and confessed himself truly repentant was that he might be saved from burning eternally in hell, even if the law condemned him to be burned alive here on earth. The use of secret informers, the confronting of the unconfessed heretic with the confessed heretic, the promise of pardon

On 9th May, she was taken to the great tower where he (Cauchon) was awaiting her with Lemaitre and nine Doctors. The instruments of torture were shown to her, and next to them the torturers, Mauger, Leparmentier, and his assistants. Also present was the usual array of *greffiers de douleurs* and the *notaires d'angoisse*, trained in the indispensable art of picking confessions from the incomprehensible shrieks of the victims.

Monsieur de Beauvais gave her sufficient time to take in the nature of the assembled implements, the pullies and cords, the winches and the rack, the malles and the funnels, the hooks, the gridirons, the knives, the spikes, the boot, the pincers, and the braziers glowing in the shadows. "Then," as he says in his account of the scene, "Joan was required and advised to make true answer" to a number of different points, on pain of "being delivered" to the officers, who "by our order are here ready to put you to the torture, and thus force you to return into the way of truth, and to acknowledge it, that thus the salvation of your soul and body may be assured which by your inveterate errors you have put in a great peril."

after confession—which could later be withdrawn—were all known; and dungeons insured the necessary physical debilitation. Very few persons were, however, burned alive compared with those who hastened to confess and accept the beliefs and penances imposed by the Church, the victims of the stake being usually heretics who had been pardoned but later relapsed.

The Methodists of the eighteenth century showed similar zeal and power in the art of indoctrination. Their devoted preachers nobly accompanied legally condemned persons on their last dreadful ride in open carts from Newgate Prison to a public hanging at Tyburn, and successfully abolished all fear of death in many of them. *The Life of Mr. Silas Told,* an autobiography, first published in 1786,[130] gives a graphic account of such events:

> The next account I shall give, is that of Mary Pinner, who was sentenced to death for setting fire to her master's house. At the same time, three or four men were cast for death, with whom Mary showed herself very wanton . . . I strove to make this young woman the greatest and first object of my visit, but experienced various repulses from her. I was grieved to behold her heedless conduct, especially as the death-warrant had just arrived, wherein she was included.

Told now proceeds to use the method learned after his own sudden conversion by Wesley:

> Therefore, I took her aside, and said to her, "Mary, how is it that you, above all the other malefactors, are so regardless about your precious and immortal soul? Do not you well know that God's all-seeing eye penetrates your every action? Are you not afraid of going to hell, seeing you are in a short

time to appear before the great Jehovah, against whom you have sinned with a high hand? Are you determined to destroy your own soul? Are you in love with eternal perdition and God's wrath, that you so madly pursue it? Do you long to be involved in the bottomless pit, and the lake that burns with fire and brimstone which will never be quenched? O! remember, if you die in your present condition, you will die eternally under the wrath of an offended Saviour; and all these miseries will be your portion for ever!"

Perceiving a change in her countenance, and finding out that she had often listened to his preaching at West Street Chapel before her imprisonment, Told reports that he did not afterwards "hear one unbecoming expression, or observe an indiscreet action in her, to her last moment." But he went on to consolidate his initial success:

The night prior to her execution, I importunately besought her to spend every moment in wrestling mightily with God for pardon through His dearly beloved Son. . . . Similar advice I gave to all the rest of the malefactors, one of whom espoused the like resolution.

He also used group suggestion to obtain his remarkable results; for he goes on:

I then desired the inner keepers (of Newgate) to lock them all up in one cell, that they might pour out their joint supplications to the awful and tremendous Judge of the quick and the dead, in whose presence they must all unavoidably appear in a few fleeting moments. This was readily granted; so they accordingly devoted that night to an inexpressible advantage, by praying, singing hymns, and rejoicing, the Lord God Himself being evidently in the midst of them.

When I returned to them the next morning, after having received this soul-reviving information, I begged the keepers to unlock the cells, and lead them down into the press yard.

The results certainly justified the group psychotherapy used:

The first that came out was Mary Pinner. I was struck with delight when I beheld the happy change in her countenance. As she came out of the cell, she appeared to be filled with the peace and love of God, and, clapping her hands together, she gave a triumphant shout, with these words, "This night God, for Christ's sake, has forgiven me all my sins; I know that I have passed from death unto life, and I shall shortly be with my Redeemer in glory."

Told describes his gruesome journey to Tyburn with the prisoners in an open execution cart:

She continued in this happy state, singing, praising and giving glory to God without intermission, till she arrived at the gallows. . . . She then began to strengthen her fellow sufferers, beseeching them not to doubt the readiness of God to save them.

We possibly have few preachers today who, if put in Told's place, would be as successful in making ordinary men and women walk with joy to the public gallows, convinced that God approved of this long-defended British legal punishment for stealing property worth no more than five shillings, but would welcome them with open arms to His Kingdom now that they had truly repented.*[131] Yet this

---

* Even as late as 1800, England still had more than 200 crimes punishable by public hanging.

same frightening power of persuading persons to accept gladly terrible and unjustified punishments has been demonstrated again and again in recent years in the political field by materialistic atheists in Russia, Hungary and China, using what seem to be the same basic techniques.

CHAPTER 10

Consolidation and Prevention

It is one thing to make the mind of a normal person break down under intolerable stress, eradicate old ideas and behaviour patterns, and plant new ones in the vacant soil; it is quite another to make these new ideas take firm root. Every animal-trainer and schoolmaster knows this only too well—how schoolmasters resent the effects of long summer holidays on their promising pupils!—but churches and political organizations may forget it. George Whitfield, a powerful eighteenth-century Calvinist preacher, whose conversions were as spectacular as John Wesley's, and who spent much of his life in revivalist tours of England, Scotland, Wales and the United States, admitted at the close of his life:

> My brother Wesley acted wisely. The souls that were awakened under his ministry he joined in Class, and thus preserved the fruit of his labour. This I neglected, and my people are a rope of sand.[53]

For Whitfield founded no distinct sect, and though he quarrelled with Wesley in 1741 on the question of predestination, it was his patron, Selina Countess of Huntingdon, who gathered his followers into a Calvinistic Methodist group of chapels, known as "The Countess of Huntingdon's Connexion".

Wesley's class meetings deserve special attention. Having converted much of England by his use of fear-provoking and powerful forms of preaching, he consolidated his gains by highly efficient follow-up methods, which were used as soon as possible after "sudden conversion" or "sanctification" had occurred. Wesley divided his converts into groups of not more than twelve persons, who met each week under an appointed leader; problems of an intimate nature relating to their conversion and their future mode of life were then discussed in agreed secrecy. The class leader was originally required to visit all members of his class at least once a week, ostensibly to collect a small weekly contribution of money. This means of access to their home soon allowed him to decide whether a conversion was genuine or not; and he later tested his conclusions at the weekly class meetings. Members who were not found to be sincerely repentant, and set upon leading a new life, would be expelled both from the class and from the Methodist Society in general. The importance of these class meetings in maintaining the power of Methodism during the eighteenth and nineteenth centuries can hardly be overestimated. Wesley wanted to be rid of all who doubted his particular views on the correct way to salvation—he had broken, among others, with Peter Böhler who had helped to convert him, and for a time even with George Whitfield— and of all who might bring the movement into disrepute by their wrong mode of life. Wesley himself wrote:[132]

> But as much as we endeavoured to watch over each other, we soon found some who did not live the Gospel. I do not know that any hypocrites were crept in: but several grew

cold, and gave way to the sins which had long easily beset them. We quickly perceived there were many ill consequences of suffering these to remain among us. It was dangerous to others inasmuch as all sin is of an infectious nature . . .

Wesley, whose authoritarianism had aggrieved the colonists of Georgia before his conversion, now turned this stumbling-block into a stepping stone:

I called together all the leaders of the classes (so we used to term them and their companies), and desired, that each would make a particular enquiry into the behaviour of those whom we saw weekly. They did so. Many disorderly walkers were detected. Some turned from the evil of their ways. Some were put away from us. Many saw it with fear, and rejoiced unto God with reverence. As soon as possible, the same method was used in London and all other places. Evil men were detected, and reproved. They were borne with for a season. If they forsook their sins, we received them gladly; if they obstinately persisted therein, it was openly declared that they were not of us. The rest mourned and prayed for them, and yet rejoiced, that, as far as in us lay, the scandal was rolled away from the society.

The personal visitation of Methodist homes by class leaders was originally decided upon because Wesley had found, with the growth of the movement, that:

The people were scattered so wide in all parts of the town, from Wapping to Westminster, that I could not easily see what the behaviour of each person in his neighbourhood was; so that several disorderly walkers did much hurt before I was apprised of it.

The class meetings were intended for those already sensitized by their sudden and overwhelming conversion experience; the close group feeling, the communal hymns and prayers, the intimate discussion of personal problems and advice on ways of avoiding "the wrath to come" were a constant reminder of their original sanctification. Wesley personally directed the general policy of the movement, dictating what attitude his lay preachers should take to new political or social changes. The lay preachers were in frequent contact with him on his travels; periodic Methodist "conferences" were held; and class leaders were responsible to lay preachers for the discipline of smaller units.

Wesley appreciated the danger of stirring up crowds, reducing them to penitence, and then leaving others to do the work of reconditioning. While touring the Irish Catholic countryside in 1750, he was asked to preach at Mullingar, but refused because:[53]

> I had little hope of doing good in a place where I could preach but once, and where none but me could be suffered to preach at all.

In 1763, similarly, he wrote from Haverfordwest:

> I was more convinced than ever that preaching like an apostle, without joining together those that are awakened and training them up in the ways of God, is only begetting children for the murderer [the Devil].

When investigating a North Carolina religious snake-handling cult in 1947, it was easy for me to see what Wesley had meant. The descent of the Holy Ghost on these meetings, which were reserved for whites, was supposedly shown by the occurrence of wild excitement, bodily jerkings, and the final exhaustion and collapse, in the more susceptible participants.[9] Such hysterical states were induced by means of rhythmic singing and hand-clapping, and the handling of genuinely poisonous snakes—as reported in Chapter 5— brought several visitors unexpectedly to the point of collapse and sudden conversion. But a young male visitor—the "murderer" incarnate—was attending these meetings with the deliberate object of seducing girls who had just been "saved". The fact is that when "protective inhibition" causes a breakdown and leaves the mind highly suggestible to new behaviour patterns, the conversion may be non-specific. If the preacher arrives in time to preach chastity and sobriety, well and good; but the "murderer" [the devil] had learned that on the night that followed a sudden emotional disruption, a sanctified girl might be as easily persuaded to erotic abandon as to the acceptance of the Gospel message. However, on attempting to follow up his amatory successes a day or two later he found, as a rule, that the abnormal phase of suggestibility had passed, and the girl's moral standards had returned to normal. Because he had not been continuously at her side to consolidate his victory, she might now indignantly rebuff him, and say that she could not understand what had come over her on the night in question. Two very opposite types of belief or personal behaviour could, in fact, be implanted at the close of a revivalist meeting: by the preacher or by the "murderer". And Jesus himself emphasized *(Matthew* xii. 43-45) how dangerous it is for a man who has been cured of an unclean spirit and returns to find his house "swept and garnished". If his family and friends are not careful, he will then fall a victim to seven other unclean spirits and be worse off than ever.

The Wesleyan class meeting derives, of course, from earlier Christian practice; and this in turn from the Jewish. The Jewish faith was controlled by the joint presidents of the Sanhedrin, by means partly of the Temple services, partly by the synagogue system. The obligatory annual Temple feasts began with the Fast of Atonement—a confession of national guilt—followed by Tabernacles where ecstatic singing and dancing filled the whole population of Israel with the Love of God, and careful measures had to be taken against the "light-heartedness" of the women. Later came the feasts of Passover and Weeks, where the immense crowds became equally infected by religious enthusiasm. The careful sober weekly conditioning at the synagogue, with hymns, prayers, interpretations of the scripture and annual Day of Atonement confessions of sinfulness, also helped to keep the Jews together as a nation and continued to do so for two thousand years, even when they had been scattered all over the world, and their Temple desecrated.

Communists have long realized the importance of dividing converts into small groups or cells for follow-up and consolidation purposes. They are supervised by a cell leader, who is in turn responsible to higher Party of officials. At small Party meetings, current modifications of policy are discussed; members are encouraged to air their doubts, and the confession of personal "deviation" is encouraged. Thus it is easy for cell leaders, as it was for Wesley's class leaders, to know whether or not they have obtained a

devoted and industrious worker for the Cause. All successful authoritarian systems, whether political or religious, now
use follow-up conditioning and extend it from the top to
the very bottom of the movement.

Primitive societies, too, have used periodic group meetings, where emotions are aroused by dancing and drumming, to help to maintain religious beliefs and to
consolidate previously implanted religious attitudes. The
excitement may be kept going until fatigue and exhaustion occur, and a leader may then be more easily able to
implant or reinforce beliefs in a state of artificially heightened suggestibility. The West African slaves probably
brought such methods with them to America. In 1947, I
attended several Sunday evening services in a small Negro
church at Durham, North Carolina. For several hours the
congregation were encouraged to perform solo dances to
hand-clapping or to the beating of tambourines in a loud
and rhythmic manner. The dancing was of a jitterbug variety. Members of the congregation would often go into states
of trance and continue to dance to the point of collapse.
Suggestibility was greatly heightened in the participants
and the pastor would exhort the dancers with a constant
repetition of "God is good" or "Thank God for all He has
done for you!" Drained of all pent-up emotions, exhausted
by hours of dancing, and with submission and gratitude to
God reinforced by suggestion, the Negroes would return
cheerfully to live another week in over-crowded slums, seg-
regated and ignored by the white community.[9] The Methodist revival also helped to condition the English of the
early nineteenth century to accept social conditions which
would have caused revolutions in most other European

countries. Wesley had taught the masses to be less concerned with their miserable life on earth, as victims of the Industrial Revolution, than with the life to come; they could now put up with almost anything. The amount of consolidation needed to fix new patterns of thought and behaviour must depend on the particular type of higher nervous system as well as on the methods employed. Some persons seem to absorb new doctrines much more readily than others, but the slower or more obstinate types can be trusted to grasp them more securely, once accepted. And there is a type so basically suggestible and unstable that new behaviour patterns can be constantly implanted in it, and none ever stays fixed—the type popularly called "the born actor".

The different methods needed for converting persons of different temperamental types have not yet been the subject of sufficient research. But certain facts may have emerged. The normal extravert, for instance, seems to be "got at" more easily, and his new patterns maintained, by quite crude and non-specific group excitatory methods, provided that they result in a strong, continued and often repeated emotional arousal. The obsessional person, or the intravert, may be more unresponsive to such an approach; physical debilitation, an individual approach, and very strong individual pressure is then perhaps needed to change his behaviour and, in the follow-up period, repeated reinforcement and meticulous explanation of doctrine. He is the "doubting Thomas" who always demands to "thrust his hand into the wound" before believing what he is told. Some more unstable types, on the other hand, will never check details or worry about consistency in either religion or politics; but for the time being accept everything whole and without questioning.

Then there is the psychopath who, as a rule, has learned very little from his early environmental training, and whose electrical brainwave records still show marked immaturity for his age. It is very difficult indeed to condition or recondition such persons, some of whom are criminals, until later in life when their brainwave patterns become much more normal, their brain matures and seems to start to learn by experience as ordinary men do. Sooner or later a drug will be found to increase the speed of delayed brain maturation in these psychopaths, thus helping to solve a difficult social problem which is only exaggerated by the severe prison sentences and flogging that have often been advocated as treatments.

The need to vary methods of conditioning and reconditioning according to the different temperaments is clearly shown by a study of the way prison sentences affect various types. In most ordinary, and therefore reasonably suggestible people the threat of imprisonment, with its social disabilities, is a sufficient deterrent against crime; and a single experience of prison will abruptly end the criminal career of three-quarters of those who have not been so deterred. But there is a large hard core of "old lags" and those psychopaths whose abnormal patterns of brain behaviour cannot be changed by prison discipline, however rigorously or even brutally it may be applied. Tense and anxious people, as a rule, can be more efficiently conditioned than placid ones. Those of basically unstable and hysterical temperaments cannot be so easily conditioned, since they succumb so readily to either social or anti-social suggestion.

Quite obviously, further detailed research is required on many of these matters. We have seen the sort of excitatory methods that can be used in both primitive and civilized societies to increase group suggestibility, and thus maintain a common pattern of belief; and, further, to indoctrinate some individuals with entirely new beliefs. We have also seen that individuals vary in their reaction to these methods, and that if it is desired to subject them to a radical religious and political conversion, and then stabilize it, the technique will need to be modified in many cases. For instance, the conversion of John and Charles Wesley was facilitated by a preliminary "softening up" of both by Peter Böhler, the Moravian missionary; yet it was only after Peter Böhler had left the country that John's heart was finally and suddenly "warmed" in a small religious group-meeting in Aldersgate Street. And three days before this, Charles, whom illness had reduced to a state of mental and physical debility in the humble house of John Bray, a brazier, had obtained his longed-for and equally sudden conversion, lying alone in his room, in quite different circumstances. Yet Charles was able to describe himself the following day as:

> A slave redeemed from death and sin
> A branch cut from the eternal fire.
> How shall I equal triumphs raise,
> And sing my great Deliverer's praise?[133]

Research is therefore needed on group-excitatory methods, to discover how far they are applicable to all members of any group, and how far particular individuals are proof against them. It clearly must happen often that many appear to be influenced, but make mental reservations, and adopt the majority mode of behaviour from policy, not conviction.

We need to know much more about the different reactions to indoctrination methods of persons in solitary confinement, or placed in selected groups for "re-education". The physiological problem becomes further complicated with a realization that temperamental types in both man and animals are rarely pure. Pavlov found that many of his dogs were mixtures of the four basic temperaments; and the same seems to be true of humans. In primitive cultures, where life is hard and conditioning is rigorous, the survivors will probably be more temperamentally standardized than in more civilized societies and thus disciplined by less varied methods. The higher the civilization, it may indeed be suggested, the greater the number of chronically anxious, obsessional, hysterical, schizoid and depressive "normals" that the community can afford to carry. A greater number of variables in personality types should, it seems, call for a greater variation in the group and individual therapies needed for their cure, but we have as yet no certain information on this point. It may be true, as Aldous Huxley says (page 171): "Meanwhile, all we can safely predict is that, if exposed long enough to tom-toms and the singing, every one of our philosophers would end by capering and howling with the savages."[90] But we do also know that there are philosophers who are more easily converted to new behaviour patterns and new beliefs by means of solitary prayer and fasting, or even by the use of drugs such as mescalin.

However, Pavlov found that when the higher nervous system of animals was intolerably strained by various kinds of applied stress, of greater or lesser power, "transmarginal inhibition" of one kind or another (with its accompanying equivalent, "paradoxical" and "ultra-paradoxical" phases) finally supervened in all temperamental types. In the stronger types this might happen only after a long period of great and sometimes uncontrolled excitement; while in the "weak inhibitory" it might happen very quickly. It seems, therefore, that there are common final paths which all individual animals, though their initial temperamental responses to imposed stresses vary greatly, must finally take, if only stresses are continued long enough. This is probably the same in human beings, and if so, may help to explain why excitatory drumming, dancing and continued bodily movement are so much used in such a number of primitive religious groups. The efforts and excitement of keeping the dance in progress for many hours on end should wear down and, if need be, finally subdue even the strongest and most stubborn temperament, such as might be able to survive frightening and exciting talk alone for days or weeks.

The recent war also showed (see p. 26) that continual active combat experience with its noise, excitement, fear and loss of weight and sleep, eventually produced breakdown in all temperamental types. Though the early breakdown picture might differ, the final inhibitory phase of combat exhaustion, so well described by Swank (see p. 25) and many others, is fairly constant for most ordinary types of person. Therefore, if these underlying physiological principles are once understood, it should be possible to get at the same person, converting and maintaining him in his new belief by a whole variety of imposed stresses that end by altering his brain function in a similar way. Certain individuals, however, can be unexpectedly resistant to well-approved methods. In North Carolina, one heavily-built man had attended the "revival" services of his community, which included abreactive dancing, singing and group excitement, practically every Sunday for nine years, in the hope of winning the experience of sudden conversion and salvation, which nearly all his fellow-members had already obtained by these methods. Salvation had not, so far, been vouchsafed to him, despite all his efforts, but he had not lost heart. He was probably of a phlegmatic temperament, such as Pavlov found could be upset, in animals, only when he added physical debilitation or castration to other stresses.

Another subject of promising research is: which fear-provoking psychological stimuli are best suited to different temperamental types and to different environments and cultures? Few senior Oxford men, for instance, of Wesley's time seem to have been disturbed by his threats of hellfire, which left them as a whole immune to Wesley's University Sermons as a Fellow of Lincoln College. Yet with these same threats of damnation, Wesley could make many dissolute and uneducated Cornish and Gloucester miners abandon their previous solace, which was cheap gin, and live clean lives of sober service to the community. Nevertheless, nearly two hundred years later, another evangelist, Frank Buchman, achieved a certain success with some Oxford men by inviting them to small group meetings where he encouraged them to confess publicly the sexual peccadilloes which weighed on their consciences, and thus to achieve a sense of grace. Psychiatrists have also found how useful this subject may be as a means of increasing anxious tension, which can be continued if need be until the patient is more suggestible and unable to repel the final assault on the citadel of his previous beliefs. But whereas psychotherapists generally treat individuals on a couch, Buchman often worked on small well chosen groups seated informally around the tea-table. Now psychotherapists are themselves starting to use such group methods and to encourage group ventilation of their patients' sexual lives, but different interpretations are given afterwards so that different beliefs are created. Ever-present threats of being burned alive for heresy were most effective in the Middle Ages for indoctrination purposes, just as the threat of "liquidation" is in Communist states today. This particular aspect of our problem—the finding of the right sore spots—could form a whole chapter in itself because of the variabilities encountered in different groups, due in part to the educational level and previous conditioning of the persons involved.

The Prevention of Conversion, Brain-Washing and Confessions

Further research on the available means of resisting political conversion is also needed, both in Great Britain and in the United States. One cannot always oppose powerful physiological and mechanistic techniques merely by a placid intellectual acceptance of religious or philosophical doctrines.

Some statesmen and Service chiefs seem to believe that, given the necessary patriotism and proper training, a decent man can resist every assault made on the fortress of his integrity whether by Fascists, Communists, or any other deluded outlaws; which is quite untrue. We are continually paying the price of such mistaken judgments.

Certain basic principles, however, do emerge from a study of animal behaviour under stress, and seem equally relevant to man. Some of these have already been mentioned. Sutherland, for instance, has emphasized the difficulty found in breaking down animals that will not co-operate with the experimenter, as opposed to the ease in breaking down those who try nobly to carry out the tasks set them.[134] When a dog sullenly refuses to pay any attention to the flashing lights and other food signals intended for his conditioning, his brain remains unaffected; consequently Pavlov used to bring his dogs to the experimental stand in a hungry state, hoping to fix their attention on signals which might be followed by food. Human beings, like dogs, do not break down if they simply refuse to face a problem or task presented to them, or take evasive action before giving it a chance to upset their emotional equilibrium. Whoever refuses to co-operate in any technique of conversion or brain-washing and, instead of paying attention to the interrogator or preacher, manages to concentrate mentally on some quite different problem, should last out the longest. A good example is Kipling's Kim, who resisted Indian hypnosis by a desperate recollection of the English multiplication tables. Colonel R. H. Stevens, ambushed by the Gestapo in 1940 while on special duties in Holland, was chained to the wall of his German prison cell "like a dog" for two whole years in an attempt to destroy his morale. He found it valuable to set his memory the task of reconstructing his childhood home "room by room to the very minutest details, the patterns on the curtains, the ornaments on the mantelpiece, the books in the library".[135] Both British and American Service authorities rightly insist that prisoners of war shall refuse to co-operate militarily or politically with their captors, or answer any questions at all after giving their name, rank, service number and date of birth. Any uncertainty about the amount of legitimate co-operation desirable with the enemy leads to trouble and often to breakdown. Colonel Stevens found "the thing they seemed to dislike was a cold, dignified sort of air, rather expressing a certain amount of contempt for everything". The adoption of this attitude helped him to survive not only his period chained to the wall in solitary confinement, but three further years in Dachau concentration camp.

An eminent medico-legal expert has been saying, off the record, for the last twenty years: "If suspects, when questioned by the police, would undertake to answer only those questions submitted to them in writing through their solicitors, and no one else—which is no more than their legal right—there would be very few police convictions indeed." And lawyers have long known how much more difficult it is to convict anybody who cannot be persuaded to talk. Yet, far too many normally law-abiding, even if guilty, suspects are easily persuaded to sign the most damaging confessions voluntarily because of an initial over-eagerness to co-operate with the police, and to answer all sorts of difficult and searching questions without a lawyer at hand to say: "My client reserves his explanation of the alleged incident."

The degree of physiological "co-operation" or "transference" that can be established between the police examiner and the citizen under questioning, or the preacher and his congregation, or the political speaker and his audience, is vital to the problem. Whoever can be roused either to fear or anger by politician, priest or policeman, is more easily led to accept the desired pattern of "co-operation", even though this may violate his normal judgment. The obstacles that the religious or political proselytizer cannot overcome are indifference or detached, controlled and continued amusement on the part of the subject at the efforts being made to break him down, or win him over, or tempt him into argument. The safety of the free world seems therefore to lie in a cultivation not only of courage, moral virtue and logic, but of humour: humour which produces the well-balanced state in which emotional excess is laughed at as ugly and wasteful.

In bull-fighting, the early efforts of the matador and his assistants are directed towards exciting, annoying and frustrating the bull, in order to wear him out and thus make him more suggestible and responsive. The matador must "dominate" the bull into doing what is required of him in the final stage: namely, to follow the movements of the red *muleta* with trance-like obedience. A "good" bull who earns popular applause when finally dragged off dead from the ring is one that "co-operates" by getting as aggressive as possible when baited with capes, and stabbed in the shoulder muscles with the picador's lance and the barbed darts of the banderillero. He is kept constantly on the move until emotionally and physically exhausted, and only when he can no longer hold up his head does the matador give the *coup-de-grace* with a lunge of his rapier between the relaxed shoulder blades.

A "bad" bull—unless some physical defect, such as partial blindness, prevents him from following the movements of the cape or the *muleta*—is one that refuses to get excited and so contrives to avoid both exhaustion and suggestibility. Until recently, the cure for phlegmatic bulls was *banderillas de fuego*—a type of dart, with an explosive at the point, which made them buck and leap all over the ring—but these are now prohibited. The matador's terror therefore is the bull that cannot be panicked by the traditional means, that seems to continue to think for himself and so is unpredictable in his responses. When eventually killed, often after having sent his matador to the infirmary or the grave, or ordered out of the ring by a prudent President, whistles and groans and curses follow him. The "good" bull, in fact, is the bull that might consider himself (to credit him with human feelings) immune to the ordeal facing him, confident in his courage, his quick anger in the face of things he dislikes, his great physical strength, his capacity for fighting to the very end. The "bad" bull is one with a stronger sense of self-preservation than bull-headed duty.

One should not carry such an analogy too far; but it serves to emphasize the fact that some persons become converted against their will because they insist on doing what they consider to be the "right thing" and go out to fight what is more wisely avoided or ignored. Their energies should be devoted instead to maintaining a policy of total non-co-operation, despite their pride and a natural inclination to test their courage and strength against those trying to provoke them.

Those reported as among the best able to preserve their standards and beliefs in the German concentration camps during World War II were members of the sect of Jehovah's Witnesses. This pacifist religious group has many strange beliefs, but these were implanted with such strength and certainty by their religious leaders as to remain operative when continued debilitation and psychological degrada-tion had reduced most other people of the highest ideals, but no specific loyalties, to accept the very lowest concepts of individual and group morality. A safeguard against con-version is, indeed, a burning and obsessive belief in some other creed or way of life. History shows that well indoc-trinated and trained soldiers can be just as brave and stub-born as Jehovah's Witnesses. One of Wesley's converts, stout-hearted John Evans, "when the cannon ball took off both his legs at the Battle of Fontenoy, called all about him, as long as he could speak, to praise and fear God, and honour the King as one who feared nothing but lest his last breath should be spent in vain".[55] In groups of persons, morale is of supreme importance, as when individuals get fatigued they usually become much more suggestible to the brave or cowardly group attitudes of others.

It will already be obvious that the victim of attempted brain-washing or the eliciting of a confession should do his best, when possible, not to lose weight by worrying, or cause himself unnecessary fatigue; and he should learn to snatch sleep whenever possible. Persons of phlegmatic tem-perament and strong, heavy body-build, who are also mentally well adjusted with a settled, happy viewpoint on life, are likely to hold out longer than those who have few or none of these assets.

It is a fallacy that intellectual awareness of what is happening can always prevent a man from being indoctrinated. Once he becomes exhausted and suggestible, or the brain enters the "paradoxical" or "ultra-paradoxical" phases, insight can be disturbed; even the knowledge of what to expect may be of little help in warding off breakdown. And afterwards, he will rationalize the newly-implanted beliefs and offer his friends sincere and absurd explanations of why his attitude has changed so suddenly. Mental depressives are well aware, in their lucid periods, that as soon as a new attack occurs they will lose all rational insight into the foolishness of their depressive ideas. And political prisoners should equally realize that, after an induced failure in brain function, their normal judgment will be impaired or altogether lost, and that, as soon as they find themselves growing suggestible, they should make every effort to evade further stress. Above all, they must remember that anger can be as potent a means of increasing suggestibility as fear and guilt.

In stressing the importance of further research on this whole problem, it must be emphasized once again that the concept of will-power and of any individual's power to resist for an indefinite period the physiological stresses that can now be imposed on both body and brain, have found little scientific support either in peace or war. We only delude ourselves if we think that any but the most rare individuals can endure unchanged to the very end. This does not mean that all persons can be *genuinely* indoctrinated by such means. Some will give only temporary submission to the demands made on them, and fight again when strength of body and mind returns. Others are saved by the supervention of madness. Or the will to resist may give way, but not the intellect itself.

As mentioned in a previous context, the stake, the gallows, the firing squad, the prison, or the madhouse, are usually available for the failures.

CHAPTER 11

General Conclusions

Since the purpose of this book has been to discuss possible physiological aspects of political and religious conversion, no apology need be given for its limited mechanistic approach. Pavlov's experiments are only one way of throwing light on a fascinating problem. There are other means available, including biochemical and electrical studies of normal and abnormal brain function. Much experiment is still needed before final conclusions can be drawn and meanwhile viewpoints must be constantly revised as fresh knowledge comes in. Much also remains to be learned by the use of other approaches,[*][136] including the study of the same phenomena from philosophical and spiritual bases; the author is well aware, for instance, that the eating of a large supper and the supine posture in bed do not explain all that needs to be known about the subsequent nightmare. But none of this research falls within the scope of the present book, which admittedly raises many new problems in trying to solve old ones.

It is, nevertheless, a modern paradox that rapid scientific progress often results when a field of experimental research is deliberately limited. For centuries medicine was, in ef-

---

* For instance J. A. M. Meerloo in *The Rape of the Mind* has recently studied the phenomena of political brain-washing from both a Pavlovian and a psycho-analytical viewpoint.

fect, controlled by those using a broad and comprehensive system of scholastic metaphysics to explain all forms of sickness; yet little progress resulted in the diagnosis or treatment of disease.

Then from the moment when the medical profession decided to forget its metaphysical preoccupations—which had meant concentrating on the whole man in his environmental and religious setting—and simply set about examining the functional mechanism of the lungs, the heart, the liver, and finally the brain itself, its present stupendous practical progress began. For hundreds of years before that, even the study of anatomy was thought unnecessary as an aid to medicine; scholastic philosophers claimed to explain satisfactorily the supposed workings of the body as well as those of the mind. The medical attitude of the Middle Ages, in fact, recalls some contemporary psychological views, such as that a satisfactory knowledge of metapsychology suffices to explain what may often be the varied results of normal and abnormal brain function. From time to time, the varied parts do have to be reassembled into a new whole; but this is where the dangers of wrong generalization so often arise.

Newton, being a philosopher at heart and more interested in Biblical prophecy and alchemy than in the mechanical laws of gravitation, thought that his discoveries had contributed little to the stock of human knowledge. Towards the end of his life he reproached himself with having dallied on the shores of a wide ocean of knowledge, and there played with a few pebbles and shells. Yet, more than two centuries later, we still find ourselves without any philosophical understanding of gravitation, though its simple mechanical formulae, framed by Newton, have proved of inestimable practical benefit. And we are still faced with Newton's problem: where best to concentrate research on problems concerning the mind of man. Many thinkers bravely navigate too broad a philosophical ocean, only to find themselves caught in a Sargasso Sea of tangled weed or on unsuspected reefs of ineluctable physical fact. This book is mere beachcombing, yet an examination of the pebbles and shells collected may suggest the value of sometimes concentrating more on the workings of the brain itself in psychiatric research, rather than scouring the metaphysical ocean for hidden mysteries. By an assemblage of relatively simple mechanistic and physiological studies, it has been shown here that not only certain methods of religious and political conversion—whether practised on groups or individuals—but also some of the results of psychoanalysis, of drug abreaction and of shock therapies in the treatment of sick patients, may start to be better understood in relation to one another.[8]

Must a new concentration on brain physiology and brain mechanics weaken religious faith and beliefs? On the contrary, a better understanding of the means of creating and consolidating faith will enable religious bodies to expand much more rapidly. The preacher can rest assured that the less mysteriously "God works His wonders to perform," the easier it should be to provide people with an essential knowledge and love of God. Man cannot and should not try to exist without some form of religion, but let us add, that although it is quite possible to indoctrinate people with ideas based on an out-of-date economic or historical tradition, or even on deliberate lies, and keep them fixed in these beliefs, a nation's health and efficiency depends on a close relation between social practice and religious belief. Any contradiction between them can only help to breed mental stress and impair judgment. No alternative exists to Christianity as the religion of the Western world, but it will probably become necessary to put the incidents of the New Testament into less ambiguous historical perspective; consolidate the lessons of Christ's sacrifice for the sins of His people; reinforce the prime texts of "Fear God" and "Love thy neighbour as thyself"; give these real social and political validity; and thus make it unnecessary for the businessman, or labourer, or priest to be the victim of a dissociation between his acts and his profession.

Boswell, in his *London Journal*,[137] reports a conversation between himself and Dr. Johnson about Wesley:

> We talked of preaching and of the great success that the Methodists have. He [Johnson] said that was owing to their preaching in a plain, vulgar manner, which was the only way to do good to common people. . . . He said that talking of drunkenness as a crime, because it debases reason, the noblest faculty of man, would do no service to the vulgar. But to tell them they might have died in their drunkenness and show how dreadful that would be, would affect them much.

Dr. Johnson was right; to secure such converts one has to try to overwhelm them emotionally. But this is no longer the eighteenth century. Then it did not seem to matter what the common people believed because they exercised no political power and were supposed only to work, not think; and because they read no books or papers. But religious conversion to fundamentalism seems out of date now; in a healthy modern nation everyone needs to have a mind that is no "divided house of faith and reason," as Pope Pius XI so aptly called the phenomenon of religious dissociation, and cannot afford to reject, as mischievous lies, the agreed facts of geology, archaeology and biology.

If this book has offended the religious or ethical susceptibilities of any reader, despite my efforts to avoid doing so, let me plead in extenuation the need for a greater understanding, by as many intelligent readers as possible, of the power and comparative simplicity of some of the methods here discussed. If we are to promote true religion, preserve our democratic ways of life and our hard-won civil liberties, we must learn to recognize that these same methods are being used for trivial or evil purposes instead of noble ones.

Yet science, however exploited by soldiers, merchants and politicians, is often a negative discipline; religion, ethics and politics should be strongly positive ones. Therefore, once doctors have learned how to indurate the human brain against strains and stresses, how to make it better able to think and learn from experience, and how to redirect it, when disorientated, into religious or ethical balance, they will doubtless be glad to sit back and watch the priests and politicians carrying out their own proper work, and with, we hope, much less need than at present for so many prison warders and policemen. Doctors—if I may speak for my profession—certainly do not claim that they are capable of formulating a new religious or political dispensation; it is merely their function to learn how to provide the health that will enable the most suitable of such dispensations to be fought for and won.

Though men are not dogs, they should humbly try to remember how much they resemble dogs in their brain functions, and not boast themselves as demigods. They are gifted with religious and social apprehensions, and they are gifted with the power of reason; but all these faculties are physiologically entailed to the brain. Therefore the brain should not be abused by having forced upon it any religious or political mystique that stunts the reason, or any form of crude rationalism that stunts the religious sense.

References

1. W. Sargant—"The Mechanism of Conversion"—*Brit. Med. J.*, II, 311; 1951.
2. P.O.W.—*The Fight Continues After the Battle*. Report of the Secretary of Defense's Advisory Committee on Prisoners of War—U.S. Government Printing Office, Washington; 1955.
3. A. Koestler—"The God that Failed"—*Six Studies in Communism*—Hamish Hamilton, London; 1950.
4. I. P. Pavlov—*Lectures on Conditioned Reflexes, Vol. 2. Conditioned Reflexes in Psychiatry*. Trans. with Introduction by Horsley Gantt—Lawrence & Wishart, London; 1941.
5. H. Fabing, in a personal communication.
6. W. Sargant and H. J. Shorvon—"Acute War Neuroses: Special Reference to Pavlov's Experimental Observations and Mechanism of Abreaction"—*Arch. Neurol. Psychiat. Chicago*, LIV, 231; 1945.
7. J. S. Horsley—"Narco-Analysis: A New Technique in Short-cut Psychotherapy. A Comparison with Other Methods"—*Lancet*, I, 55; 1936.
8. W. Sargant—"Some Observations on Abreaction with Drugs"—*Dig. Neurol. Psychiat.*, XVI, 193; 1948.
9. W. Sargant—"Some Cultural Group Abreaction Techniques and their Relation to Modern Treatment"—*Proc. Roy. Soc. Med.*, XLII, 367; 1949.
10. W. Gordon—*Soviet Studies*, III, 34—University of Glasgow; 1951-52.
11. Y. P. Frolov—*Pavlov and His School*. Trans. by C. P. Dutt—Kegan Paul, Trench, Trubner, London; 1938.
12. B. P. Babkin—*Pavlov. A Biography*—Gollancz, London; 1951.
13. J. Wortis—*Soviet Psychiatry*—The Williams & Wilkins Co., Baltimore; 1950.
14. E. A. Asratyan—*I. P. Pavlov. His Life and Work* (English translation)—Foreign Languages Publishing House, Moscow; 1953.
15. I. P. Pavlov—*Selected Works* (English translation)—Foreign Languages Publishing House, Moscow; 1955.

16. G. Ekstein, in a personal communication.

17. C. Symonds—"The Human Response to Flying Stress"—*Brit. Med. J.*, II, 703; 1943.

18. R. L. Swank—"Combat Exhaustion"—*J. Nerv. Ment. Dis.*, CIX, 475; 1949.

19. R. R. Grinker and J. P. Spiegel—*War Neuroses in North Africa. The Tunisian Campaign (January-May, 1943)*—Josiah Macy, Jr. Foundation, New York; 1943.

20. R. L. Swank and B. Cohen—"Chronic Symptomatology of Combat Neurosis"—*War Med.*, VIII, 143; 1945.
R. L. Swank and E. Marchand—"Combat Neurosis. Development of Combat Exhaustion"—*Arch. Neurol. Psychiat.*, LV, 236; 1946. See also note 18.

21. See note 20, Swank and Marchand.

22. E. L. Spears—*Prelude to Victory*—Jonathan Cape, London; 1939.

23. W. Sargant—"Physical Treatment of Acute War Neuroses: Some Clinical Observations"—*Brit. Med. J.*, II, 574; 1942.

24. H. B. Craigie—"Physical Treatment of Acute War Neuroses" (Correspondence)—*Brit. Med. J.*, II, 675; 1942. See also note 23.

25. *Proc. Roy. Soc. Med.*, XXXIV, 757; 1941.

26. Suetonius—*History of Twelve Caesars*. Trans. by Philemon Holland (1610)—Broadway Translations, Geo. Routledge, London.

27. W. Gordon—"Cerebral Physiology and Psychiatry"—*Journ. Ment. Sci.*, XCIV, 118; 1948.

28. R. R. Madden—*Phantasmata or Illusions and Fanaticisms of Protean Forms Productive of Great Evils. Vols.* I *and* II—T. C. Newby, London; 1857.

29. J. Breuer and S. Freud—*Studies in Hysteria*. 1893. Trans. by A. A. Brill—Nerv. and Ment. Dis. Publishing Co., New York; 1936.

30. W. S. Sadler—*Theory and Practice of Psychiatry*—Henry Kimpton, London; 1936.

31. M. Cuplin—*Psychoneuroses of War and Peace*—Cambridge University Press; 1920.

32. W. Brown—*Psychological Methods of Healing. An Introduction to Psychotherapy*—University of London Press; 1938.

33. H. A. Palmer—"Abreactive Techniques—Ether." *J. Roy. Army Med. Corps*, LXXXIV, 86; 1945.

34. D. P. Penhallow—"Mutism and Deafness due to Emotional Shock cured by Etherisation." *Boston Med. & Surg. J.*, CLXXIV, 131; 1915.

35. A. Hurst—*Medical Diseases of War*—Edward Arnold, London; 1940.

36. H. J. Shorvon and W. Sargant—"Excitatory Abreaction: Special reference to its Mechanism and the use of Ether." *J. Ment. Sci.*, XCIII, 709; 1947.

37. P. Janet—*Principles of Psychotherapy*—Macmillan, London; 1925.

38. C. H. Rogerson—"Narco-Analysis with Nitrous Oxide"—*Brit. Med. J.*, 1,811; 1944.

39. L. J. Meduna—*Carbon Dioxide Therapy*—Chas. C. Thomas, Springfield, Illinois; 1950.

40. J. L. Simon and H. Taube—"A Preliminary Study of the use of Methedrine in Psychiatric Diagnosis"—*J. Nerv. Ment. Dis.*, CIV, 593; 1946.

41. B. G. M. Sundkler—*Bantu Prophets in South Africa*—Lutterworth Press, London; 1948.

42. V. Cerletti and L. Bini—"L'elettroshock"—*Arch. Gen. Neurol. Psichiat. Psicoanal.*, XIX, 266; 1938.

43. M. Sakel—*The Pharmacological Shock Treatment of Schizophrenia* (Nerv. & Ment. Dis. Monogr. Series No. 62)—Nervous and Mental Disease Publishing Co., New York; 1938.

44. W. Sargant—"Indications and Mechanisms of Abreaction and its Relation to the Shock Therapies"—*Internat. Psychiat. Congr.* (1950) *Proc.*, IV, 192—Hermann et Cie, Paris; 1952.

45. Robert Graves, in a personal communication.

46. E. Moniz—*Tentative opératoires dans le traitement de certaines psychoses*—Masson et Cie, Paris; 1936.

47. R. Ström-Olsen and P. M. Tow—"Late Social Results of Prefrontal Leucotomy"—*Lancet*, I, 87; 1949.

48. G. Rylander—"Personality Analysis before and after Frontal Lobotomy" in *The Frontal Lobes*—Williams & Wilkins, Baltimore; 1948.

49. J. Pippard—"Personality Changes after Rostral Leucotomy: A comparison with standard leucotomy"—*J. Ment. Sci.*, CI, 425; 1955.

50. J. Wesley—*The Journal of John Wesley*, Vol. II. Standard edition edited by N. Curnock—Charles H. Kelly, London; 1909-16.

51. H. Nicolson—*Good Behaviour*—Constable, London; 1955.

52. R. A. Knox—*Enthusiasm; A Chapter in Religious History*—Clarendon Press, Oxford; 1950.

53. W. L. Doughty—*John Wesley—Preacher*—Epworth Press, London; 1955.
    Wesley's *Journal*, Vol. V. See note 50.

54. Wesley's *Journal*, Vol. II.

55. L. Tyerman—*Life and Times of Rev. John Wesley, M.A.* 3 vols.—Hodder & Stoughton, London; 1871.

56. Tyerman's Life of Wesley quoted by W. James in *The Varieties of Religious Experience*—Longmans, Green, London; 1914.

57. C. Smyth—*Simeon and Church Order*—Cambridge University Press; 1940.

58. A. Koestler—*Arrow in the Blue*—Hamish Hamilton, London; 1952.

59. A. Koestler—*The Invisible Writing*—Hamish Hamilton, London; 1954.

60. P. Verger—*Dieux d'Afrique*—Paul Hartmann, Paris; 1954.

61. M. Deren—*Divine Horsemen. The Living Gods of Haiti*—Thames and Hudson, London; 1953.

62. Mrs. R. Chilver, in a personal communication.

63. G. Bolinder—*Devilman's Jungle*. Trans. by M. A. Michael—Dennis Dobson, London; 1954.

64. J. G. Frazer—*The Golden Bough. A Study in Magic and Religion.* Abridged edition—Macmillan, London; 1950.

65. George Fox—*The Journal of George Fox.* Everyman edition—Dent, London.

66. H. Harrer—*Seven Years in Tibet.* Trans. by Richard Graves—Rupert Hart-Davis, London; 1953.

67. T. Butts, quoted by W. L. Doughty. See note 53.

68. Ben Jonson—*Plays.* Everyman Edition—Dent, London; 1948.

69. A. D. dePirajno—*A Cure for Serpents: A Doctor in Africa.* Trans. by Kathleen Naylor—André Deutsch, London; 1955.

70. See note 56. (The italics are the author's.)

71. D. Hill—Chapter IV in W. Sargant and E. Slater's *Physical Methods of Treatment in Psychiatry.* 3rd edition—E. & S. Livingstone, Edinburgh; 1954.

72. A. Huxley—*The Doors of Perception*—Chatto & Windus, London; 1954.

73. L. Alexander—*Treatment of Mental Disorders*—W. B. Saunders, Philadelphia; 1953.

74. G. Salmon—*The Evidence of the Work of the Holy Spirit.* (With an appendix on the Revival Movement in the North of Ireland.)—Hodges, Smith, Dublin; 1859.

75. P. F. Kirby—*The Grand Tour in Italy 1700-1800*—S. F. Vanni, New York; 1952.

76. J. F. C. Hecker—*The Epidemics of the Middle Ages.* Trans. by B. G. Babington—Sydenham Soc., London; 1844.

77. E. L. Backman—*Religious Dances in the Christian Church and in Popular Medicine*—Allen & Unwin, London; 1952.

78. J. Edwards—*A New Narrative of the Revival of Religion in New England with Thoughts on that Revival.* With an Introduction Essay by John Pye Smith, D.D.—Wm. Collins, Glasgow; 1829.

79. F. Youssoupoff—*Lost Splendour.* Trans. by A. Green and N. Katkoff—Jonathan Cape, London; 1953.

80. G. R. Taylor—*Sex in History*—Thames and Hudson, London; 1953.

81. H. Leuba—*Amer. J. Psychology*, VII, 345; 1895.

82. F. W. Farrar—*Eternal Hope*—Macmillan, London; 1878.

83. Article on Dr. Billy Graham in *Time* magazine, LXIV, 38; 1954.

84. E. Wilson, in a review of *The Rungless Ladder; Harriet Beecher Stowe*, by C. H. Forster, Duke University Press—*The New Yorker*, XXXI, 125; 1955.

85. C. G. Finney—*Lectures on Revivals of Religion.* (13th edit.)—Simpkin, Marshall, London; 1840.

86. W. B. Sprague—*Lectures on Revivals of Religion.* With an Introductory Essay by Rev. G. Redford and Rev. J. Angell. 2nd edition—Wm. Collins, Glasgow; 1833.

87. Apuleius—*The Golden Ass.* Trans. by R. Graves—Penguin Books, London; 1950.

88. G. Orwell—*Nineteen-Eighty-Four*—Secker & Warburg, London; 1949.

89. S. Maugham—*Don Fernando*—Heinemann, London; 1950.

90. A. Huxley—*The Devils of Loudun*—Chatto & Windus, London; 1952.

91. L. S. B. Leaky—*Defeating Mau Mau*—Methuen, London; 1954.

92. *The Times*, September 1st, 1955.

93. *The Times*, November 1st, 1955.

94. Han Suyin—*A Many Splendoured Thing*—Jonathan Cape, London; 1952.

95. *Time* magazine, March 5th, 1956.

96. R. L. Walker—*China Under Communism*—Allen & Unwin, London; 1956.

97. *The Times*, May 16th, 1956.

98. G. Thomson—*Aeschylus and Athens.* 2nd edition—Lawrence & Wishart, London; 1946.

99. J. E. Harrison—*Prolegomena to the Study of Greek Religion*—Cambridge University Press; 1922.

100. V. Magnion—*Les Mystères d'Eleusis*—Paris; 1950.

101. Pausanias—*Description of Greece*, Vol. I. Trans. with a commentary by T. D. Frazer—Macmillan, London; 1898.

102. Plutarch—"A Discourse concerning Socrates's Daemon" in *Plutarch's Miscellanies and Essays.* Trans. from the Greek by several hands. Corrected and revised by William Goodwin. 6th edition, Vol. II—Little, Brown, Boston, Mass.; 1889.

103. Strabo IX, 418.

104. Suetonius—*Caligula*, XXIX.

105. Dioscorides—*De Materia Medica*, IV, 148-9.

106. Pausanias—X, 361.

107. Pliny—*Natural History*, XXV, 27.

108. Idem, XXV, 23.

109. A. Weissberg—*Conspiracy of Silence*—Hamish Hamilton, London; 1952.

110. Z. Stypulkowski—*Invitation to Moscow*—Thames and Hudson, London; 1951.

111. Full text quoted in *The Observer*—London, June 10th, 1956.

112. L. E. Hinkle, jnr. and H. G. Wolff. "Communist Interrogation and Indoctrination of 'Enemies of the State'." *Archives Neurol. & Psychiat.*, 76, *115*, 1956.

113. *The Observer*, London, July 29th, 1956. ·

114. C. D. Lee—*The Instrumental Detection of Deception. The Lie Test.* A monograph in The Police Science Series. Edited by V. A. Leonard—Charles C. Thomas, Springfield, Illinois; 1953.

115. *Police Magazine*, III, 5. September, 1925. (The italics are the author's.)

116. D. W. Winnicott—"Mind and its Relation to the Psyche-Soma."—*Brit. J. of Med. Psychol.*, XXVII, 201; 1954.

117. E. Jones—*Sigmund Freud: Life and Work.* 2 Vols—Hogarth Press, London; 1955.

118. A. Farrar-Hockley—"The Spirit in Jeopardy." B.B.C. broadcast script, January 2nd, 1955.

119. *Malleus Maleficarum.* Trans. with an Introduction, Bibliography and Notes by Rev. Montague Summers—Pushkin Press, London; 1948.

120. J. Caulfield—*Portraits, Memoirs and Characters of Remarkable Persons.* 2 Vols.—R. S. Kirby, London; 1813.

121. Pennethorne Hughes—*Witchcraft*—Longmans, London; 1952—who also quotes from *The Witch Persecutions* ed. by G. L. Burt in "Translations and Reprints", Univ. of Pennsylvania.

122. J. S. Henderson—*Report of Inquiry into Conviction of Timothy Evans*, and *A Supplementary Report*—H.M. Stationery Office, London; July and September, 1953. Permission for quotations from the White Paper in this chapter has been obtained from the Controller of H.M. Stationery Office.

123. M. Eddowes—*The Man on Your Conscience*—Cassell, London; 1955.

124. Lord Altrincham and I. Gilmour—*The Case of Timothy Evans*—Special *Spectator* Publication, 1956.

125. The full transcript of the trial finally became available to the public in 1957 in the *Trials of Evans & Christie*, edited by F. Tennyson Jesse and published by William Hodge & Co., Edinburgh, after this book had been completed. Recently another interesting book on the Evans and Christie controversy, *Ten Rillington Place*, has been written by Ludovic Kennedy and published by Gollancz.

126. *The Times*, London, May 18th, 1956.

127. F. Beck and W. Godin—*Russian Purge and the Extraction of Confession.* Trans. by E. Mosbacher and D. Porter—Hurst & Blackett, Lonton; 1951.

128. R. Sabatini—*Torquemada and the Spanish Inquisition.* 7th edition—Stanley Paul, London; 1929.

129. L. Fabre—*Joan of Arc*—Odhams Press, London; 1954.

130. S. Told—*The Life of Mr. Silas Told Written by Himself.* With a note to the serious and candid reader by John Wesley, A.M. 1786—Reprinted Epworth Press, London; 1954.

131. See A. P. Herbert—*Mr. Gay's London*—Ernest Benn, London; 1948.

132. M. Piette—*John Wesley in the Evolution of Protestantism*—Sheed & Ward, London; 1938.

133. M. R. Brailsford—*A Tale of Two Brothers; John and Charles Wesley*—Rupert Hart-Davis, London; 1954.

134. G. Sutherland, in a personal communication.

135. R. H. Stevens—"The Spirit in the Cage." B.B.C. broadcast script, March, 1947.

136. J. A. M. Meerloo—*The Rape of the Mind. The Psychology of Thought Control Menticide and Brain-washing*—World Publishing Co., New York; 1956.

137. *Boswell's London Journal* 1762-3. Edited by F. A. Pottle—Wm. Heinemann, London; 1950.

Bibliography

These further references do not include those already annotated in the text.

Andrews, E. D.—*The People Called Shakers*—Oxford University Press, New York; 1953.

Barrett, W. P.—*The Trial of Jeanne d'Arc: a complete translation of the text of the original documents, with an introduction by W. P. Barrett*—Routledge, London; 1931.

Bartemeier *et al.*—"Combat Exhaustion"—*J. Nerv. & Ment. Dis.*, CIV, 358; 1946.

Bromberg, W.—*The Mind of Man*—Hamish Hamilton, London; 1937.

Cadbury, H. J.—*George Fox's Book of Miracles: edited, with an introduction and notes, by H. J. Cadbury: foreword by Rufus M. Jones*—Cambridge University Press; 1948.

Culpin, M.—*Recent Advances in the Study of the Psychoneuroses*—J. & A. Churchill, London; 1931.

Curran, D., and Partridge, M.—*Psychological Medicine*—E. & S. Livingstone, Edinburgh; 4th edition, 1955.

Davies, R. T.—*Four Centuries of Witch Beliefs (with special reference to the Great Rebellion)*—Methuen, London; 1947.

Debenham, G., Hill, D., Sargant, W., and Slater, E.—"Treatment of War Neuroses"—*Lancet*, I, 107; 1941.

Eysenck, H. J.—"A Dynamic Theory of Anxiety"—*J. Ment. Sci.*, CI, 28; 1955.

Fabing, H.—"Combat Experience of a Soldier with Narcolepsy"—*Arch. Neurol. Psychiat.*, LIV, 367; 1945.

Fabing, H.—"Narcolepsy, Theory of Pathogenesis of Narcolepsy—Cataplexy Syndrome"—*Arch. Neurol. Psychiat.*, LV, 353; 1946.

Fermor, P. Leigh—*Traveller's Tree*—John Murray, London; 1950.

Finney, C. G.—*Finney of Revival: an abbreviation of the Sermons on Revival, arranged by E. E. Shelhamer*—Oliphants, London; 1954.

Freud, S.—"The Psychic Mechanism of Hysteria Phenomena" in *Selected Papers on Hysteria and other Psychoneuroses*—J. Nerv. Ment. Dis. Publishing Co., New York; 1893.

Gantt, W. H.—*The Origin and Development of Behaviour Disorders in Dogs* (Psychosomatic Med. Monographs)—P. B. Hoeber, New York; 1943.

Gantt, W. H.—*Experimental Basis for Neurotic Behaviour*—P. B. Hoeber, New York; 1944.

Gantt, W. H.—*Russian Physiology and Pathology*—Amer. Assoc. for Advancement of Science, Washington, D.C.; 1952.

Gelhorn, E.—"Is Restoration of Inhibited Conditioned Reactions by Insulin Coma Specific for Pavlovian Inhibitions? Contributions to the Theory of Shock Treatment"—*Arch. Neurol. Psychiat.,* LVI, 2, 216; 1946.

Gibson, W.—*The Year of Grace: A History of the Ulster Revival of 1859*—Andrew Elliott, Edinburgh; 1860.

Grinker, R. R., and Spiegel, J. P.—*Men Under Stress*—Balkiston, Philadelphia; 1945.

Horsley, J. S.—*Narco-analysis*—Oxford University Press; 1943.

Hunter, E.—*Brain-washing in Red China*—Vanguard Press, New York; 1953.

Hunter, E.—*Brain-washing: the Story of Men who defied it*—Farrar, Straus and Cudahy, New York; 1956.

Hurston, Z.—*The Voodoo Gods: an Inquiry into Native Myths and Magic in Jamaica and Haiti*—Dent, London; 1939.

Kardiner, A.—*The Traumatic Neuroses of War* (Psychosomatic Med. Monographs)—P. B. Hoeber, New York; 1941.

Leuba, H.—*The Psychology of Religious Mysticism*—Kegan Paul, Trench, Trubner, London; 1929.

Lewis, N. D. C.—*A Short History of Psychiatric Achievement*—Chapman and Hall, London; 1942.

Liddell, H. S.—"Conditioned Reflex Methods and Experimental Neurosis" in *Personality and Behaviour Disorders*, Vol. I, edited by J. McV. Hunt—The Ronald Press, New York; 1944.

Liddell, H. S.—"Experimental Induction of Psychoneuroses by Conditioned Reflex with Stress" with postscript by Horsley Gantt, in *Biology of Mental Health and Disease*—Cassell, London; 1952.

Lifton, R. J.—"Thought Reform in Western Civilians in Chinese Communist Prisons"—*Psychiatry*, XIX, 173; 1956.

Lindemann, E.—"Pathological Effect of Sodium Amytal"—*Proc. Soc. Exp. Biol. N.Y.*, XXVIII, 864; 1931.

Little, A. M. G.—*Pavlov and Propaganda Problems of Communism*, Vol. 2—Internat. Information Administration, Washington, D.C.; 1953.

McDougall, W.—*An Outline of Abnormal Psychology*—Methuen, London; 1926.

Masserman, J.—*Behaviour and Neurosis*—University Press, Chicago; 1943.

Meerloo, J. A. M.—"Pavlovian Strategy as a Weapon of Menticide"—*Am. J. Psychiat.*, CX, 809; 1954.

Miller, E.—*The Neuroses in War*—Macmillan, London; 1940.

Moran, Lord—*The Anatomy of Courage*—Constable, London; 1945.

Mowrer, O. H., Light, B. H., Luria, Z., and Zeleny, M. P.—"Tension Changes during Psychotherapy with special reference to Resistance" in *Psychotherapy, Theory and Research*: edited by O. H. Mowrer—The Ronald Press, New York; 1953.

Pavlov, I. P.—*Lectures on Conditional Reflexes: the Higher Nervous Activity (Behaviour) of Animals*, Vol. 1, translated by Horsley Gantt—Lawrence and Wishart, London; 1928.

Piddington, W. E. R.—*Russian Frenzy*—Elek Books, London; 1955.

Rattenbury, J. E.—*The Conversion of the Wesleys*—Epworth Press, London; 1938.

Roth, M.—"Changes in E.E.G. under Barbiturate Anaesthesia produced by Electroconvulsive Treatment and their Significance for the Theory of E.C.T. Action"—*Electroenceph. and Clinical Neurophysiol.*, III, 261; 1951.

Roth, M.—"A Theory of E.C.T. Action and its Bearing on the Biological Significance of Epilepsy"—*J. Ment. Sci.*, XCVIII, 44; 1952.

Rylander, G.—"Therapeutic Effects of the Lobotomies"—*Internat. Psychiat. Cong.* (1950) Proc., IV, 357—Hermann et Cie, Paris; 1952.

Sargant, W.—"Physical Treatment of Acute Psychiatric States"—*War Med.*, IV, 577; 1953.

Sargant, W.—"Ten Years Clinical Experience of Modified Leucotomy Operations."—*Brit. Med. Jour.*, II, 800; 1953.

Sargant, W., and Craske, N.—"Modified Insulin Therapy in War Neuroses"—*Lancet*, II, 212; 1941.

Sargant, W., and Slater, E.—"Acute War Neuroses"—*Lancet*, II, 1; 1940.

Sargant, W., and Slater, E.—"Treatment of Obsessional Neurosis"—*Proc. Roy. Soc. Med.*, XLIII, 1007; 1950.

Sargant, W., and Slater, E.—"Physical Methods of Treatment in Psychiatry"—*Brit. Med. J.*, I, 1315; 1951.

Sargant, W., and Slater, E.—"Influence of the 1939-45 War on British Psychiatry"—*Internat. Psychiat. Cong.* (1950) *Proc.*, VI, 180—Hermann et Cie, Paris; 1952.

Schein, E. H.—"The Chinese Indoctrination Program for Prisoners of War"—*Psychiatry*, XIX, 149, 1956.

Sherrington, C.—*Man and his Nature: the Gifford Lectures*—Penguin Books, London; 1955.

Shorvon, H. J.—"Abreaction"—*Proc. Roy. Soc. Med.*, XLVI, 158; 1953.

Smollett, T.—*Travels through France and Italy*, 2 Vols.—London; 1766.

Spectator, London; 1954—Articles and correspondence on "Physical Treatments of the Mind and Spiritual Healing."

Times, The, London; 1955—Leading article and correspondence on "Fundamentalism: a Religious Problem."

Walter, E. Grey—*The Living Brain*—Duckworth, London; 1953.

Whittingham, R.—*The Whole Works of Rev. John Berridge, M.A. with a Memoir of his Life*—Ebenezer Palmer, London; 2nd edition, 1864.

Zilboorg, G.—*A History of Medical Psychology*—W. W. Norton, New York; 1941.

Index

salivary secretion, experiments with, 7-8, 12

Salmon, Rev. George, on group excitation, 133; on religious revivals, 135-7

Salvation Army, militancy of, 113

Samothracian Mysteries, 193

sanctification, suddenness of, 93

"sanguine" temperament, 4

Saul, conversion of, 119-21

schizophrenia, reversal of conditioning in, 44; examples of, 129-31; treatment of, 71-3

Selina, Countess of Huntingdon, Connexion of, 248

sensitivity, religious exploitation of, 167

sesamoides, use of, 201

shakers, 147

Shakespeare, 20

Sherrington, on Christian martyrs, 20

shock therapy, insulin, 71

shock treatments, value of, 71; variety of, 69-72

Shorvon, Dr. H. J., and ether, 49

sleep, deprivation of, 233, 235

Smollet, on religious excitation, 134-5

Smyth, Charles, on methods of conversion, 95

snake-handling cult, results of conversion in, 251-2

social degradation, use of, in eliciting confessions, 236

Songhay, tribe of, 105

Southey, on Berridge's conversion techniques, 95

Spiritual Exercises, W. S. Maugham on, 168-70; use in Jesuit training, 168-70

Spiegel, on narcosynthesis, 49

Sprague, William, B., on Finney's conversion methods, 165

Stephanus of Byzantium, on cures at Anticyra, 200

stereotypy, 50, 52-4; dispersal of, 52; of movements, 20

stimuli, need for research in power of various, 260-1

stool pigeons, use of in eliciting confessions, 236

Stowe, Harriet Beecher, theological ordeal of, 160

stress, Taoist avoidance of, 43; effects of, 37, 151-2; use of in eliciting confessions, 236-7

Ström-Olsen, on leucotomy, 78-9

"strong excitatory" temperament, 4, 6, 16, 37